Microsoft® Windows® Movie Maker

FOR DUMMIES®

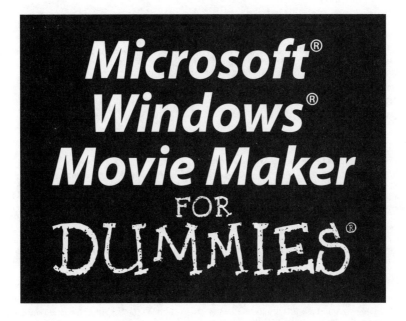

Microsoft® Windows® Movie Maker FOR DUMMIES®

by Keith Underdahl

IDG BOOKS WORLDWIDE

IDG Books Worldwide, Inc.
An International Data Group Company

Foster City, CA ◆ Chicago, IL ◆ Indianapolis, IN ◆ New York, NY

Microsoft® Windows® Movie Maker For Dummies®

Published by
IDG Books Worldwide, Inc.
An International Data Group Company
919 E. Hillsdale Blvd.
Suite 400
Foster City, CA 94404
www.idgbooks.com (IDG Books Worldwide Web Site)
www.dummies.com (Dummies Press Web Site)

Library of Congress Control Number: 00-103651

ISBN: 0-7645-0741-9

Printed in the United States of America

10 9 8 7 6 5 4 3 2 1

1O/QW/QZ/QQ/IN

Distributed in the United States by IDG Books Worldwide, Inc.

Distributed by CDG Books Canada Inc. for Canada; by Transworld Publishers Limited in the United Kingdom; by IDG Norge Books for Norway; by IDG Sweden Books for Sweden; by IDG Books Australia Publishing Corporation Pty. Ltd. for Australia and New Zealand; by TransQuest Publishers Pte Ltd. for Singapore, Malaysia, Thailand, Indonesia, and Hong Kong; by Gotop Information Inc. for Taiwan; by ICG Muse, Inc. for Japan; by Intersoft for South Africa; by Eyrolles for France; by International Thomson Publishing for Germany, Austria and Switzerland; by Distribuidora Cuspide for Argentina; by LR International for Brazil; by Galileo Libros for Chile; by Ediciones ZETA S.C.R. Ltda. for Peru; by WS Computer Publishing Corporation, Inc., for the Philippines; by Contemporanea de Ediciones for Venezuela; by Express Computer Distributors for the Caribbean and West Indies; by Micronesia Media Distributor, Inc. for Micronesia; by Chips Computadoras S.A. de C.V. for Mexico; by Editorial Norma de Panama S.A. for Panama; by American Bookshops for Finland.

For general information on IDG Books Worldwide's books in the U.S., please call our Consumer Customer Service department at 800-762-2974. For reseller information, including discounts and premium sales, please call our Reseller Customer Service department at 800-434-3422.

For information on where to purchase IDG Books Worldwide's books outside the U.S., please contact our International Sales department at 317-572-3993 or fax 317-572-4002.

For consumer information on foreign language translations, please contact our Customer Service department at 1-800-434-3422, fax 317-572-4002, or e-mail rights@idgbooks.com.

For information on licensing foreign or domestic rights, please phone +1-650-653-7098.

For sales inquiries and special prices for bulk quantities, please contact our Order Services department at 800-434-3422 or write to the address above.

For information on using IDG Books Worldwide's books in the classroom or for ordering examination copies, please contact our Educational Sales department at 800-434-2086 or fax 317-572-4005.

For press review copies, author interviews, or other publicity information, please contact our Public Relations department at 650-653-7000 or fax 650-653-7500.

For authorization to photocopy items for corporate, personal, or educational use, please contact Copyright Clearance Center, 222 Rosewood Drive, Danvers, MA 01923, or fax 978-750-4470.

 is a registered trademark under exclusive license to IDG Books Worldwide, Inc. from International Data Group, Inc.

About the Author

Keith Underdahl is a writer and electronic publishing specialist residing in Albany, Oregon. He has written or contributed to numerous books from IDG Books Worldwide, including *Teach Yourself Microsoft Word 2000, Teach Yourself Office 97,* and *Internet Bible* 2nd Edition. Keith works full time as a project manager and graphics designer for Ages Software, where he produces electronic libraries of classic Christian texts. When he is not goofing around with computers, Keith is also a senior editor for *Street Bike Magazine,* a magazine serving motorcyclists in the western United States.

ABOUT IDG BOOKS WORLDWIDE

Welcome to the world of IDG Books Worldwide.

IDG Books Worldwide, Inc., is a subsidiary of International Data Group, the world's largest publisher of computer-related information and the leading global provider of information services on information technology. IDG was founded more than 30 years ago by Patrick J. McGovern and now employs more than 9,000 people worldwide. IDG publishes more than 290 computer publications in over 75 countries. More than 90 million people read one or more IDG publications each month.

Launched in 1990, IDG Books Worldwide is today the #1 publisher of best-selling computer books in the United States. We are proud to have received eight awards from the Computer Press Association in recognition of editorial excellence and three from Computer Currents' First Annual Readers' Choice Awards. Our best-selling *...For Dummies®* series has more than 50 million copies in print with translations in 31 languages. IDG Books Worldwide, through a joint venture with IDG's Hi-Tech Beijing, became the first U.S. publisher to publish a computer book in the People's Republic of China. In record time, IDG Books Worldwide has become the first choice for millions of readers around the world who want to learn how to better manage their businesses.

Our mission is simple: Every one of our books is designed to bring extra value and skill-building instructions to the reader. Our books are written by experts who understand and care about our readers. The knowledge base of our editorial staff comes from years of experience in publishing, education, and journalism — experience we use to produce books to carry us into the new millennium. In short, we care about books, so we attract the best people. We devote special attention to details such as audience, interior design, use of icons, and illustrations. And because we use an efficient process of authoring, editing, and desktop publishing our books electronically, we can spend more time ensuring superior content and less time on the technicalities of making books.

You can count on our commitment to deliver high-quality books at competitive prices on topics you want to read about. At IDG Books Worldwide, we continue in the IDG tradition of delivering quality for more than 30 years. You'll find no better book on a subject than one from IDG Books Worldwide.

IDG BOOKS WORLDWIDE

John Kilcullen
Chairman and CEO
IDG Books Worldwide, Inc.

VIII WINNER

Eighth Annual
Computer Press
Awards ≥1992

IX WINNER

Ninth Annual
Computer Press
Awards ≥1993

X WINNER

Tenth Annual
Computer Press
Awards ≥1994

XI WINNER

Eleventh Annual
Computer Press
Awards ≥1995

IDG is the world's leading IT media, research and exposition company. Founded in 1964, IDG had 1997 revenues of $2.05 billion and has more than 9,000 employees worldwide. IDG offers the widest range of media options that reach IT buyers in 75 countries representing 95% of worldwide IT spending. IDG's diverse product and services portfolio spans six key areas including print publishing, online publishing, expositions and conferences, market research, education and training, and global marketing services. More than 90 million people read one or more of IDG's 290 magazines and newspapers, including IDG's leading global brands — Computerworld, PC World, Network World, Macworld and the Channel World family of publications. IDG Books Worldwide is one of the fastest-growing computer book publishers in the world, with more than 700 titles in 36 languages. The "...For Dummies®" series alone has more than 50 million copies in print. IDG offers online users the largest network of technology-specific Web sites around the world through IDG.net (http://www.idg.net), which comprises more than 225 targeted Web sites in 55 countries worldwide. International Data Corporation (IDC) is the world's largest provider of information technology data, analysis and consulting, with research centers in over 41 countries and more than 400 research analysts worldwide. IDG World Expo is a leading producer of more than 168 globally branded conferences and expositions in 35 countries including E3 (Electronic Entertainment Expo), Macworld Expo, ComNet, Windows World Expo, ICE (Internet Commerce Expo), Agenda, DEMO, and Spotlight. IDG's training subsidiary, ExecuTrain, is the world's largest computer training company, with more than 230 locations worldwide and 785 training courses. IDG Marketing Services helps industry-leading IT companies build international brand recognition by developing global integrated marketing programs via IDG's print, online and exposition products worldwide. Further information about the company can be found at www.idg.com.   1/26/00

Dedication

To my mother, Carol, for the love, support, and strength she has given me throughout my life.

I also wish to dedicate this work to the memory of my dear friend Jim Novak. His time here was short, and I thank him for so many good times.

Author's Acknowledgments

Many friends, associates, and loved ones came together to help me complete this project, and it can truly be said that this book would not have come to completion without the help of these people. First and foremost I want to thank my family who has patiently stood by as I worked day and night to complete my work. My wife Christa provided invaluable support during this project, and my sons Soren and Cole sacrificed many hours of Daddy time to let me do this.

Soren and Cole deserve further thanks for the inspiration and subject matter they provide for my many film projects. They appeared in many of the projects featured in this book, and were excited to do so on each occasion.

Billy O'Drobinak wrote chapter 20, *Ten Tips From a Pro Videographer*, and did an outstanding job of it. His extensive professional video and film experience made him perfect for the task, and he did a great job writing tips that any camcorder owner can understand and use. I also wish to thank Bill Heald for introducing me to Billy.

Of course, credit for the high quality of *Windows Movie Maker For Dummies* lies with the ever-enthusiastic editorial team assembled by IDG Books. Susan Christophersen helped keep me on schedule, make sense of my submissions, and provided timely feedback and ideas throughout the process. This is my first *...For Dummies* book, so I know I caused Susan to work extra hard to ensure that this project met IDG's high standards.

A special thank you goes out to my technical editor, Buddy Morel. In spite of being pulled in on this project at the last moment, he did an outstanding job of reviewing the text and provided many excellent tips and ideas along the way. The book has truly benefited from his involvement.

Many other people at IDG worked tirelessly to make this book what it is. I wish to thank David Mayhew for giving me this opportunity and Ed Adams for overseeing the project.

Finally, gratitude is owed to Microsoft and the Windows Movie Maker development team for producing such a fun and exciting new product. The developers worked long hours poring over feedback and bug reports, and up to now their only appreciation has come in the form of rants and screeds from myself and other beta testers in the Movie Maker newsgroup.

Publisher's Acknowledgments

We're proud of this book; please register your comments through our IDG Books Worldwide Online Registration Form located at http://my2cents.dummies.com.

Some of the people who helped bring this book to market include the following:

Acquisitions, Editorial, and Media Development

Project Editor: Susan Christophersen

Acquisitions Editor: Ed Adams

Copy Editor: Susan Christophersen

Proof Editor: Teresa Artman

Technical Editor: Buddy Morel

Editorial Manager: Constance Carlisle

Production

Senior Project Coordinator: Regina Snyder

Layout and Graphics: Brian Drumm, LeAndra Johnson, Barry Offringa, Tracy K. Oliver, Erin Zeltner

Proofreaders: Laura Albert, Marianne Santy, Toni Settle, York Production Services, Inc.

Indexer: York Production Services, Inc.

General and Administrative

IDG Books Worldwide, Inc.: John Kilcullen, CEO

IDG Books Technology Publishing Group: Richard Swadley, Senior Vice President and Publisher; Walter R. Bruce III, Vice President and Publisher; Joseph Wikert, Vice President and Publisher; Mary Bednarek, Vice President and Director, Product Development; Andy Cummings, Publishing Director, General User Group; Mary C. Corder, Editorial Director; Barry Pruett, Publishing Director

IDG Books Consumer Publishing Group: Roland Elgey, Senior Vice President and Publisher; Kathleen A. Welton, Vice President and Publisher; Kevin Thornton, Acquisitions Manager; Kristin A. Cocks, Editorial Director

IDG Books Internet Publishing Group: Brenda McLaughlin, Senior Vice President and Publisher; Sofia Marchant, Online Marketing Manager

IDG Books Production for Branded Press: Debbie Stailey, Director of Production; Cindy L. Phipps, Manager of Project Coordination, Production Proofreading, and Indexing; Tony Augsburger, Manager of Prepress, Reprints, and Systems; Shelley Lea, Supervisor of Graphics and Design; Debbie J. Gates, Production Systems Specialist; Steve Arany, Associate Automation Supervisor; Robert Springer, Supervisor of Proofreading; Trudy Coler, Page Layout Manager; Kathie Schutte, Senior Page Layout Supervisor; Janet Seib, Associate Page Layout Supervisor; Michael Sullivan, Production Supervisor

Packaging and Book Design: Patty Page, Manager, Promotions Marketing

◆

The publisher would like to give special thanks to Patrick J. McGovern, without whom this book would not have been possible.

◆

Contents at a Glance

Cartoons at a Glance

By Rich Tennant

page 7

page 103

page 45

page 247

page 181

Fax: 978-546-7747

E-mail: richtennant@the5thwave.com

World Wide Web: www.the5thwave.com

Table of Contents

Part V: The Part of Tens *247*

Chapter 19: Ten Movie Maker Film Projects *249*

Chapter 20: Ten Tips from a Pro Videographer *261*

Introduction

- -

*I*s film dead? Have mega-budget Hollywood blockbusters stifled the movie-making art, banishing the independent filmmaker deeper into the recesses of obscurity? Or is the realm of small-screen movie making on the verge of a creative boom, as high-tech video cameras and video-editing tools become affordable and more accessible? I believe the latter to be the case.

To date, two major revolutions have occurred in personal video production:

- ✔ In the 1950s, motion-picture cameras became widely available, putting the possibility of home movies into the hands of the average consumer.

- ✔ In the 1970s, videotape recorders and cameras meant that consumers could easily record sound and video together. No special film processing was required, tapes were cheap and could be reused many times, and all that was needed to watch the movie was a television set.

Today we stand on the crest of a third great revolution in personal video. Personal computers have become widespread and have finally become powerful enough to handle the demands of video editing. With your modern PC and a digital camcorder, you can quickly and easily edit the video you shoot; and, with Internet access, you can share your videos almost instantaneously with distant friends, relatives, and associates. The bar for personal video quality has been raised.

Why This Book?

Windows Movie Maker is the latest entry into the field of PC video-editing software. It comes free with Windows Millennium Edition (Windows Me). Movie Maker differs substantially from other video-editing programs in two significant ways:

- ✔ Movie Maker is generally simpler.
- ✔ The program places an emphasis on sharing videos online.

Microsoft Windows Movie Maker For Dummies is your no-nonsense guide to this exciting new program. The book includes detailed yet easy-to-follow instructions on performing every task that Windows Movie Maker can perform. I've left no feature uncovered. In the pages that follow, you'll find step-by-step instructions, pictures, tips, and ideas to help you create the best possible movies using your digital camcorder. And if you don't have a digital camcorder yet, that's okay, too. I show you how to use other kinds of cameras with Movie Maker, and even how to make movies when you have no camera at all.

In case you have trouble with the Movie Maker program, this book shows you how to solve or avoid those problems in a candid and straightforward way that Microsoft's own documentation simply won't do.

But that's not all! This book is more than just a manual for using Windows Movie Maker. It contains instructions to help you complete the movie-making process. I show you how to publish your movies on the Internet and even create a simple Web page to serve as your online screening room. You can also find out how to distribute your movies in other ways, such as on video-tapes or compact discs.

If you need some help with your photographic skills, *Microsoft Windows Movie Maker For Dummies* is here for you. I've brought in professional videographer and cinematographer Billy O'Drobinak to show you what to do and what not to do when you're using your digital camcorder. Billy has been shooting film and video for a long time and has served as camera operator on such movies as *Starship Troopers*, *Bowfinger*, *The Parent Trap*, and *Austin Powers: The Spy Who Shagged Me*.

If you're just getting started with editing your own videos, Windows Movie Maker may be your most important tool. And *Microsoft Windows Movie Maker For Dummies* is your ultimate guide to both the program and the entire video production experience!

Foolish Assumptions

We've all heard the old saying about what happens when we assume things, but sometimes a few basic assumptions are necessary. Here are a few that I have made about you:

- ✔ You're no dummy. You just want to learn how to make great movies without a lot of fuss and technical hoops to jump through.
- ✔ You have a computer running Windows Me and your computer meets the minimum system requirements for using Movie Maker (see Chapter 3 to find out what those requirements are).
- ✔ You are reasonably familiar with Windows 95 or later.

✓ You think movies are cool and can't wait to create your own and share them with whoever cares to watch.

✓ You're not ready to go professional just yet. Video editing is a new thing for you.

If this sounds like you, congratulations! You're reading the right book!

Conventions Used in This Book

Microsoft Windows Movie Maker For Dummies can answer just about any question you may have about Windows Movie Maker. It serves as a comprehensive reference to this program, and because Movie Maker is a computer program, you will find that this book is a bit different from other kinds of texts you have read. The following are some unusual conventions that you will encounter in this book:

✓ Filenames or lines of computer code look like THIS or this. This style of print usually indicates something you should type in exactly as you see it in the book. (Occasionally you'll find text in **bold**, which also indicates something to type exactly as it appears.) The only "code" you will find in this book is HTML, and most of that can be found in Chapter 16.

✓ Internet addresses look something like this: www.dummies.com. Notice that I've left the http:// part off the address, because you never actually need to type it in your Web browser anymore.

✓ I frequently instruct you to access commands from the menu bar in Movie Maker and other programs. The menu bar is that strip that lives along the top of the Movie Maker program window and includes menus called File, Edit, View, Clip, Play, and Help. When I'm telling you to access the Save command in the File menu, for example, the sequence appears like this: File⇨Save.

✓ You'll be using your mouse a lot. Sometimes you're asked to click something to select it. This means that you should click *once* on whatever it is you are supposed to click, with the *left* mouse button. Other times, you're asked to *double-click* something; again, you double-click with the *left* mouse button. Finally, I'm a big fan of *shortcut* menus (also called *context* menus by some people), so you'll often see instructions to right-click something. If you are told to right-click something, click *once* with the *right* mouse button.

How This Book Is Organized

If you saw my desk, you would find it hard to believe that I even know what the word "organized" means. But, sure enough, there is a certain order to things in this book as described hence.

Part I: Lights, Camera . . .

Movie making is more than just pointing the camcorder in the general direction of your subject and pressing the Record button. A bit of preparation beforehand will make your movies far better, and Part I helps you prepare. You begin by touring the Movie Maker program and getting familiar with its tools and basic features. Next I give you some pointers for shooting better video, followed by some things you can do to ensure that Movie Maker and the rest of your computer is ready to edit your video.

Part II: Action!

Can you guess where this is going? Here you find out how to use Movie Maker to record video from cameras attached to your computer and other video devices. You see how to import video from other electronic video files and from your digital camcorder. Audio recordings get their own chapter, as do still images. Still graphics have many uses in your movie projects, and you can even use Movie Maker to create slideshows using nothing but stills.

Part III: Cut!

After you've imported, recorded, pushed, and pulled source material into your computer and Windows Movie Maker, it's time to get down and dirty with editing. You see how to trim video clips, join them together into a movie, change your mind and take them out again, and maybe add a soundtrack. In case some of your video doesn't turn out quite as nicely as you hope, I show you what you can do (and what you can't) in Movie Maker to fix it. And to give your movies that professional, finished look, you use Microsoft Paint — another tool that comes free with Windows Me — to create title screens to show the title of your movie and give credit to the people who helped create it.

Part IV: And the Award Goes to . . .

You may think that after you've edited your movie project, all the work is done, but you would be wrong. Next you need to make a final review to make sure that everything is just right; then, you need to distribute it. I show you how to create a basic Web page to link to your movies, how and where to upload the movie, and how to send out movies via e-mail (there's more to it than you might think). And in case you want to record your movie onto a videotape or CD, I cover that, too.

Part V: The Part of Tens

Everyone loves a Top Ten list, right? Well, this part is full of them. I provide a top ten list of Movie Maker project ideas, ten useful online resources, ten software tools (other than Movie Maker) that you'll want to have handy, and almost-but-not-quite ten special effects. Also, of course, this part includes ten tips from pro videographer Billy O'Drobinak. Even if you've been shooting video for a while, Billy can surely show you a trick or two to make your video even better.

Appendix

Making movies requires more than just software; you need some pretty high-tech hardware as well. The appendix shows you how to choose, install, and use many of the devices you need in your personal movie studio, including digital camcorders, FireWire cards, TV tuner cards, microphones, and more.

Icons Used in This Book

Occasionally, you find some icons in the margins of this book. The text next to these icons includes information and tips that deserve special interest, and some warn you of potential hazards and pitfall you may encounter. Icons in this book include:

Tips are usually brief instructions or ideas that aren't always documented but that can greatly improve your movies and make your life easier. Tips are among the most valuable tidbits in this book.

Heed warnings carefully. Some warn of things that may merely inconvenience you, whereas others tell you when a wrong move may cause expensive and painful damage to your equipment or person.

Computer books are often stuffed with yards of techno babble, and if it's sprinkled everywhere, this stuff can make the whole book a drag and just plain difficult to read. As much as possible, I try to pull some of the deeply technical stuff out into these icons. This way, the information is easy to find if you need it, and just as easy to skip if you already have a headache.

The topic of discussion in a computer book often turns lengthy and runs off on some tangent that is only vaguely relevant to the current subject. Try as I may to avoid rambling on so, it happens. Don't get me wrong; everything in this book is useful and you'll be hanging on every word. But if I ever run off on a tangent in an attempt to give you "extra" information and it is not techno babble, you see this icon.

Windows Movie Maker isn't perfect. It has a few bugs and minor aggravations that myself and other testers have identified. If you're likely to encounter one of these annoyances, you may see this icon. This icon helps reassure you that you're not alone, and whenever possible, I provide information for getting around the problem. By the way, these are the kinds of things you're not likely to find in Microsoft's own documentation.

I wish I could cover everything in one book, but I can't. A Dummies Plug icon points you to another book that can help you out if you want more information on a subject.

Where to Go From Here

You are about to enter the mad world of video production. Exciting, isn't it? We stand at the dawn of a new revolution in personal video production, and you are at the very forefront of it. Now you're ready to begin. If you still need to set up your movie studio or need some equipment, I suggest that you start off with Appendix A, *Equipping Your Movie Maker Studio*. Otherwise, you should go ahead and familiarize yourself with Windows Movie Maker, beginning with Chapter 1.

Part I
Lights, Camera . . .

The 5th Wave   By Rich Tennant

"I'VE GOT SOME IMAGE EDITING SOFTWARE, SO I TOOK THE LIBERTY OF ERASING SOME OF THE SMUDGES THAT KEPT SHOWING UP AROUND THE CLOUDS. NO NEED TO THANK ME."

In this part . . .

This is your big chance to be in pictures! The chapters in this part introduce you to Windows Movie Maker, show you how to shoot better video, and help you pre-pare Movie Maker and the rest of your computer for some movie magic!

Chapter 1

Making Your Way Around in Movie Maker

· ·

In This Chapter

▶ Launching Movie Maker

▶ Getting to know Movie Maker

▶ Customizing the program

▶ Closing Movie Maker

· ·

omputers are cool, no doubt about it. With a personal computer, you can play games, browse the Internet, type memos, design a personal rocket-propulsion system, edit home movies, and figure out how much you owe in taxes. Well, okay, maybe paying taxes isn't so cool, but you've got to admit that being able to edit home movies on your PC is swell.

Today the PC is indispensable to filmmakers, and thanks to programs such as Windows Movie Maker, it can be pretty useful to you, too. In fact, with your modern PC, you have more computing power at your fingertips than did the makers of *Gone With the Wind, 2001: A Space Odyssey,* and *Star Wars* combined. But first you have to know your way around the program. This chapter helps you get up and running with Windows Movie Maker so that you'll be prepared to make some movie magic of your own.

Launching Movie Maker

If you already have Windows Millennium Edition installed on your computer, Movie Maker should be ready to go. Yes? No? Not sure? No biggie; it's easy to check.

1. **Click the Windows Start button to open the Start menu.**

2. **Move the mouse pointer over Programs, and in the Programs menu, choose Accessories.**

You should see Windows Movie Maker listed in the Accessories menu, as shown in Figure 1-1.

3. **Click the listing for Windows Movie Maker.**

The program should open.

The first time you launch Movie Maker, you should see a Movie Maker Tour window. The tour shows you the various features in Movie Maker and even provides some brief tutorials on performing a few tasks. Click Exit in the lower-right corner of the tour window to close it. If you didn't see the tour or want to review it again later, simply choose Help⇨Tour.

Don't like the Start menu? Create a shortcut!

If you can't find a program in the Windows Start menu, it probably isn't installed on your computer. The Start menu is handy, organizing all your programs into logical little menus and submenus, alphabetized and categorized to make each item easy to find.

Click to open the progam.

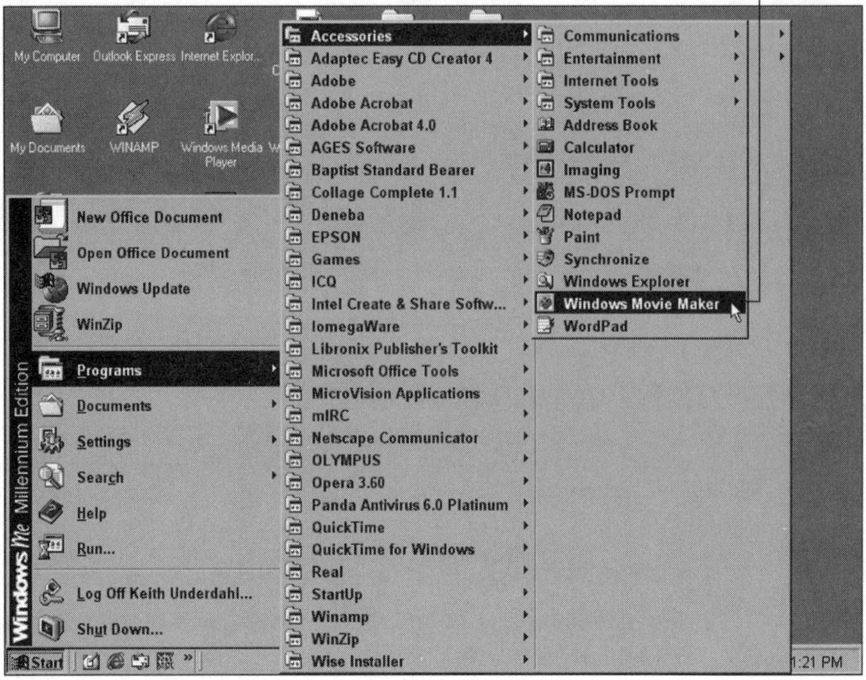

Figure 1-1: Windows Movie Maker can be found in the Accessories menu.

You want to use Movie Maker on a what?

If you plan to use Windows Movie Maker a lot, you should make sure that your computer meets the minimum system requirements for using the program. They are as follows:

✔ Pentium II processor — 300mHz or faster

✔ 64MB (megabytes) of system memory (RAM)

✔ 2GB (gigabytes) of free space on your hard drive

These are Microsoft's recommendations, of course, but I have installed and used Windows Movie Maker on lesser systems. The slowest system I tried it on was running a Cyrix 6x86 PR-200 processor, which is roughly equivelant to a 200mHz Pentium. The program worked, but barely. Not surprisingly, Movie Maker likes fast processors and lots of RAM. To avoid frustration, don't bother with a lot of video editing on a system that doesn't meet Microsoft's minimum recommendations.

But other than being handy and useful, the Start menu is a bit of a pain, especially if you use a program hidden within it frequently. Are you the kind of PC user who prefers to open your favorite programs by double-clicking an icon on the Windows desktop? It would be nice if there was a desktop icon for Movie Maker, huh? Fortunately, you can quickly create your own by following these steps:

1. **Open the Start menu as if you were going to launch Movie Maker the old-fashioned way.**

2. **In the Start menu, choose Programs⇨Accessories to display the Accessories menu.**

3. **Wait! Don't click Windows Movie Maker yet; instead, *right*-click Windows Movie Maker to display the shortcut menu, shown in Figure 1-2.**

4. **Choose Send To from the menu.**

   A submenu appears.

5. **Choose Desktop from the submenu.**

   The Start menu and all its related submenus disappears and a new shortcut for Windows Movie Maker appears on your desktop.

Now you have a new icon on your desktop called Windows Movie Maker. To open Movie Maker, all you have to do is double-click it. You can drag the icon around the desktop to place it wherever you want.

Figure 1-2:
Choose
Sent To
from this
menu.

Open
Add to Zip
Add to Moviemk.zip
Panda Antivirus
Send To ▶
Cut
Copy
Create Shortcut
Delete
Rename
Sort by Name
Properties

A quick way to neatly arrange all the icons on your Windows desktop is to right-click a blank area of the desktop and choose Arrange Icons⇨By Name (or choose another arrangement option if you wish). Doing this lines up all the icons in whatever order you choose.

Create a desktop archive for your projects

If you prefer to organize the stuff on your computer using the Windows desktop, you may want to create an archive for your Movie Maker projects and clips on the desktop, too. You do this by creating a new desktop folder. Just follow these steps:

1. **Right-click an empty area of the Windows desktop.**

   A shortcut menu (also called *context menu*) should appear.

2. **In the shortcut menu, choose New⇨Folder.**

   A new folder icon appears on the desktop and is called — what else? — New Folder.

3. **Type a more descriptive name, such as** Movies **or something.**

   You can always rename a desktop folder by right-clicking it and choosing Rename from the shortcut menu.

Using a desktop folder as your film archive makes it easy to re-open projects without having to dig through a bunch of folders and menus. To do so, just double-click the desktop folder to open it and then double-click a project listed there.

Save projects in your desktop archive

A desktop film archive isn't too handy if you don't actually save your film projects there. When you save a project in Movie Maker, the default folder that the program wants to use is called My Movies and it's located in the My Documents folder. But if you want to save the project in a desktop folder, try this:

1. **In Movie Maker, click File⇨Save As.**

   This action opens the Save Project dialog box, shown in Figure 1-3.

Figure 1-3:
Locate the desktop folder that will serve as your film archive.

2. **In the Save In list on the left side of the dialog box, click Desktop.**

   The contents of your Windows desktop should appear to the right.

3. **Double-click the desktop folder where you want to save the project.**

4. **When the folder opens, name the project in the File Name box and click Save.**

   The project is saved in your desktop archive.

Tooling Around in Movie Maker

Windows Movie Maker is jam-packed with handy tools to help you make better movies. But that knowledge doesn't do you much good if you can't figure out what's what in the program window. The following steps give you a tour. Open Windows Movie Maker so that you see a window similar to that shown in Figure 1-4.

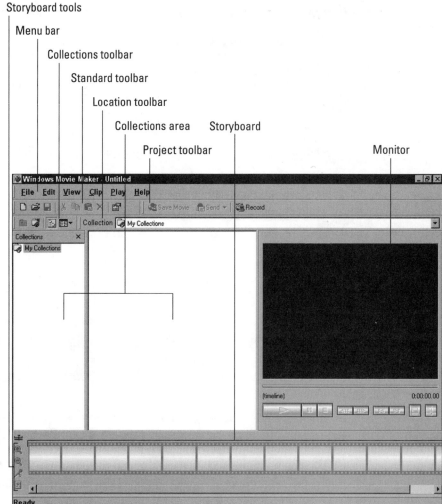

Storyboard tools

Menu bar

Collections toolbar

Standard toolbar

Location toolbar

Collections area   Storyboard

Project toolbar   Monitor

Figure 1-4:
Knowing
your way
around the
Movie
Maker
window is
critical to
using the
program.

1. **Click a menu name in the menu bar.**

   A menu containing various program tools and options should open. Press the Esc key on your keyboard to close the menu.

2. **Move your mouse pointer over some of the tools on the Standard toolbar.**

   A small identifying label, called a *ToolTip*, should appear when you hold the pointer still over a button. ToolTips describe the purpose of the button you are pointing at.

3. **Now hover over the tools on the Project toolbar.**

   These tools let you record a clip or save or send a movie. The buttons on the Project toolbar are self-explanatory, so you won't see any ToolTips appear over them.

4. **Hover the mouse over the Collections toolbar.**

   The Collections toolbar helps you manage your collections of sound and video clips.

5. **Click My Collections in the list on the left side of the Collections area.**

   When you create new collections, they are listed below My Collections. The Location toolbar tells you which collection folder is currently displayed.

6. **Hover the mouse pointer over the controls in the Monitor.**

   Notice that these controls are similar to those used on a VCR.

7. **Finally, hover the pointer over the Storyboard controls to the left of the Storyboard.**

   The Storyboard is where you arrange clips and modify them, and the controls let you change the view of the Storyboard.

Does your Movie Maker window look different from the one shown in Figure 1-4? If the Storyboard is missing, you probably have your screen area set at 640 x 480 pixels. To view the entire Movie Maker window, you really need to work with a screen area of 800 x 600 pixels or greater. Use the Display tool in the Windows Control Panel to adjust your screen area.

Customizing the Program

One of the really great things about Windows programs is that almost all of them can be bent, folded, stapled, and mutilated into virtually any shape and form you want. Yes, you can also change the way Windows Movie Maker looks, but for now, take a look at ways you can change the way it *works*.

Start by opening the Options dialog box. Open Movie Maker if it isn't already, and on the menu bar, click View⇨Options. You should see an Options dialog box similar to that shown in Figure 1-5.

The first thing you see in the dialog box is someone's name — yours, I hope. If it's not yours, feel free to change the name so that you get proper director credit for your clips and movies.

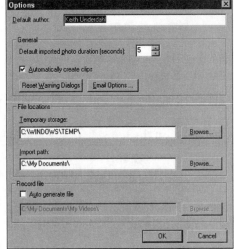

Figure 1-5:
The Options
dialog box
lets you
change
important
program
settings.

Below the director's name is the General options section. Specify how long you want still images to "play" in your movies, specify whether you want Movie Maker to automatically create clips from movies that are played, and reset the various program warning dialog boxes.

I suggest that you leave the Automatically create clips option checked. With this option selected, Movie Maker creates a new clip every time it detects a new scene in a movie. Separating clips in this manner makes it easier for you to use and edit the clips later on.

The E-mail Options button doesn't actually lead to much in the way of options. If you have more than one e-mail program installed, you can specify which one you use for e-mailing movies here. The default setting is (surprise) your default e-mail program.

At the bottom of the Options dialog is a section called Record File. If you want Movie Maker to automatically generate and save a file every time you record, place a check mark next to "Auto generate file" and choose a path underneath. I suggest that you leave this option unchecked for now.

Telling Movie Maker where to store your clips

The Options dialog box (click View➪Options to see it) contains a section that lets you specify a default location where your clips and related Movie Maker files are stored. The default Temporary directory is C:\WINDOWS\TEMP\, and this is where files are temporarily stored as you record and edit.

C:\WINDOWS\TEMP\ is a good place to store files as you record, as long as you have a lot of free space on your C drive. By "a lot," I mean at least a few gigabytes of unused space. More free space is always an Official Good Thing because video eats up gigabytes like there's no tomorrow, and the more free space you have, the more video you can capture. If you have a second or third hard drive with more space, consider using it for your Temporary directory by clicking Browse and navigating to it.

The Import Path is the location where Movie Maker imports video files from when you open the program. This should be the folder that you work out of the most, and again, it should be located on a hard drive that has a lot of free space. If you want to use a folder other than the one specified — say, a desktop film archive that you created on the Windows desktop — click Browse and navigate to the folder. A desktop folder can be found in the C:\ WINDOWS\Desktop directory.

Avoid using network drives to store your Movie Maker files. Data traveling over your network moves slower than molasses in January, resulting in poor performance as you attempt to import and edit video over the network. If you really need external storage space, consider an external hard drive that runs on an IDE, SCSI, or IEEE-1394 bus.

Resizing the Movie Maker window

So you say you don't want Movie Maker to take up your whole screen? You can reduce the size of it, but this solution has limitations. Movie Maker has a built-in minimum size that keeps all the program tools in view. If, for instance, you want to make the window shorter, you won't be able to change it at the expense of pushing the Storyboard out of view.

To see what I mean, try this:

1. **In the upper-right corner of the Movie Maker window, click the Restore button (it's just to the left of the Close button).**

   The window shrinks a bit so that it no longer takes up the whole screen.

2. **Hover the mouse pointer over a window border so that it becomes a double-headed arrow.**

3. **Click and hold the left mouse button and drag the window to a new size.**

   If you hold the mouse pointer over a corner, you should be able to adjust two borders at one time.

4. **Release the mouse button when you have reached the desired new size.**

5. **To make Movie Maker fill the whole screen again, click the Maximize button in the upper-right corner (the Restore button turned into the Maximize button).**

6. **To temporarily hide the Movie Maker window altogether, click the Minimize button to the left of the Restore/Maximize button.**

   Movie Maker disappears, but it should still be shown on the Windows taskbar at the bottom of the screen. Click it there to view the program again.

If your screen area is set at 800 x 600 pixels or less, you probably won't be able to shrink the height of the Movie Maker window at all. The higher your screen area settings, the more you will be able to shrink Movie Maker. If you want to experiment with different screen area settings, use the Display icon in the Windows Control Panel.

Hiding and displaying components

If you find that you never use some parts of the Movie Maker window, you can get rid of them to make more room for the parts you actually do use. You control the various screen elements using the View menu on the menu bar. Click View and then hold the mouse pointer over Toolbars. You should see a list of the toolbars, each with a check mark next to it. If you click one of the toolbar names to remove the check mark, the related toolbar disappears. AHH!! Where did it go? Don't worry, just click View⇨Toolbars and click the toolbar name again to return it to view.

Take a look at the rest of the View menu. Notice that each of the various screen elements, such as the Collections list and Storyboard, are listed. The ones that are currently displayed should have their little icon depressed in the menu. You can click items in this menu to toggle them on or off.

You can also change the way that clips are displayed in the Collections area. You have three basic display options:

- **List:** Clips and Collections are displayed in a basic list with small icons. This view is best if you want to see the most possible clips without scrolling down.

- **Details:** A single-column list displays the name of each clip, the director, the date it was created, the rating, a description, the source path for the clip, and the length of the clip along with start and end times if it was taken from a movie. You may have to scroll left or right to see all the detail columns.

> ✔ **Thumbnails:** Large icons are used, each showing a small "thumbnail" sample of the clip. The picture will actually be the first frame of the clip. This view takes up a lot of screen space but makes finding a desired clip easier.

Another view option to take note of is the ability to toggle the bottom area of the screen — also called the Workspace — between the Storyboard and Timeline. The Storyboard and Timeline let you control different aspects of a project's playback.

Closing Movie Maker

When you are done touring the Movie Maker window, close it just as you would any other Windows program by clicking the Close (X) button in the upper-right corner of the screen. If you've been working on projects or clips, you should be prompted to save your work before exiting the program.

If you like menus, you can also close Movie Maker by choosing File⇨Exit from the menu bar.

Chapter 2

Photography Primer

● ●

In This Chapter

▶ Composing your scene and preparing your subjects

▶ Working with tripods

▶ Lighting your scenes

▶ Shooting moving subjects

▶ Dealing with poor situations

● ●

*W*indows Movie Maker is a pretty amazing tool, but there is only so much that it can do to help you make great movies. Many things affect the quality of your video, beginning with the way you hold the camera. If you shoot video that is too dark or distorted, or has the camera wiggling too much, no amount of editing in Movie Maker or any other program will help. By following a few simple rules of videography, you can shoot better video for all your movie projects.

In addition to the great stuff you'll find here, you can find more videography wisdom in Chapter 20, *Ten Tips from a Pro Videographer*.

Composing Your Scene

Everyone wants the best possible view at an event, including you and your camera. But positioning your camera can be tricky because camcorders just don't adapt very well. Sure, modern digital camcorders are technological wonders compared to the bulky, low-tech cameras of just a few years ago, but they still can't come close to the human eye's ability to adjust to varying light levels, harsh climates, and the really tall person sitting right in front of you.

When you are choosing a spot to photograph from, ask yourself several important questions about the scene:

✔ **Where is most of the light coming from?** If you are outdoors, avoid shooting in the direction of the sun. Also, be aware that shadows that you hardly notice with your eye will be intensified on video. Diffused light from all directions is best, and try not to let any strong light sources (such as a light bulb or the sun) shine directly on your lens.

✔ **Is anyone likely to walk in front of the camera?** Try to position the camera higher than passing foot traffic, or use an assistant to keep people out of the way.

✔ **Should I be using a tripod?** Tripods provide smoother video, and I recommend that you use one whenever possible. If the tripod is going to be a trip hazard for you and other passers-by, keep the legs folded in and use it like a monopod (you'll have to hold onto it, of course).

✔ **What kind of sound will I record?** You probably plan to use the microphone built into the camcorder. Will it be able to record the sound of your child's choir concert, or will it pick up only the distracting chatter of other audience members? Consider getting an external microphone with a long cable for use when you can't get the camcorder close enough to record good audio. Finally, be wary of loud ambient noise sources in the background, such as roadways, waterfalls, and large crowds.

Note: Don't take this personally, but the person holding the camera can be an annoying source of sound as well. If you are relying on the microphone mounted to the camcorder, anything the videographer says will be significantly louder than anything else. So, either use an external microphone or turn the personal volume level down a bit, okay?

✔ **What's in the background?** It's easy to overlook the background when you're filming a subject, so always take a moment to survey what's back there. Is the background distracting? Can you position your subject in front of something illustrative, such as a sign or landmark? If there is a lot of movement in the background, make it out of focus a bit by shooting closer to your subject (thus shortening your depth of field).

Dressing Your Subjects for Successful Video

If you are filming subjects who are participating in a sporting event or other activity that requires a uniform, you won't have much (or any) control over the clothing they wear when you film them. However, if you *do* have some control, here are some fashion tips for the people who will appear in your video:

✔ **Avoid stripes or other clothing patterns with a lot of parallel lines.** These often cause waviness and distortion called moiré patterns in your video.

✔ **Limit intense colors, such as red or bright blue.** Some very bright colors may bleed into other areas of the video, or your camera may compensate incorrectly.

✔ **Choose colors that differ somewhat from the background.** A dark-gray shirt jacket tends to blend in with a dark-gray background and cause your subject to get somewhat "lost."

Tripods: Friend or Foe?

Virtually all digital camcorders today have a built-in image-stabilization feature that helps make your video image appear more stable. Unfortunately, these features simply can't compensate for all the movement that occurs when you hold the camera by hand, so I strongly suggest that you use a tripod whenever possible.

Practice using your tripod so that you can set it up quickly and use it properly when you are filming. If you plan to pan across a scene by swiveling your camera on the tripod, make sure that the adjustment screws are loose enough that you can pan the camera smoothly.

If you are panning across a scene while recording, start panning slowly, speed up in the middle of the pan, and slow down again before you stop.

One of the benefits of using a tripod that isn't often mentioned is that it can help you get yourself into more of your video. How many hours of video have you shot of your family, yet you don't actually appear in any of it? Sometimes you can ask others to shoot some video for you, but sometimes you can't.

Certainly, sometimes a tripod may not be desirable:

✔ In busy, crowded environments, someone is likely to kick or bump the tripod. This causes a very unsettling series of shakes and shimmies in what may be an otherwise smooth video picture.

✔ If you are trying to suggest motion or movement with the video, you probably don't want to bother with a tripod. For instance, you may shoot some video that is meant to depict your dog's view of the backyard as he wanders from tree to tree. In this case, you would probably want to walk quickly along while holding the camera close to the ground below waist-level.

✔ Thinking about making your own *Blair Witch* spoof? Leave the tripod at home, but please do try to remember to bring a map.

> ✔ Sometimes you need to be able to move quickly so that you can get out of the way of approaching subjects or reposition the camera. A tripod can be too much of a hindrance in these situations, but a *monopod* (which is like a tripod, but has only one leg) may be perfect.
>
> ✔ If the "floor" is not stable — say, in a moving car or van — the tripod may transmit every road shock or vehicle movement to the camera.

When you go shopping for a tripod, get one that includes a quick-release mechanism for the camera. This feature allows you to quickly switch the camera between the tripod and your hand.

Let There Be Light!

Light can be your greatest ally or your worst enemy. Pro videographers tell you that you want soft, diffuse light with just the right amount of contrast. What does that mean, in English?

Perhaps the best way to define "soft, diffuse light" is to explain what it isn't. Imagine your subject sitting in the middle of a dark room and you're shining a bright spotlight directly in his or her face. This kind of light is neither soft nor diffuse. *Soft* light should not be too intense or bright. If the light source reflects off your subject's cheek, it's probably too bright.

Diffuse means that the light is spread out and seemingly everywhere. Many household lamps face up so that their light is reflected from the white ceiling, thus *diffusing* the light throughout the room. If you are lighting a scene, try to position light sources so that the light is reflected around the room rather than focused just on the spot where you will be shooting.

Now all you need is the right amount of contrast. One way to diffuse light is to reflect it with white surfaces or even mirrors. But if too much light is on your subject, especially if your subject is a person, features can wash out because not enough shadow exists to provide contrast. Monitor shadows — especially those cast across facial features — using your camcorder's viewfinder, and try to balance the shadows out before you begin recording.

Compensating for backlit subjects

Sometimes the major light source in a scene is behind your subject rather than you and there is nothing you can do about it. This situation is called *backlighting* because the main light source is in the background.

Consider Figure 2-1, which shows some video I shot of Mount Rushmore in South Dakota. This video was shot in the evening because that is when we arrived at the mountain. Unfortunately, the mountain faces east, and when I arrived on the scene, the sun was almost directly behind it. The sky directly behind the mountain was so bright that the mountain itself looked like a big, black blob. I basically had three options:

- ✔ Wait until morning when the sun would be at my back, illuminating the mountain.
- ✔ Take advantage of backlighting to compose dramatic scenes in which the subject is washed out into a silhouette by the light behind.
- ✔ Deal with the situation and try to compensate for the backlighting.

Figure 2-1:
This clip of Mount Rushmore was shot in an extremely backlit situation. The operator wasn't holding the camera very straight, either.

Many camcorders have a control that allows you to compensate for backlighting. The backlighting control automatically increases the exposure setting so that the backlit object shows up a little better. Looking at Figure 2-2, you can see that I have adjusted for backlighting while filming Mount Rushmore.

As you can see in the figure, details are much easier to pick up from the mountain now. Unfortunately, the sky is overexposed and the mountain, although better, still is not as colorful and brilliant as I would like. Backlight compensators can help only so much. If I had really wanted a better picture of Mount Rushmore, I would have had to wait until morning.

Figure 2-2:
I have compensated for the backlighting situation at Mount Rushmore.

Dealing with improper colors

Your camcorder automatically focuses for you, adjusts lighting exposures, and even helps soften some of your movements when you hand-hold the camera. Did you know that your camcorder is also constantly adjusting color balance and levels?

Different lighting situations have different effects on colors. For instance, if you are in a room lit by incandescent light bulbs, the warm light output by those bulbs creates a slight orange tint in your video. Likewise, fluorescent light casts a slight greenish hue on everything. Daylight is usually the "whitest" lighting situation, but even that is not perfect.

If you aren't happy with the way your camcorder is picking up colors, try adjusting the white balance. Digital camcorders usually adjust white balance automatically, so all you should have to do is the following:

1. **Find a piece of blank, white paper.**

   The kind in your printer or copy machine will work, but make sure that it's really, really white.

2. **Turn on your camcorder in the room or setting where you intend to film.**

   If necessary, adjust the current lighting to where it will be when you begin filming.

3. **Begin recording but immediately press Pause.**

   The camcorder should now be in Record mode but the tape should not be rolling.

4. **With recording paused, hold the white sheet of paper in front of the lens so that it fills the viewfinder.**

After several seconds, the camcorder should reset itself and balance its levels based on your white balance test.

Try to carry a clean sheet of paper with you everywhere you go. If it's handy, you are more likely to use it to set white balance every time you prepare to record.

Keeping Up with Moving Subjects

Filming moving subjects may be a bit tricky but is possible nonetheless. You'll almost inevitably end up shooting some moving subjects, so the following sections look at a few common problems and explore the solutions.

Keeping your subject in view

Keeping a moving subject in view can be difficult. This is especially true if you are shooting a distant subject and have zoomed in to get a better view. Looking at Figure 2-3, you can see that some of the action is being missed because I have zoomed in too much. It is not even clear what is happening on-screen, and as the action moves off-screen, viewers crane their heads to see around the picture tube to get a better view.

Figure 2-3: If you zoom in too close, you may miss some of the action.

Unfortunately, the best solution is usually to zoom out a bit (or physically back up if you can't zoom out). When you are shooting action, having unused space at the edges of the screen is usually more acceptable, especially if this space allows you to see more of the subject. You'll just have to accept the fact that you aren't going to capture every grimace and detail. As shown in Figure 2-4, I have improved the view of my own action movie by zooming out.

Figure 2-4: Zooming out a bit has helped tremendously. At least viewers can see that the subjects are flying in an airplane.

Panning smoothly with the subject

If you intend to pan with your subject as it moves across the screen, endeavor to do so as smoothly as you can. If possible, mount the camera on your tripod and use the tripod's handle to pan the camera. Also, practice panning to ensure that you won't trip over the tripod or anything else when you record the shot.

When you do pan across a scene, try to keep the subject in the same spot in your viewfinder through the entire shot. In other words, don't pan faster or slower than the subject you are filming.

Here's another Official Good Thing. Limit yourself to one pan per shot. Don't pan with a subject and then quickly pan the camera back to the beginning position while the tape is rolling. This looks very tacky.

Maintaining focus and exposure control

As you film a moving subject, it may move closer to or farther from the camera, and it could move from dark areas into light (or from light into dark). These constant changes confound the little computer chips in your camcorder as it struggles to keep your subject in focus and properly exposed. Poor thing. Inevitably, the camera just can't keep up, resulting in an auto-focus feature that hunts back and forth, with your subjects getting plunged into darkness when a light background suddenly comes into view.

Anticipate this problem and use manual focus and exposure controls on your camera if necessary. It's pretty easy to make some reasonable settings before you make your shot, realizing that you may have to compromise a bit to maintain the overall integrity of the shot.

This doesn't mean that you should always turn off auto-focus and auto-exposure controls when shooting action. If the subject will move along a predictable and steady path, you may want to leave auto focus on but turn off auto exposure. In a situation like the one shown in Figure 2-5, doing this will help keep the subject in focus throughout the shot.

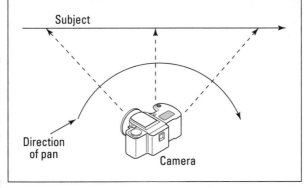

Figure 2-5:
Auto focus can be helpful as you pan across this scene.

The subject starts out far away but gradually the distance between it and the camera decreases. Eventually the *apex* is reached where the depth of field is shortest, and then the distance begins to increase again. This situation is best resolved by the auto-focus feature on your camcorder.

Following moving subjects

Sometimes you may actually want to walk alongside, lead, or trail your subject as he or she walks along. This is one of those rare instances when holding the camera by hand may be preferable. You'll shake and move the camera a bit as you walk, but if it's not too bumpy, the movements will actually add to the sense of motion. Just keep two things in mind:

- ✔ Avoid trailing (walking behind) your subjects as much as possible. Their backsides are usually not all that interesting.

- ✔ Try a practice walkthrough whenever possible. Your eyes will be glued to the camcorder's viewfinder when you are filming, meaning that you won't see the trip hazards, tree branches, and other obstacles in your path.

Holding a camera steadily

Camcorders don't like to stay still. When you hold them in your hand and attempt to shoot video, every bump, wiggle, and vibration of your body is transmitted directly to your video image. Blechh. You can buy some really fancy (that is, expensive) sling systems, and in Chapter 20 I even tell you how to make your own, but the fact is that there is nothing that will completely eliminate all the gyrations that occur when you hand-hold the camera.

Or is there? Well, no, there isn't, but one trick seems to work pretty well for me: Pretend that your camcorder is a bowl of hot tomato soup that you're holding over an expensive, light-colored carpet. Be careful!

Chapter 3

Getting Movie Maker Ready to Perform Movie Magic

• •

• •

*T*he PC industry experts have been peering into their crystal balls for a couple of years now and predicting that "soon" anyone with a personal computer would be able to create and edit top-notch movies on his or her own desktop. Well, seeing as how you are reading this right now, it would appear that "soon" is now.

Can you create and edit top-notch movies on your own desktop? Yes, if you have the right hardware. You also need to make sure that Movie Maker — along with Windows Millennium Edition (Windows Me) — is configured properly and ready to go. This chapter shows you what you need to have and to do to make those great desktop movies.

Is Your Computer Up to Snuff?

We all would have liked to start editing home video on our PCs a long time ago. But until recently, the powerful computer hardware needed to handle digital video has been way too expensive. Now it is only slightly expensive and getting cheaper every day.

Hardware you need

Microsoft's minimum system requirements for using Windows Movie Maker are a little vague; they don't tell you why you need each item or which equipment best meets your needs. Still, they do provide a basic picture of what you need. The following gives you a closer look at the requirements:

- ✔ **Pentium II – 300:** Microsoft recommends that your computer have at least a Pentium II processor running at 300 MHz (megahertz). Movie Maker actually runs on much slower systems, but the movies it creates on slower processors don't turn out very well.

- ✔ **64MB (megabytes) of RAM:** As with all things PC related, when it comes to system memory (RAM), more is better.

- ✔ **Hard drive space:** The party line from Microsoft is that you need 2GB (gigabytes) or more of free hard disk space. This number is pretty arbitrary because the only thing you really need it for is storing digital video files. The more free space you have, the more video you can store.

- ✔ **An audio source:** You actually don't need this unless you plan to record audio at the computer, in which case a microphone hooked up to your sound card should be sufficient.

- ✔ **A video source:** If you want to edit video with Movie Maker, you need to get the video into your computer. This can be a digital camcorder, a digital camera attached to your PC, a TV tuner card, a video capture device, or perhaps even a video file that you downloaded from the Internet.

Hardware you want

Okay, so you have the bare minimum of gear to make use of Movie Maker. You can make simple, low-quality movies with that gear. But if you want to make better films, you want to have:

- ✔ **The fastest processor you can afford:** Movie Maker requires a much faster processor than many other digital video editing programs because it compresses video on-the-fly as you capture it. The nice thing about this on-the-fly compression is that the files are much smaller than those produced by other programs. Unfortunately, it also means that if you have anything less than a 600 MHz Pentium II (or equivalent processor), you may have a hard time capturing acceptable video from a camcorder.

- ✔ **At least 128MB of RAM:** What I said about processors goes for memory, too.

✔ **Digital camcorder:** Good digital camcorders are now available for as little as $650 if you shop around. Modern digital camcorders provide far better image quality than do analog camcorders, and many are packed with features such as image stabilization and exposure controls previously found only in much more expensive units.

✔ **FireWire (IEEE-1394) adapter:** A FireWire adapter card allows you to download video from your digital camcorder quickly and without quality loss. Unlike newer Macintoshes, most Windows PCs don't come with a FireWire adapter pre-installed, so you'll have to buy and install your own.

✔ **A good microphone:** Eventually you'll want to record some narration for your video, and those cheap little microphones that come with most sound cards aren't worth their own weight in polymer.

Where do you store all this stuff?

Video files can gobble up hard disk space faster than even Windows itself. Fortunately, monster-sized hard drives are ridiculously cheap these days, so giving yourself a bit more space is easy on the wallet.

My number-one suggestion for storage: Get a second hard drive that you use exclusively for video storage. Most computers can have more than one hard drive installed, so consider buying a big one (20GB or more) exclusively for digital video storage. Hard disks are so cheap right now that computer retailers seem almost to be giving them away.

Avoid using an external storage device, such as a Zip drive, for Movie Maker files. External storage devices are usually a lot slower than hard drives, meaning that you'll end up with jerky video and poor sound when you try to work with files stored there.

Not all hard drives are created equal

When you buy a hard drive, speed is just as important as sheer capacity. Imagine for a moment that your hard drive is connected to your computer by a straw. No matter how big the drive is, it still has to transfer data to and from the rest of the computer through that straw. Almost everything you do on your computer uses the hard drive, so if your drive's straw is too small, it will bog down the whole system.

Windows Movie Maker uses the hard drive a lot, and if the drive isn't fast enough (that is, the straw is too small) the quality of your movies will suffer. How fast is fast enough for Movie Maker? I suggest that you get a hard drive that can transfer at least 66.6 MB/s *(megabytes per second)*. The 33.3 MB/s hard drives that were common just a year or two ago are not adequate for handling top-quality video.

Not surprisingly, faster hard drives usually cost more. SCSI hard drives are the fastest (transfer rates usually exceed 100 MB/s) but are also the most expensive. Furthermore, a SCSI hard drive must be attached to a special SCSI adapter, and chances are your PC doesn't have one. But if you're running Windows Me, I can virtually guarantee that you have an interface for EIDE hard drives, probably built right into the motherboard. EIDE drives are the cheapest, but you have to be careful to get one that can transfer data at 66.6 MB/s. When you're checking the specs, keep in mind that 66.6 MB/s EIDE drives are usually said to run at 7200 RPM *(revolutions per minute)*.

All the usual disclaimers apply here: If you've never messed around with computer hardware or aren't sure what kind of hard drive you currently have, consult a professional, your PC's documentation, or both. It's a lot easier to ruin delicate computer components and void your warranty than you might realize.

Movie Maker Is Already Installed, But Is It Ready?

Windows Movie Maker is a pretty simple program, but you should still spend a few minutes making sure that everything is set and ready to go before you dive into video editing.

Checking the all-important Options dialog box

Almost every Windows program has a dialog box called Options that contains important (and some not-so-important) program options. Movie Maker is no exception:

1. In Movie Maker, choose <u>V</u>iew⇨<u>O</u>ptions.

The Options dialog box appears, as shown in Figure 3-1. Thankfully, this dialog box has only one tab's worth of options.

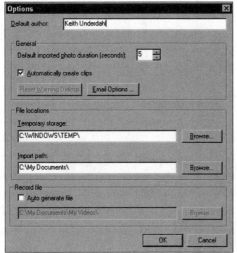

Figure 3-1:
Movie
Maker's
Options
dialog box is
pretty
simple
compared to
some other
Windows
programs.

2. **Make sure that the correct Default Author is listed.**

   This should be you, but if you have a special nickname such as "MovieDawg" or "FilmFreak123," you can enter it here.

3. **Review the default duration for still picture.**

   If you place a still image in a movie, this is the amount of time that picture will be shown. I suggest that you just leave the default value of five seconds, because you can always customize the duration for individual pictures when you create your movies.

4. **Leave the Automatically create clips option checked unless you find this feature really annoying.**

   This subject is covered in greater detail in Chapters 4 and 5.

5. **Review the file locations for Temporary storage and the Import path.**

   It's usually a good idea to leave the temporary storage thing alone, but if you have a special folder that you use just for storing audio and video files, you may want to specify it under Import path. Click Browse and locate the desired folder.

6. **At the bottom of the Options dialog box, decide whether you want Movie Maker to automatically generate a file every time you record some audio or video.**

   This feature can be handy if you record frequently and don't like having to deal with the Save dialog box every single time you record something. If you choose this option (under normal circumstances, I suggest that you don't), specify a folder to save your auto-generated files in.

7. **Click OK when you are done making changes, or click Cancel to close the dialog box and reject any changes that you made.**

If you're returning to Movie Maker after a long absence, or if someone else who uses your computer has already used it a lot, open the Options dialog box and click Reset Warning Dialogs. Doing this ensures that you get the most on-screen help possible as you learn or relearn the program.

Setting e-mail options

When you open Movie Maker's Options dialog box (View➪Options), you'll notice a button that says "E-mail Options." Click it. You should see a small "E-mail Movies" dialog box similar to that shown in Figure 3-2.

Figure 3-2: Movie Maker lets you specify an e-mail program to use when mailing out movies.

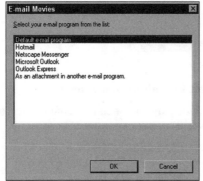

Usually, you're best off leaving Default e-mail program selected here, but if you want to specify one particular e-mail program to use for e-mailing movies, select it here and click OK.

What about other Windows components?

Windows Me comes with a few other programs (sometimes called *applets* because they're like baby versions of bigger applications) that you may find useful:

✔ **Paint:** Paint (see Figure 3-3) allows you to create and edit title slides or just about any other kind of picture you want. It's a fun program for kids to play with, and you may want to include some of their cute artwork with your movies. Or maybe you want to include your own cute artwork; it's up to you. Paint saves pictures in Bitmap (.BMP) format, which you can easily import into Movie Maker as stills. You can find Paint by clicking Start➪Programs➪Accessories➪Paint.

Figure 3-3:
Windows comes with this handy tool that lets you paint pictures for use as stills in your movies.

✔ **Sound Recorder:** Record audio and save it as .WAV files with this simple yet handy tool. Open Sound Recorder by choosing Start⇨Programs⇨Accessories⇨Entertainment⇨Sound Recorder.

✔ **Windows Media Player:** This is the program that you and others will use to watch the movies you create with Movie Maker. Choose Start⇨Programs⇨Windows Media Player to open it, and make sure that you test all your movies before sending them out into the world.

✔ **WordPad:** A mini word processor that you can find by choosing Start⇨Programs⇨Accessories⇨WordPad, this program is a good place to edit text for titles in your movies, which you can then copy-and-paste into the actual title slides that you create in Paint.

Installing a Windows component

If you can't find one of these Windows components, it might not be installed. To install a Windows component, follow these steps:

1. **Place your Windows Me CD into your CD-ROM drive and choose Start⇨Settings⇨Control Panel.**

   The Windows Control Panel opens.

2. **Double-click the Add/Remove Programs icon to open the Add/Remove Programs Properties dialog box.**

3. **Click the Windows Setup tab to bring it to the front, as shown in Figure 3-4.**

Figure 3-4:
Windows
components
can be
installed or
uninstalled
here.

4. **Select a category name, such as Accessories (most Windows components are hidden inside categories), and click Details near the bottom of the dialog box.**

   A dialog box just for that category appears, as shown in Figure 3-5.

Figure 3-5:
Paint is one
of the
components
you'll find
in the
Accessories
category.

5. **To add a component, just place a check mark next to it.**

   Components with a check mark next to them are already installed.

6. **Click OK once to close the category dialog box; click OK again to close the Add/Remove Programs dialog box.**

   Windows installs the components you are adding and probably asks you to insert your Windows Me CD to continue.

Is Your Hardware Supported?

Back in the bad old days, configuring pieces of hardware in Windows was about as easy as starting a fire by rubbing two sticks together. But today, the modern wonder of *Plug-and-Play* hardware brings matches and lighter fluid to the hardware setup process, with little effort required on your part to get everything burning properly. Just install the hardware, turn on the computer, and let Windows Me do the rest.

I have found that, in general, any audio or video devices that works in other Windows programs works in Movie Maker as well. But there is a list of hardware that is "officially" supported by Movie Maker, which you can easily find:

1. **In Windows Movie Maker, choose Help⇨Windows Movie Maker on the Web.**

   Internet Explorer opens to the Windows Movie Maker Web site, as shown in Figure 3-6.

2. **At the top of the window, click Support⇨Knowledge Base.**

   A Knowledge Base Search page opens, allowing you to search Microsoft's database for help on Movie Maker.

3. **Choose Windows Movie Maker from the list of Microsoft products; then, in the last box, enter the question, "What hardware is supported by Windows Movie Maker?"**

   An article or list of articles should appear with an answer to your question.

4. **Close Internet Explorer when you are done.**

Note: As new hardware is tested by Microsoft and support for it is added, updates to Windows Me are made available to you for free downloading. To make sure that you have the latest and greatest version of Windows, choose Start⇨Windows Update periodically and download the updates.

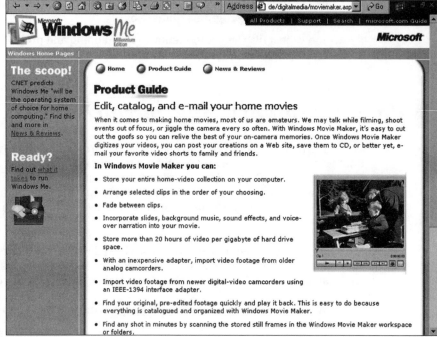

Figure 3-6:
The Windows Movie Maker Web page is your first stop for program information and updates.

Getting Movie Maker to recognize your equipment

If your equipment is supported byMicrosoft for Windows Movie Maker, getting the program to recognize it should be easy. If the device is a camera or microphone attached to a USB (Universal Serial Bus) port, parallel port, serial port, or your sound card, try this:

1. **Turn the power on for the device (if applicable) and then launch Windows Movie Maker.**

2. **Click Record.**

   Movie Maker detects your hardware automatically. However, if you don't turn the device's power on, you may (or may not) see a warning similar to that shown in Figure 3-7. Otherwise, you should see the Record dialog box with your devices listed in the upper-left corner.

3. **If you saw the warning shown in Figure 3-7, click OK to proceed to the Record dialog box.**

Figure 3-7:
You might
see this
warning if
your device
isn't turned
on.

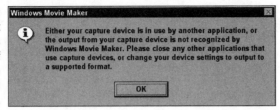

4. **Close the Record dialog box, close Movie Maker, restart Windows, turn on the device, and then start over at Step 1.**

5. **Close the Record dialog box if you don't want to record at this time.**

If you are trying to get Movie Maker to recognize a FireWire (IEEE-1394) device such as a digital camcorder, try this:

1. **Plug the device into a FireWire cable attached to your FireWire adapter and turn the device's power on.**

    After a few seconds, you should see a little dialog box similar to the one shown in Figure 3-8.

Figure 3-8:
You should
see this
dialog box
shortly after
plugging in
a new
FireWire
device for
the first
time.

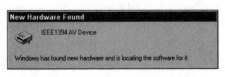

2. **Wait while Windows does some things; then, when Windows appears to be done doing things, open Movie Maker.**

3. **Click Record.**

    The Record dialog box should open and your FireWire device should be listed in the upper-left corner.

4. **Close the Record dialog box if you don't want to record anything right now.**

Restart: The Windows cure-all

A chemist, an electrician, and a programmer were on a road trip together when suddenly their car broke down. The trio mulled over their predicament. "Perhaps we got some bad fuel," suggested the chemist. "Maybe I should try putting some properly formulated gas in the tank."

"No," replied the electrician. "I think the problem is electrical. I should check the spark plug wires."

The chemist and the electrician then turned to the programmer and asked whether he had any bright ideas. The programmer said, "I think we should try getting out of the car and then get back in."

But seriously, as much as Windows has evolved over the years, one thing that has not changed is the fact that simply restarting a program or even your whole computer can cure a cornucopia of PC ailments. This remains true with Movie Maker, especially when it comes time to try to get your hardware to work. If a camera that once worked now does not, check all the obvious things (cables attached, power on, seat backs and tray tables upright and locked, and so on) and then close and re-open the program. If that doesn't solve the problem, restart Windows by closing all open programs and choosing Start➪Shut Down.

What to do if your equipment is unsupported

Companies are always coming out with newer, better things. The digital video market in particular is growing by leaps and bounds, and it's inevitable that some new equipment will appear that Microsoft did not anticipate when it first created Movie Maker.

So, you've bought a camera or some other device that isn't on Microsoft's official list of supported devices. Have you tried to actually use it yet? Go ahead, install the device according to the manufacturer's instructions, open Movie Maker, and try to use it. I have found that many devices that Microsoft does not claim to support work just fine with Movie Maker anyway. If it doesn't work, check the Movie Maker Web site (Help➪Windows Movie Maker on the Web) to see whether drivers for your new hardware have become available from Microsoft.

As a last resort, use the software that came with your hardware. Many digital video devices come with Windows software to help you capture audio and video. Use that software to save the material in a format that can be imported into Movie Maker. Table 3-1 lists audio and video formats that Movie Maker can import.

Table 3-1	File Formats Supported by Movie Maker	
Audio	*Video*	*Still Graphics*
.AIF	.ASF	.BMP
.AIFC	.AVI	.DIB
.AIFF	.MPEG	.GIF
.AU	.MPG	.JFIF
.MP3	.M1V	.JPE
.SND	.MP2	.JPEG
.WAV	.MPA	.JPG
.WM	.MPE	
.WMA	.WMV	

Of course, in many cases, the software that comes with digital video devices has many of the same video-editing capabilities as Windows Movie Maker. In that case, why bother importing the content back into Movie Maker at all? Although many third-party video-editing programs can produce superior quality video, few can produce video files that are as small as those created by Windows Movie Maker. If you plan to exchange your movies online, Windows Movie Maker may prove to be indispensable.

Keep Movie Maker on Its Toes with Online Updates

One of the most important but often overlooked features of Windows Me is the ability to keep the operating system up-to-date with free, downloadable updates. This ensures that if Microsoft develops fixes for any bugs that may dwell inside Windows, or develops drivers for new hardware, you can get them quickly and easily.

Because Movie Maker is part of Windows Me, it is updated automatically when you perform an online update. It's a good idea to do an update periodically — say, once a month — to keep your system running smoothly. To do an online update, perform the following steps:

1. **Close all open programs — including Movie Maker — and choose Start⇨Windows Update.**

   Internet Explorer opens and dials your Internet connection (if applicable) to display a Web page similar to Figure 3-9. Because Web pages change frequently, the actual page you see may differ slightly from this one.

2. **Find the link for Product Updates and click it.**

   A dialog box appears, telling you that your computer is being checked (but no information is being sent to Microsoft). After the check, a catalog customized to your computer is shown.

3. **Review each update category and place a check mark next to each item you want to download.**

   Be especially on the lookout for any Windows Movie Maker or Windows Media Player upgrades, as well as updated device drivers for your hardware.

4. **Click the Download button.**

   The updates are downloaded and installed.

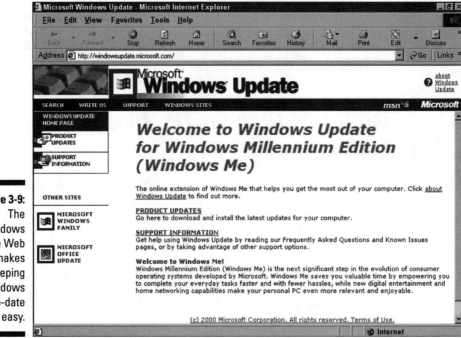

Figure 3-9:
The
Windows
Update Web
site makes
keeping
Windows
up-to-date
easy.

Part II
Action!

The 5th Wave   By Rich Tennant

"NO, THAT'S NOT A PIE CHART, IT'S JUST A CORN CHIP THAT GOT SCANNED INTO THE DOCUMENT."

In this part . . .

*I*t's time to get some video into your computer so that you can begin working with it. This part of *Microsoft Windows Movie Maker For Dummies* is all about source material. The first chapter in this part guides you through the process of recording video right from the comforts of your PC. Next you'll see how to import video into Windows Movie Maker from outside sources. Finally, you record some audio to go along with your videos, and you import still images for use in your movie projects.

Chapter 4

Recording Video from the Comforts of Your Own PC

In This Chapter

▶ Preparing the camera

▶ Recording video

▶ Taking snapshots of video

*W*hen Microsoft developed Windows Movie Maker, it had more than just camcorders in mind. Let's face it: Digital camcorders can get pretty expensive, and may be overkill if all you want to do is take a few snapshots of yourself. So Movie Maker supports more than just those ultra-expensive camcorders connected to FireWire ports. It also allows you to use simpler cameras, such as those offered for video conferencing. These cameras are usually small and designed to rest on top of your computer monitor, and they usually connect to a USB *(universal serial bus)* port or a special adapter card. Small USB cameras are widely available with prices ranging on either side of $100.

Capturing video with Movie Maker from cameras connected to your computer is extremely easy. If you have one of these simple little cameras attached to your computer, this chapter is for you.

Getting Your Camera Ready to Record

Before you can even think aboutrecording video of yourself sitting in front of the computer, the camera needs to be installed and working properly. How you do this depends on the instructions that came with the camera. Some cameras come with their own adapter card and must be plugged into that card. Others simply plug into a USB port on the back of your computer.

Note: Before you buy a USB video camera, make sure that your computer has a USB port. Virtually all modern PCs have them, but if your computer is more than two years old or has not been configured adequately, it may not have one.

Whatever the connection, follow the manufacturer's instructions for installing it on your computer before trying to use it in Movie Maker. The camera almost certainly came with some video conferencing software and maybe even some programs to help you capture crude little videos. Figure 4-1 shows a test of my Intel USB camera using the included Video Phone software.

Figure 4-1:
Make sure
that your
camera
works with
its own
software
before using
it in Movie
Maker.

Setting up the camera

Testing your camera to make sure that it works properly is not enough. You also need to make sure that it is positioned properly to shoot the kind of video you want. The kinds of cameras I'm talking about here are low-tech items and their video quality can't begin to compare with that of a DV camcorder with their poor color, exposure control, low resolution, and slow capture rates. Still, you can do some things to make sure that the camera shoots better video:

✔ If you are filming someone other than yourself, try to position the camera so that your subject cannot see the monitor while you are recording. This will help your subject look at the camera instead of the screen. If possible, place yourself directly behind the camera.

✔ Try to sit still while you record, and tell your subjects to do the same. Many small cameras cannot track movement adequately, creating jerky video. Movie Maker may misinterpret the jerky video and create separate clips in the middle of a scene.

✔ Carefully consider the camera angle and its effect on how the viewer perceives the subjects. If you are showing a person working on a computer and the camera is slightly above that person's head level, the viewer will assume that the person working at the computer is a subordinate performing a routine job. But if the camera is positioned at the desktop level so that it actually looks up slightly, the viewer will assume that the subject is authoritative and is "taking charge" of the computer.

✔ When filming yourself, don't sit too close to the monitor. Screen glare will reflect off your face and you will have a harder time keeping your eyes on the camera. Furthermore, the camera's automatic exposure control can be upset if the subject suddenly moves closer to the camera.

All the room is a stage

Look around. Do you really want your audience to see the *Night Ranger* and Bruce Lee posters hanging up on the wall in the background, or do you think the video might look nicer if you took them down? What about that pile of dirty laundry? Go ahead and take care of it, but come back when you're done.

Finished? Good. Now you need to turn your office (or whatever the room is that you are working in) into a sound stage so that the audio you record along with your video sounds good. If Windows Movie Maker detects that your camera records only video, it sets your computer's sound card as the default audio recording device. Virtually all modern sound cards have microphone jacks on them, and you can get cheapo microphones for less than $10 at many computer stores.

Feel like getting really fancy? Set up a backdrop for your subjects. For instance, when I was recording narration for my road trip to the Black Hills, I positioned a large map of the American west behind the narrator. This provides a more *complete* look to my video; it also eliminates distractions that may otherwise hide in the background.

Finally, you need to provide some lighting. Different cameras handle light differently, but some general rules include:

✔ Provide as much light as possible. Leave the camera on while you adjust lighting to see how your changes affect the image.

✔ Avoid strong light sources in the background, including exterior windows.

✔ If you are recording a face, light the person's face but avoid having the light source too close, to prevent squinting and skin glare.

✔ Have your subject sit in position for a few minutes before you begin recording. This will help train the person's eyes to the light levels, to reduce squinting.

✔ Light your backdrop, if you have one. Lighting from directly above eliminates shadows that your subject may cast on the background.

✔ Try to have multiple light sources coming from many different angles. This helps eliminate shadows, but only if each light has the same brightness.

✔ If you can put lights only above your subject, try placing a mirror on the desk surface to reflect some light back up toward the subject's face.

Scripting your movie

No matter what kind of movie you are recording — be it narration for a mini-documentary or a simple video letter for Mom — you should plan what you want to say ahead of time. In many cases, I recommend against writing a script that you use word for word because, inevitably, the words don't sound like natural conversation. They sound, well, like you're reading from a script.

Instead, consider making an outline of the points you plan to cover. Use bigger print so that the outline is easy to read from a distance, and position the outline on a document holder behind or right next to the camera. Keep outline points brief but descriptive, like this:

Introduction

> Say hello; introduce "Black Hills Road Trip 2000"
>
> Introduce myself — name, hometown, career
>
> Introduce rest of cast — CJ, Cole, Christa

Describe itinerary

> Montana Rockies
>
> Miles City bucking horse sale
>
> Minneapolis visit
>
>> Family picnic
>>
>> Mall of America
>>
>> Twins baseball game

Mount Rushmore

Reptile Gardens

Devil's Tower — Mention camping!

Conclusion — "Thanks and enjoy the show!"

An outline like this — which I used when creating a narrated introduction clip for the beginning of one of my movies — helps you cover all the important points while still speaking in a conversational manner, in case that is the style you are looking for.

Recording Video in Movie Maker

As long as your camera is configured properly, recording video from it in Movie Maker should be a piece of cake. Just click the Record button on the Project toolbar, or choose File⇔Record. The Record dialog box appears, as shown in Figure 4-2.

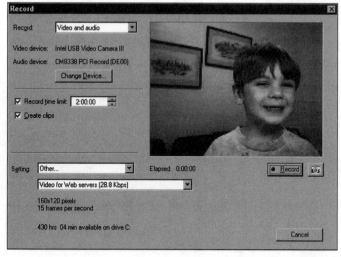

Figure 4-2: The Movie Maker Record dialog box contains controls to let you record video.

Before you begin recording, get the camera, microphone, and all your lighting configured, as described earlier in "Getting your camera ready to record," in this chapter.

Choosing input devices

Sometimes when you open the Record dialog box, the wrong input devices are selected. They are listed in the upper-left corner of the Record dialog box, and changing to a different device is easy:

1. **In the Record dialog box, click Change Device.**

   The Change Device dialog box appears, as shown in Figure 4-3.

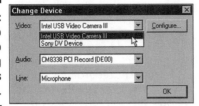

Figure 4-3:
Select audio and video recording devices here.

2. **In the upper portion of the Change Device dialog box, click the down arrow to open the list of video recording devices and choose the one you want to use.**

   Depending on which device you choose, the Audio recording device may change automatically.

   If Windows Movie Maker can't seem to find your camera, try closing the program, turning on the camera, and reopening Movie Maker.

3. **Click Configure.**

   If you chose a USB camera as your video device (as I did), you will probably see a Properties dialog box, similar to the one shown in Figure 4-4. Here you can adjust various aspects of the camera's recording quality. You may have to experiment a bit with the various settings before you get an image that you're happy with.

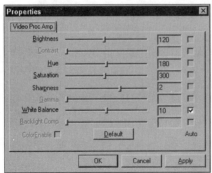

Figure 4-4:
Adjust video quality settings here. This may require some experimentation.

Note: If your Properties dialog box has digital VCR controls rather than controls like those shown in Figure 4-4, the device you have chosen is probably your digital camcorder. See Chapter 5 for more on capturing video from that type of source.

4. **Click OK to close the Properties dialog box.**

5. **In the Change Device dialog box, choose an Audio device.**

   You will probably use the recording device that is part of your sound card, as I do (Figure 4-4).

6. **If your audio device can record from different sources, choose the correct one in the Line box.**

   You'll probably want to record from the microphone, but you can also choose to record from an audio CD, a .WAV file, a synthesizer, or an auxiliary input.

7. **Click OK to close the Change Device dialog box.**

By default, Movie Maker records both sound and video together, but if you want to record only one or the other, use the Record menu in the upper-left corner of the Record dialog box. There you can choose to use just audio, just video, or audio and video together.

Setting the quality

You need to decide on a recording quality before you begin recording. This decision is important because you want the highest quality possible but you don't want to take up too much space. Because you will be able to specify a file when you save your movie later on, I suggest that you make your recording with the highest quality possible. Just make sure that you have enough disk space to save it!

You set the recording quality in the lower-left corner of the Record dialog box. There are three basic quality settings — Low, Medium, and High — but if you choose Other in the Setting list, you will see a second menu, as shown in Figure 4-5.

The quality setting you choose will determine how much disk space the video takes up. Table 4-1 lists the average size of one minute of video at each of Movie Maker's available settings.

Movie Maker estimates how much recording time is available on your hard disk.

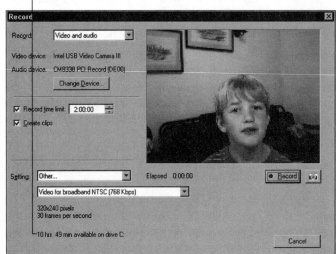

Figure 4-5:
Choose a quality setting carefully before you begin to record.

The quality setting you choose will determine how much disk space the video takes up. Table 4-1 lists the average size of one minute of video at each of Movie Maker's available settings.

Table 4-1	Video File Sizes
Quality Setting	*Average File Size* *(1 minute of video)*
Broadband NTSC (768 Kbps)	4.75MB (megabytes)
Broadband NTSC (384 Kbps)	2.3MB
Broadband NTSC (256 Kbps)	1.5MB
E-mail and dual-channel ISDN (128 Kbps)	760KB (kilobytes)
Single-channel ISDN (64 Kbps)	390KB
Web servers (56 Kbps)	230KB
Web servers (28.8 Kbps)	150KB

The numbers shown in Table 4-1 are only estimates, of course, but you do get an idea of how much more disk space is required at higher-quality settings. Movie Maker tries to provide you with an estimate of its own, telling you roughly how many minutes and hours you can record using the free space left on your hard drive. If you change to a different recording quality, the time estimate changes accordingly.

Movie Maker also tells you how big the picture will be (the higher-quality images are recorded at 320 x 240 pixels) and how many frames per second (fps) will be recorded (30 fps for all the broadband settings, 15 fps for the others). Thirty fps is the same frame rate used in standard television broadcasts, as well as movies on film. Video recorded at 15 fps doesn't look as smooth but does take up a lot less storage space.

Adjusting the Record Time Limit option

The Movie Maker Record dialog box has a few options that can only be categorized as "miscellaneous." One of them is a limit on the record time for your video. This is useful only if you just want to leave the camera running to record everything that happens in front of it. For instance, suppose that you train the camera on a bird's nest in a tree outside your window. If you believe that the eggs will hatch soon, you can aim your camera at the nest and set it to record. With any luck, you'll capture that magic moment when the chicks finally hatch.

Placing a limit on a recording like this is important because eventually your hard drive will fill up. If you set a limit of, say, five hours, the camera will automatically stop recording after five hours have elapsed. If you do not want a limit placed on the recording, remove the check mark next to the Record Time Limit option.

I urge you to leave the time limit option checked, even if that limit is a very long period of time. I also suggest that your time limit be less than Movie Maker's estimate of free space remaining on your hard drive. If you fill up your hard drive with video recordings, Windows may not run efficiently and may crash.

To create clips or not to create clips?

You can specify whether Movie Maker should automatically create clips as it records video. Movie Maker creates a new clip every time it identifies what it thinks is a new scene. Unfortunately, it doesn't always identify these points perfectly, and I have found that, when I am recording video with my USB camera, I end up with a lot of extra clips where there shouldn't be. If you have a problem with Movie Maker creating too many clips, remove the check mark next to this option.

If your problem with Movie Maker creating too many clips is ongoing, consider disabling the feature by default. Just choose View➪Options and, in the Options dialog box, remove the check mark next to "Automatically Create Clips."

Clicking the Record button

After you have the Record dialog box open and the camera set up and ready to go, recording video in Movie Maker can't get much easier. Just click Record and voilà! The camera is rolling.

When you are done recording, click Stop. Pretty tough, huh? After you click Stop, you'll see the Save Windows Media File dialog box, as shown in Figure 4-6. Type a name for the file and click Save. Movie Maker takes a few seconds to create clips from your video and places those clips in a collection with the name you gave the file.

Figure 4-6:
The filename you give your movie is also its collection name in Movie Maker.

Movie Maker normally saves video that it captures in .WMV format, but Windows developers left a backdoor in the program that allows you to save files in .ASF format if you prefer. Just choose "All Files" in the Save as type menu, and add the .ASF extension to the end of the filename. The file is saved in .ASF format.

A Moment in Time: Taking Snapshots of Video

Besides capturing video, Movie Maker helps you take snapshots with your digital video camera, too. You may find this handy, although the image quality is not very good. If you have a digital camera or a scanner, I suggest using one of those tools to get your still pictures into the computer and then simply importing the stills as described in Chapter 7.

Taking the picture

Snapping a picture in Movie Maker is a lot like shooting video:

1. **Set up the camera and the scene just as if you were going to shoot some video.**

2. **In Movie Maker, click once on the collection in the Collections list where you want to save the picture you are about to take.**

3. **Turn on the camera and click Record (or choose File⇨Record).**

   The Record dialog box appears.

4. **Set a recording quality for the photo.**

   Stills don't require a lot of disk space (compared to video), so I recommend choosing the highest-quality setting possible.

5. **Set up the scene the way you want it and position the mouse pointer over the Take Photo button, as shown in Figure 4-7 (but don't click it yet!).**

Take Photo

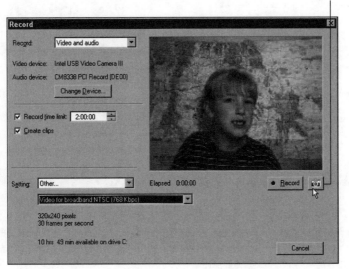

Figure 4-7:
Use the
Take Photo
button next
to the
Record
button to
snap a
picture.

TIP

Be aware of where you are looking. If you are looking at the on-screen preview rather than the camera, your gaze will be "off camera" in the picture.

6. Click the mouse button to take the photo.

The snapshot is taken instantly without any delay whatsoever.

7. Name and save the picture.

Movie Maker saves it as a jpeg (.jpg) file, making it easy to use in Web pages and other documents.

8. Close the Record dialog box when you are done.

The still appears as a clip, as shown in Figure 4-8.

When you save the still, Movie Maker creates it as a clip in whatever collection you opened back in Step 2 of the preceding steps. You can move it around, of course, by simply dragging it to a new location.

I just took this photo.

Figure 4-8:
The photo you snapped becomes a clip in Movie Maker.

How long is this photo, anyway?

When you use a photo in one of your movies, Movie Maker "plays" the picture for a certain period of time. The default time is five seconds. Why? If the picture were inserted as a single frame of video, it would flash by in 1/30th of a second and you wouldn't see it.

If you don't like that default value of five seconds, you can change it:

1. **In Movie Maker, choose View⇨Options.**

   The Options dialog box appears, as shown in Figure 4-9.

This is how many seconds the clips will play.

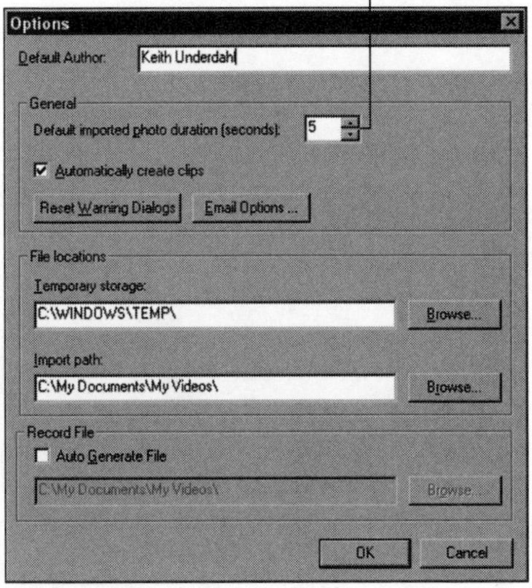

Figure 4-9:
Change the
default
"play" time
for still
photos here.

2. **Under General options, click the up or down arrows next to "Default imported photo duration" to change the default time.**

3. **Click OK to close the Options dialog box.**

Although you may be tempted to choose a shorter time frame, remember that when you show a still photo in a movie, it will take a few seconds for the picture to "sink in" to the brains of your viewers. And, of course, you can always customize the playback time for any still photo using the Timeline when you are creating your movie.

Chapter 5

Importing Video Clips from Any Source

*W*indows Movie Maker helps you create interesting movies and send them to people. You create those movies by beginning with source material. This source material can include video, sound files, and still graphics. Movie Maker even helps you get some of this source material by allowing you to record audio and video and take snapshots.

Still, much of your source material will probably originate somewhere outside the Movie Maker program. Maybe you recorded some video with your digital camcorder, or downloaded some video files from the Internet, or have some previously recorded music; or maybe you simply want to use some still photos. Movie Maker can easily import your source material and, once imported, that material can be used in any movie you create.

Importing Video Clips in Movie Maker

Importing media into Movie Maker is an important first step to performing movie magic. When you import some media, whether it be audio, video, or a still graphic, Movie Maker reviews it and adds a picture of it to a collection. However, the source file itself is not affected. Movie Maker still relies on the original source material when you create a movie.

Double-check Movie Maker's clip collections before deleting any audio or video files from your hard drive. I know, I know, they're huge files and you want to clear some space for more important stuff, but if you delete a file that you imported into Movie Maker at some point, it will become unavailable for your movie projects. Just because it appears in Movie Maker's collections, do not assume that it is preserved forever.

Which formats are supported?

Many (but not all) of the most common audio, video, and picture file formats are supported by Movie Maker. If the format is supported, that means that Movie Maker can import it and you can use it in your movies. Supported formats include:

- **Audio:** .AIF, .AIFC, .AIFF, .AU, .MP3, .SND, .WAV, .WMA
- **Video:** .ASF, .AVI, .M1V, .MP2, .MPA, .MPE, .MPEG, .MPG, .WMV
- **Stills:** .BMP, .DIB, .GIF, .JFIF, .JPE, .JPEG, .JPG

Any files that you have that are in one of these formats (look at the three- or four-digit file extension). The list is fairly comprehensive, but there are a few significant file types that cannot be imported into Movie Maker:

- **.CDA:** Music from audio CDs like those you play in your home stereo cannot be imported directly into Movie Maker. However, you can play a music CD in Windows Media Player and record the audio with the Windows Sound Recorder. Doing so allows you to save the music as a .WAV file.
- **.TIFF, .PCX:** A fewcommon image file formats, such as .TIFF and .PCX, are not supported. If you have an image in one of these formats that you want to use in a movie, you have to convert it to a supported format using a graphics-editing program such as PhotoDraw or Adobe PhotoDeluxe.

Importing video from a digital camcorder

If you have a digital camcorder, you import video from it into Windows Movie Maker using the Record dialog box. So, in a way, importing video from a camcorder is a lot like recording video from another type of camera that is connected directly to your PC. Still, the process is unique enough to really be considered importing rather than recording.

First you need to connect your camcorder to your computer. You'll probably do this with a FireWire (IEEE-1394) adapter card. Most PCs still don't come with FireWire adapters built in, which means that you have to buy and install your own. Appendix A shows you how to do this.

Your computer already has a parallel port, and some manufacturers (such as Panasonic) offer a few digital camcorders that can connect to it. Why bother with a camera that can use only a FireWire port? FireWire ports are blazingly fast compared to parallel ports (they can transfer up to 400 million bits of data per second, roughly 400 times as fast as a parallel port) because they were designed specifically for digital video. The parallel port is just too slow, and you will not be able to capture acceptable video from a parallel port using Windows Movie Maker.

One of the really nice things about the FireWire port is that it is "hot swappable." This means that you can connect or disconnect the FireWire cable that connects to your camcorder whenever you want. In the bad old days, you usually had to shut the computer down and turn off all power before you connected or disconnected any peripherals.

Although FireWire devices are "hot swappable," don't disconnect your camcorder while you are in the middle of doing something (such as capturing video). This can cause corrupted data and even damage to the camera. Just to be safe, stop capturing and turn the camera's power off before you disconnect it from the computer.

Capturing video from your digital camcorder is easy:

1. **Use the controls on the camera to rewind or fast forward as appropriate to get to the point where you want to begin importing.**

2. **Connect your camcorder to your FireWire adapter using a FireWire cable.**

   Note: FireWire cables can have 6-pin connectors, 4-pin connectors, or a combination of the two. In most cases, you need a cable with a 6-pin connector on the end that plugs into the FireWire adapter and a 4-pin connector on the end that plugs into your camera.

3. **Launch Windows Movie Maker and click Record.**

   The Record dialog box should open, although in some cases you might first see a warning dialog box similar to that shown in Figure 5-1.

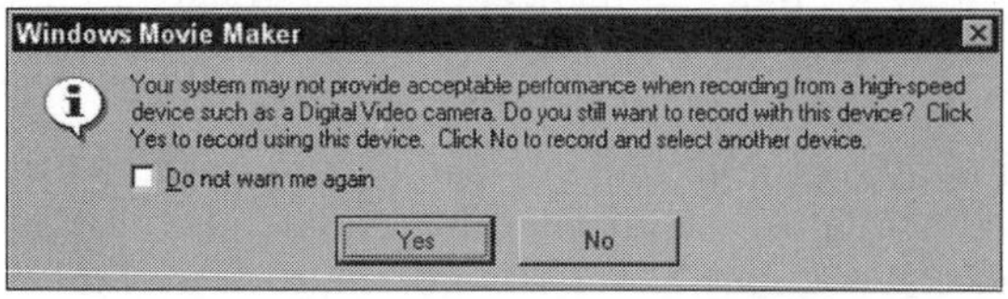

Figure 5-1: If
you see this
warning,
click Yes to
proceed and
use the
camcorder
anyway.

> **Windows Movie Maker** ☒
>
> ⓘ Your system may not provide acceptable performance when recording from a high-speed device such as a Digital Video camera. Do you still want to record with this device? Click Yes to record using this device. Click No to record and select another device.
>
> ☐ Do not warn me again
>
> [Yes]   [No]

4. **In the Record dialog box, make sure that your camcorder is listed in the upper-left corner, as shown in Figure 5-2.**

   If it isn't listed, click Change Device and select it in the Change Device dialog box.

Choose a quality setting.

Make sure your camcorder is shown here.

> **Record** ☒
>
> Record: [Video and audio ▾]
>
> Video device: Sony DV Device
> Audio device: Sony DV Device
>
> [Change Device...]
>
> ☑ Record time limit: [2:00:00 ⬍]
> ☑ Create clips
>
> ☐ Disable preview while capturing.
>
> Setting: [Other... ▾]   Elapsed 0:00:00   ● Record 🎦
>
> [Video for broadband NTSC (384 Kbps) ▾]
>
> 320x240 pixels
> 30 frames per second
>
> 30 hrs 58 min available on drive C:
>
> Digital video camera controls
> [▷] [‖] [■] [◁‖] [‖▷] [◁◁] [▷▷]
>
> [Cancel]

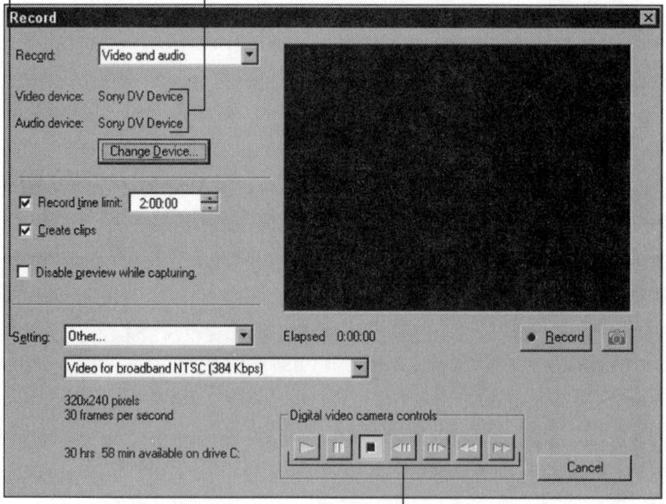

Figure 5-2:
Check all
the settings
in the
Record
dialog box
before you
begin
recording.

Control the camera here.

If your camcorder is not available in the Change Device dialog box, close the Record dialog box and Movie Maker, make sure that your camera is properly connected and the power is on, and try again.

5. Choose a quality setting for your video.

I usually suggest that you import video at the highest quality possible because you can save your movies at a lower quality (that is, with a smaller file size) later on. However, if your computer has a hard time importing video at the highest or lowest settings, you may want to experiment a bit.

6. Use the Digital video camera controls to adjust the camera as necessary.

These controls include Play, Pause, Stop, Previous and Next Frame, Rewind, and Fast Forward. These buttons send commands through the FireWire cable to your camera and can be used in place of the controls on the camera.

7. When you are ready to begin importing the video, click Record. Depending on your camera, you may also need to press the Play button on the camcorder.

After a delay of a second or two, video from the camcorder begins playing in the preview screen (Figure 5-3) and Movie Maker begins recording it.

Figure 5-3:
The video previews as Movie Maker imports it.

8. When you are done importing video from the camcorder, click Stop.

Recording stops, and Movie Maker sends a command to the camcorder to cease playback. Also, the Save Windows Media File dialog box appears.

9. Name the video you just imported and click Save.

Movie Maker saves it and then creates clips in a collection that shares the name you gave the video file. Clip creation may take a few minutes, depending on the length of the video.

After the video is imported from your camcorder, you're ready to start using it in your movie projects!

Dealing with poor audio and video

You imported from your camcorder, but the sound is choppy and the video looks like it is playing back in fast motion. What went wrong?

Windows Movie Maker is not the only video-editing software on the market. In fact, chances are pretty good that when you bought your digital camcorder or FireWire adapter, it came with a CD containing another video-editing program. But in a growing crowd of video editors, Movie Maker is unique because it produces much smaller video files than most of the other programs. This feature makes Movie Maker ideally suited for creating movies that you plan to publish online, whereas the huge .AVI or .MPEG files produced by other programs are too big to be practical.

How does Windows Movie Maker create such small movies? Movie Maker compresses video on-the-fly as you import it, which makes imported video take up a lot less disk space. For instance, when I imported a five-minute video using Movie Maker, the file was 8.5 megabytes. But when I imported the exact same video using Ulead's VideoStudio Basic SE, the five-minute video consumed more than 1 *gigabyte* (that's 1,000 megabytes) on my hard disk. When it comes to producing video files that have a manageable size, Movie Maker has a clear advantage.

Not surprisingly, some clear disadvantages to Movie Maker's on-the-fly system of importing video also exist. The first disadvantage is that the quality of video imported by Movie Maker is much lower than that provided by other programs. Movie Maker's video quality may be acceptable for short, online videos, but you won't be producing any professional-quality video with this program.

The other main disadvantage is that Movie Maker is extremely processor intensive. Compressing video makes your computer's processor work very hard, and because Movie Maker is forcing it to compress the video at the same time that it imports it, any processor that is slower than a 600MHz Pentium II will probably not be fully up to the task.

If your sound is choppy and the video looks like a fast-motion foot chase from an episode of *The Benny Hill Show,* your PC's processor probably isn't fast enough. Before you began recording, you probably saw a warning dialog box like the one shown back in Figure 5-1.

What can you do? The most obvious and expensive solution is to buy a faster computer. The other thing you should do is reduce the load on your processor as much as possible before importing video from your camcorder. Several things you can do to reduce the processor's load are as follows:

✔ Close all programs except Windows Movie Maker.

✔ Disable as many of the little icons in the Windows System Tray as possible (see Figure 5-4), including anti-virus programs. You can usually find a disable command by right-clicking the various icons and checking the shortcut menu that appears.

✔ In the Movie Maker Record dialog box, place a check mark next to "Disable preview while capturing" (see Figure 5-5). Checking this option disables the preview screen while you are recording, so use the viewfinder or display screen on the camcorder to see where you are in the video.

Figure 5-4:
Disable as many of these little icons as possible before importing video.

One last solution to poor audio and video is to import the video using another program, such as the software that came with your FireWire adapter or camcorder. After the video is imported, save it in a format that can be easily imported into Movie Maker, such as .AVI or .MPEG. Of course, that other program probably has just as much (or more) video-editing capability as Movie Maker, so you may decide to forgo using Windows Movie Maker at all. But if you want to share your videos online and need smaller files, Movie Maker is still your best bet.

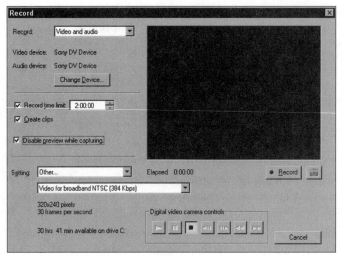

Figure 5-5:
Disabling
the preview
screen
while you
import video
will take
some load
off your PC's
processor.

Identifying clips

When you import a long video from your camcorder (or just about anywhere, for that matter) Windows Movie Maker automatically breaks the video into clips. It does this by "watching" the video, and every time the program identifies what it thinks is a new scene, it creates a new clip. A new scene usually happens when you stop recording, reposition the camera, and begin recording again. Movie Maker watches for these "cuts" between scenes and creates clips accordingly.

All the clips are organized in a collection, and that collection is named using whatever filename the video had when it was imported. For instance, when I imported video from my camcorder of an event at my son's preschool, I named the file using the name of his school ("Maple Lawn"). Movie Maker created clips from that video and placed them in a collection called MapleLawn, as shown in Figure 5-6.

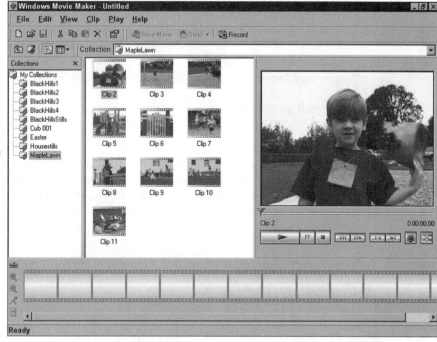

Figure 5-6:
The "Maple-Lawn" collection contains clips from the Maple Lawn preschool video I imported.

Clips are useful because they ease the editing process. When Movie Maker creates them, clips are identified numerically beginning with "Clip 1," followed by "Clip 2," and so on. If you want to give a clip a more useful name, do this:

1. **Right-click a clip and choose Properties.**

    A Properties dialog box for the clip appears, as shown in Figure 5-7.

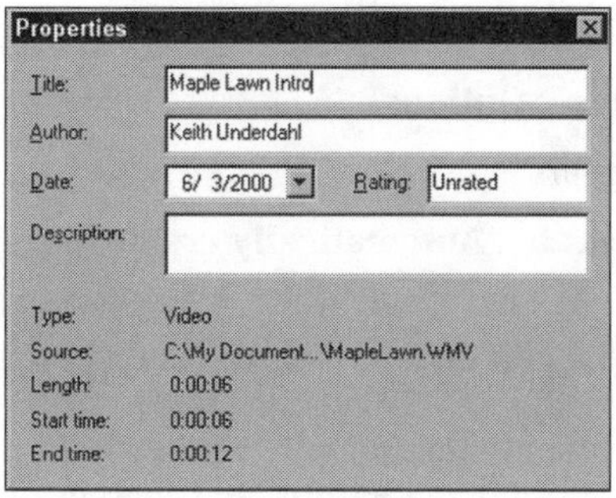

Figure 5-7:
This dialog box lets you give a clip a more descriptive name.

2. **Type a new name in the Title box.**

   You can also modify other information about the clip, including the author, its date, and the rating. A description box text box is available, but in most cases you probably won't use this.

3. **Click the Close (X) button to close the Properties dialog box.**

Note: If all you want to do is rename the clip, you can also choose "Rename" rather than "Properties" from the shortcut menu when you right-click the clip.

Identifying the clips more descriptively like this is especially useful if you plan to make a movie with clips from several different collections. As shown in Figure 5-7, I named the clip "Maple Lawn Intro" so that, in the future, I will always know which collection the clip was sourced from.

Stopping Movie Maker from breaking a video into clips

Clips are handy, but some times you'll prefer that Movie Maker not create them. Two very good reasons for not creating clips include:

- ✔ If you do not intend to edit the video and just want to publish it exactly the way it is, having the entire video as a single clip will speed up the movie-creation process.

- ✔ Sometimes Movie Maker doesn't break the clips up correctly. Clips may be created in the middle of a scene, and clips often have erroneous remnants from an adjacent scene. If you routinely have a problem with inappropriate clip creation, disabling this feature may make your life a bit easier.

Fortunately, you can disable clip creation pretty easily:

1. **In Movie Maker, choose <u>V</u>iew⇨<u>O</u>ptions.**

   The Options dialog box appears.

2. **Remove the check mark next to "Automatically create clips" and click OK.**

   The dialog box closes and the clip creation feature is disabled.

If you want to disable clip creation only temporarily while you import one video, remove the check mark next to "Create Clips" in the Record dialog box.

Importing source material from a disk

If you are importing video from your digital camcorder, you do it using Movie Maker's Record dialog box. But if you are importing source material from anywhere else, such as a CD-ROM or your hard drive, you use the Import dialog box. But the procedure is a little different, depending on whether it is material that Movie Maker will break into clips (video) or simply import as-is (everything else).

Importing video files

To import a video file that is stored on your hard drive or other disk:

1. **Launch Windows Movie Maker if it isn't already open and choose View⇨Options.**

   The Select the File to Import dialog box appears.

2. **Navigate to the disk and/or folder that contains the video.**

   In Figure 5-8, I am importing an .AVI video file called Cub 001.AVI.

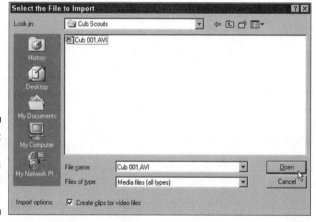

Figure 5-8:
Select a video file to import and click Open.

3. **Select the file and click Open.**

   The "Creating Clips" dialog box appears, similar to Figure 5-9. If the video file is large, this will probably take several minutes.

Figure 5-9: It
may take
several
minutes for
Movie
Maker to
import your
video and
create clips.

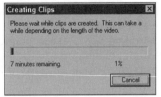

After the video is imported, it appears in a collection that shares the name of the original file you imported.

Importing audio and still files

Importing other kinds of files is a bit different. If Movie Maker doesn't create individual clips from it, the imported material is simply imported as one single clip. In this case, Movie Maker does *not* create a new collection for the material, so you need to decide where you want the clip stored before you import it.

For example, I have a collection of MP3 music files that I would like to use in the soundtracks of some of my movies. To keep the music organized, I have created a collection in Movie Maker called "Music," and that is where I store all my MP3s (see Figure 5-10). If I have a lot of MP3s and want to get really fancy, I can even create subcollections within the "Music" collection to organize each song by artist.

To import "single clip" files such as stills or audio, do this:

1. **In Movie Maker, decide which collection you want to store the imported file in and then click the collection once to select it.**

2. **Choose File⇨Import to open the "Select the File to Import" dialog box.**

3. **Navigate to the disk or folder where the file is located and click Open.**

    The file is imported and stored in whichever collection you selected in Step 1.

Note: If you are importing a file from another computer on your network, simply click My Network Places in the Select the File to Import dialog box and navigate to the appropriate computer and folder where it is located.

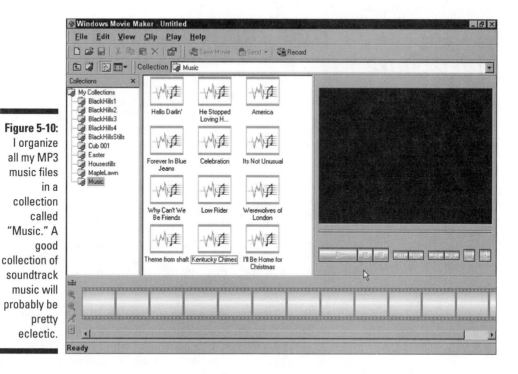

Figure 5-10:
I organize all my MP3 music files in a collection called "Music." A good collection of soundtrack music will probably be pretty eclectic.

Working with Media Files over a Network

If there is one PC trend that is growing even faster than digital video, it is home networking. Are you one of the growing number of people who have a small network of computers in their home or small office? If so, you may find that some of the files you want to use are scattered throughout the various computers on your network.

Usually, this scattering isn't a problem as long as the other computers on your network are left on all the time. But if you import media into Movie Maker from another computer on your network, it can become unavailable if that computer is shut down. This becomes a real problem if you've been working on a project but have not yet saved your movie. If the clip becomes unavailable, you won't be able to use it in that project anymore.

The safest bet, then, is to save all the material you plan to use in your movie projects on a local hard drive. This is especially true with video files, because your network connection might be too slow to import the video with acceptable quality.

Getting Video from the World-Wide Video Store

It has often been said that if you can't find it online, it can't be found. Although that might be a slight exaggeration, it is certainly true that a lot of source material can be had online. Much of it is in a format that you can easily download and then import into Movie Maker for use in your own movies.

Knowing your copyrights

Before you download anything with the intention of using it in your own movies, you need to make sure that you are not violating any copyright laws and that you are not using any of the material in a way that was not intended by the original owner.

First, assume that all material you find — whether it be video, audio, or still graphics — is copyrighted. According to international copyright laws, the producer of a work is assumed to own it, regardless of whether a copyright symbol (©) is displayed or the work is registered with a government trade-mark office. This means that the person or company who produced the material is the sole owner and has exclusive control over its use.

In other words, you have to get permission before you can use any material that was produced by someone else.

Using public domain material

The main exception to this rule is material that is in the public domain. Most of the public domain material you'll find online is government-owned material, such as video and pictures available at the NASA (www.nasa.gov) Web site. If it's owned by the government, it is generally free to use unless specifically stated otherwise.

The other main category of public domain material is stuff that is really, really old. A person owns his or her material until death, at which time ownership transfers to that person's estate for an additional 75 years, but the total copyright period shall not last more than 100 years. This means that if the artist lived an additional 50 years after he or she produced the material, the artist's estate owns it only for another 50 years.

What does this mean, really? Let's consider William Shakespeare's play *Romeo and Juliet*. It was written almost 500 years ago, so that play is generally considered public domain material. However, individual performances of that play are copyrighted, so you are not free to borrow video clips from the 1996 film *Romeo + Juliet,* starring Leonardo DiCaprio and Claire Danes, without permission from the movie studio that owns it (20th Century Fox).

Downloading material from the Web

If you find a link on a Web page to an audio or video file, you can usually click it to view or listen to it using Windows Media Player. However, if you want to save it locally so that you can use it in Movie Maker, you must:

1. **Right-click the link in your Web browser and choose Save Target As (it's "Save Link As" in Netscape) from the shortcut menu.**

   A Save As dialog box appears.

2. **Choose a location to save the file and click Save.**

   The file begins to download and you can see a download progress dialog box similar to that shown in Figure 5-11.

3. **When the download is complete, click Close.**

Figure 5-11: I am downloading an MPEG video file of a Space Shuttle launch from the NASA Web site.

After the media file has been downloaded and saved locally, you can open Windows Movie Maker and import it just like any other file. If you want to save a picture from a Web page, just right-click it and choose Save Picture As from the shortcut menu and save it locally.

Downloading media from newsgroups

Newsgroups are another good source of material for your movies. People routinely post photos, video, and audio files to newsgroups, although, as with other resources, you need to make sure that the material you are downloading is legal. Many Usenet newsgroups are a hotbed of copyright violations, so you should avoid downloading anything that the poster obviously didn't have permission to post.

Larger media files such as music and video are often posted to newsgroups in multiple parts and are usually labeled as such. For instance, if a file is posted in five separate parts, each part will be labeled "1/5," "2/5," and so on. Outlook Express does a good job of combining these multipart posts, so I suggest that you use it as a newsreader. To combine a multipart newsgroup post in Outlook Express, do this:

1. **Visit the newsgroup and locate each part of the multipart post.**

2. **Hold down the Ctrl key on your keyboard and click each part of the series once.**

   Continue until each part is selected.

3. **Right-click the selection and choose Combine and Decode from the shortcut menu.**

   The Order for Decoding dialog box appears, as shown in Figure 5-12.

Figure 5-12:
Get all the parts in the correct order before you try to combine and decode them.

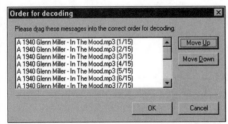

4. **Use the Move Up and Move Down buttons to assemble all the parts in the correct order.**

5. **Click OK when the parts are in the correct order.**

   Depending on the size of the file, downloading the entire series may take a while. When all the parts are combined, they open in a single message.

6. **Right-click the media file in the Outlook Express message window and choose Save As.**

   Save the file to your hard drive so that it can be imported into Movie Maker.

Chapter 6

Sounding Off with Audio Recordings

*W*hen it comes to making movies, you can easily focus your attention on the pictures that move across the screen while hardly noticing the sound that goes along with them. But bad sound — or no sound at all — can really let down an otherwise excellent film. Sure, some people would argue that silent movies can have a certain artistic appeal, but in most of your projects, you're going to want to make sound an integral part of the whole movie experience.

Sound Advice

Recording sounds can be as simple as pressing the Record button on a tape recorder. But you don't want to just record sound; you want to record audio worth listening to. Thus, a bit of preparation and thought is called for before you press that Record button.

Turn any space into a recording studio

You probably spend some time preparing a room to make it look nice before you begin to shoot video. Do you also spend some time getting the room ready to sound good, too? Good! The characteristics of a space — the shape of it, the furniture in the room, the type of floor, windows, and sources of miscellaneous noise — have a major effect on the sound it produces. Fortunately, you can do a few simple things to improve the acoustics of almost any small space:

- ✔ If possible, hang soft material, such as blankets, on the walls and other hard surfaces. This material will absorb some of the sound waves bouncing around the room and reduce echoing.

- ✔ Record in a room that does not let in a lot of outside noise, such as traffic or your neighbor's leaf blower.

- ✔ Turn off any fans or other noisy things in the room. You may also want to temporarily turn off your heater or air conditioner while you record your audio.

- ✔ Position the microphone away from clothing, but not too close to the mouth. You don't want to record the sound of your clothes rustling or your breath exhaling. Most sound studios (such as radio station booths) suspend microphones above the person speaking specifically to address these problems.

Recording audio on-scene

Recording audio outdoors or in a space that you have no control over can present special problems. You don't like the acoustics of the gymnasium at your child's school, but will the principal let you put up sound deadening material on the walls before the school play? Probably not. Still, there are some things you can do to overcome some common on-scene audio situations.

Recording with your camcorder

Most of your sound will probably be recorded using the microphone on your camcorder. Most digital camcorders claim to record high quality sound, but listening to it, what do you think?

Even the best built-in microphone can have problems. Consider the movie project that Figure 6-1 shows me working on. I am filming my son taking a verbal test at one of his Cub Scout meetings so that he can earn a badge. I'm sitting across a table from my subjects, in a small room full of hyperactive seven-year-olds.

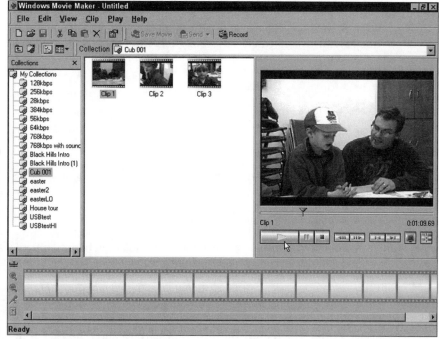

Figure 6-1:
My subjects
are sitting
across the
table, but
outside the
picture are
a bunch of
noisy,
hyperactive
kids.

You can see that I was able to capture the video of my subjects fairly well, but what you can't see is that instead of hearing my son recite the "Cub Scout Promise" and the "Law of the Pack," all I can hear are the noisy kids in the room. To deal with this, I have two basic solutions:

- ✔ **Use a "zooming" microphone.** Some newer camcorders can be equipped with a special microphone that plugs into the camera and is synchronized with the zoom lens to "zoom in" on a subject. These microphones use pretty much the same technology that the people in the black helicopters use to eavesdrop on you.

- ✔ **Use an external microphone.** This is probably the most reliable and economical decision. Virtually all camcorders have a jack for an external microphone, which you can then position closer to your subject.

If you use an external microphone, avoid ones that your subjects have to hold unless you want them to look like news reporters or sportscasters. If possible, have an assistant hold the microphone above your subjects on a boom, or use devices that clip on to your subjects' shirts.

If your camcorder has a headphone jack, consider using headphones as you record. Headphones help you get a better idea of the actual sound that is being recorded rather than some other noise that may be coming from something behind you.

Recording with other devices

Why record sound separately? You may want to record some sound effects for use with video tracks later on. Interesting sounds can be found almost anywhere:

- ✔ A forest
- ✔ Factories
- ✔ The beach
- ✔ A racetrack
- ✔ Public observation areas near the runways of major airports
- ✔ Playgrounds
- ✔ The zoo

If you plan to visit any location that you think may have some interesting sounds, drag along your audio recorder! You never know where you may be able to use the sounds later, and a well-placed sound effect — say, the sound of a lion's roar when your house cat yawns — can add a great deal of excitement to your movies.

Devices that can record audio are not hard to find. The trick is in finding one that lets you easily get that audio recording into your computer. If your recording device — be it a tape recorder or something else — has a line-out jack, you can probably plug it into the line-in jack on your computer's sound card.

Double-check the documentation that came with your sound card to make sure that it won't be damaged by plugging a tape recorder into the line in jack.

Another idea is to record your audio with an MP3 recorder. *MP3* stands for MPEG-level 3 and is an audio recording format that provides near-CD quality sound while using less then one-tenth of the storage space. Some MP3 players have a recording feature that lets you record audio in MP3 format right on the device. MP3 devices are always designed to interface with your computer with as little fuss as possible, and Windows Movie Maker can easily import MP3 files for use with your movies. Furthermore, most MP3 devices are extremely small and use very little battery power because they usually don't have any moving parts. Table 6-1 lists some MP3 devices that can be used to record audio.

Table 6-1	MP3 Recorders	
Recorder	*Company*	*Web site*
D'music SM-320V	Pine Technology USA	www.pinegroup.com/
eGo	i2Go	www.i2go.com/
MP-300-64	Yuan	www.yuan.com/
MP3 Cyberman	Trust	www.trust.com/
OmniPlayer	Sphere Multimedia Technologies	www.omniplayer.com/
rave:mp 2200	Sensory Science	www.sensoryscience.com/
TurboMP3	Nuvocom	www.turbomp3.com/
YEPP YP-E32	Samsung	www.samsungelectronics.com/

If you decide to buy an MP3 device for recording audio on location, get one that has a jack for an external microphone. You will probably find that the built-in microphones on most MP3 recorders are barely adequate for your needs.

Recording Sound in Windows

Most versions of Windows can record sound as long as the computer has a sound card and a microphone. Why not just record in Movie Maker? Sometimes you want to record some audio but your computer with Windows Me installed on it isn't handy. For instance, if you have an older laptop computer that you like to take with you to manage files and other work on the road, you can also use it to record audio, if it has Windows 95 or higher installed, by following these steps:

1. **Open the Start menu and choose Programs⇨Accessories⇨ Entertainment⇨Sound Recorder.**

   The Sound Recorder program opens, as shown in Figure 6-2.

   Note: Some versions of Windows hide the Sound Recorder in a menu called "Multimedia" rather than "Entertainment."

Figure 6-2:
Windows 95
and higher
versions
have this
utility for
recording
sound.

2. **Position your microphone, prepare the room, and tell everyone else to be quiet (tact may be called for here).**

   Your recording studio should now be ready.

3. **Click the Record button and begin recording your audio.**

   The green line in the middle of the program should move and the slider will slowly move to the right as you record.

4. **When you are done recording, click Stop.**

   The slider moves all the way to the right and recording stops.

5. **Choose File⇨Save and save your audio file.**

   It is saved as a .WAV file, which can be easily imported into Movie Maker later on.

Editing audio that you record with Sound Recorder is pretty easy, too. Use the Play button, Seek buttons, and slider to determine what you want to keep and then position the slider at the beginning of that point. Choose Edit⇨ Delete Before Current Position to trim everything up to that point and then move the slider to the end of the desired audio and choose Edit⇨Delete After Current Position. Don't forget to save after you are done editing!

Copying Music with Media Player

Do you have a big collection of music CDs and would love to use some of that music in the soundtracks of your movies? Unfortunately, Movie Maker cannot import CD audio (.CDA) directly, but two roundabout ways exist to get .CDA music into Movie Maker. You can either record the music using Movie Maker's Record dialog box or you can copy the music files to your hard drive using Windows Media Player 7. You may find this option more useful because you can build up a collection of music files on the hard drive and quickly import them into Movie Maker as needed. To copy the music from a CD to your hard drive:

1. **Launch Windows Media Player by choosing Start➪Programs➪ Accessories➪Entertainment➪Windows Media Player.**

   Note: This procedure works only with Windows Media Player 7 (which comes with Windows Me) or higher.

2. **Place an audio CD in your CD drive and click the CD Audio button in Media Player.**

   A list of tracks from the CD should appear, as shown in Figure 6-3.

Figure 6-3:
Select music that you want to copy to your hard drive by placing a check mark next to the desired tracks.

3. **Place a check mark next to the track or tracks.**

   By default, they will probably all be checked, so you may have to uncheck the ones you don't want.

4. **To make sense of the tracks later on, you may find it helpful to name them and list the artist; to do so, right-click a track and choose Edit.**

5. **Type the name of the track and press the Tab key on your keyboard to move to the other information fields.**

   Enter as much or as little information as you want, but keep in mind that the file will be easier to find later if you name the track, the artist, and the album.

6. Click Copy Music at the top of the CD Audio window.

Media Player takes a couple of minutes to copy the music, depending on how much music you selected.

When Media Player copies a CD audio song to your hard drive, it copies the song as a Windows Media (.WMA) file. The file can be found in the My Documents\My Music folder in a folder named for the artist. So, for instance, if you copied *Rocky Raccoon* from The Beatles' *White Album* to your hard drive and labeled it as such, the path to the song is:

```
C:\My Documents\My Music\The Beatles\White Album\Rocky
Raccoon.wma
```

This file can easily be imported into Movie Maker later on using the File⇨ Import command.

Even if you have other software that allows you to record music from a CD onto your hard drive as a .WAV file, I suggest that you use WiMP to copy it as a .WMA file instead. Why? Because .WAV files are big (about 11MB per minute of music), whereas .WMA files take up just one-tenth the disk space.

Using Movie Maker to Record Your Audio

You can use Movie Maker to record audio just as well as you can to record video. In fact, when you record video from a camera connected to your computer, Movie Maker records audio to go along with it unless you tell it otherwise. And if you import video from a digital camcorder, Movie Maker simultaneously imports the audio that was recorded with that video. Usually, this is the best way to get audio because it will be more perfectly synchronized to the video than you could ever get it through editing.

But there are times when you want to record only audio. You may want to do some narration for some existing video or a slide show that you created with Movie Maker, or you may simply be displeased with the quality of the audio that accompanies your video recording.

Note: If your computer is not quite fast enough to import video from a digital camcorder, sound quality will be the first thing to suffer. If you have this problem, record "new" sound later on using the techniques described here.

To record audio by itself in Movie Maker:

1. Prepare your recording space as described earlier in this chapter.

Make sure that your microphone is connected and working properly.

2. **Launch Windows Movie Maker if it isn't already open and select the collection where you want your audio recording to be stored.**

3. **Click Record.**

   The Record dialog box should appear.

4. **In the upper-left corner of the Record dialog box, choose Audio Only from the Record menu.**

5. **Make sure that the correct recording device is listed next to Audio Device and click Record.**

   You may have to wait a few seconds until the recording begins, but you will see the "Elapsed" time counting by when recording actually takes place.

6. **Record your audio.**

   When you are done, click Stop to stop recording. The Save Windows Media File dialog box appears (Figure 6-4).

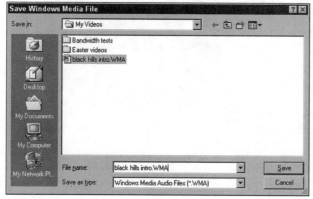

Figure 6-4:
Give your
audio file a
descriptive
name when
you are
done
recording.

7. **Name and save your audio file.**

   The file is saved and appears as an audio clip in the collection you selected back in Step 2.

If you make a mistake, continue recording but pause for a moment, say something like "Take two," and start again. It will be fairly easy to edit your audio clip later on.

Controlling the quality of your audio recordings

When you record audio in Movie Maker, the Record dialog box gives you some quality options just as it does for video. And as I recommend elsewhere in the book, I generally suggest that you make original recordings at the highest-quality setting possible. To adjust recording quality, open the Record dialog box and observe the current setting in the lower-left corner (see Figure 6-5).

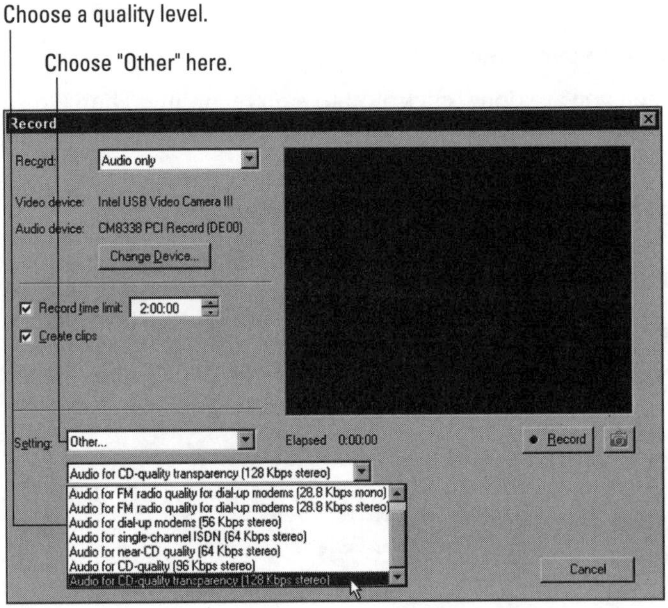

Choose a quality level.

Choose "Other" here.

Figure 6-5: In most cases, you should make your audio recording with the highest-quality setting possible.

Table 6-2 lists the approximate size of one-minute audio recordings at the various quality settings offered by Windows Movie Maker.

Table 6-2	Audio File Sizes by Quality
Audio Setting	*File size for a one-minute recording*
Low bit rate	49kb (kilobytes)
FM radio quality (mono)	150kb
FM radio quality (stereo)	150kb
Dial-up modems	240kb

Audio Setting	File size for a one-minute recording
Single-channel ISDN	360kb
Near-CD quality	480kb
CD quality	720kb
CD quality transparency	960kb

Splitting an audio clip

Inevitably, your tongue gets twisted and you goof up a bit on one of your audio recordings. Or, perhaps you have a perfectly good audio recording but want to use only a portion of it in your movie project. Whatever the case, editing audio clips in Movie Maker is pretty easy. You simply find a point at which you want to cut a clip and split it. When you split a clip, Movie Maker basically cuts it in two and turns each half into a separate clip.

To split an audio clip:

1. **Locate the audio clip you want to edit in Movie Maker.**

   It should be found in one of the clip collections.

2. **Select the audio clip and click Play in the preview area.**

   The clip begins to play.

3. **When you decide where you want to split a clip apart, click Pause to stop playback so that the slider is at the split-point.**

4. **Click Split Clip on the preview window controls.**

   Two separate clips should now appear in the Collections window, as shown in Figure 6-6.

If one of the halves you split a clip into is basically garbage, you should probably delete it from the collection so that you don't get confused later on.

Recording music from an audio CD

Music on the audio CDs in your CD collection are saved in a format called *CD Audio,* and if you view the contents of a music CD in Windows Explorer, you'll see that each song file has the extension .CDA. Unfortunately, Windows Movie Maker does not support the .CDA file format, meaning that you can't import .CDA files as you can many other kinds of multimedia files.

First part of original audio clip

Remainder of clip

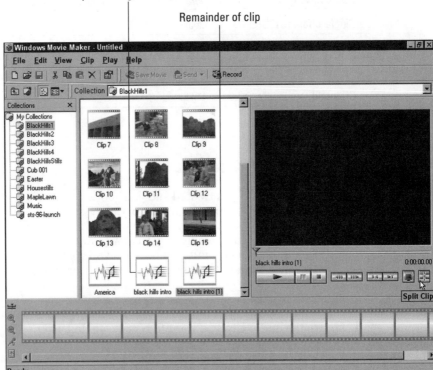

Figure 6-6:
Two audio
clips have
been
created by
splitting one
clip in two.

In spite of this, you *can* use music from your audio CDs as soundtrack music in Movie Maker movies. But rather than import the files from the CD, you record them using Movie Maker's Record dialog box. Follow these steps:

1. **Place an audio CD that you want to record some music from in your CD drive.**

2. **Launch Movie Maker and click Record to open the Record dialog box.**

3. **In the upper-left corner of the Record dialog box, choose Audio Only in the Record list box.**

4. **Under Audio Device, click Change Device.**

   The Change Device dialog box opens and probably has "Microphone" listed next to Line.

5. **Open the Line menu and choose CD Audio (see Figure 6-7).**

   You may have to scroll down the list to find it.

Figure 6-7:
Choose CD
Audio as the
line you
want to
record from.

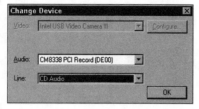

6. **Click OK to return to the Record dialog box.**

7. **Open Windows Media Player (but don't close Movie Maker!) and click the CD Audio button; then, select the track you want to record and click Play.**

8. **Quickly switch back to Movie Maker and click Record to begin recording.**

9. **Click Stop when you are done recording.**

   The Save Windows Media File dialog box appears, where you can name and save the song as a .WMA file.

After you have saved the recording, it is imported into Movie Maker as an audio clip.

Note: The procedure described here works for recording other types of audio, too. For instance, if you have a playback device connected to the Line In or Aux In ports on your sound card, you can choose one of them rather than CD Audio in the Line menu.

If you have a Sound Blaster Live! sound card, you may have to choose "What U Hear" from the audio Line menu to record audio from it. If this is the case, visit Creative Labs online (www.creative.com) to see whether an updated driver is available for your card.

Recording audio over existing video files

Although you can insert audio clips into any movie project, in some cases you may find it easier to simply record narration after you have assembled all the clips. Windows Movie Maker makes this easy to do:

1. **Assemble a movie project and click the Timeline button (or choose <u>V</u>iew⇨<u>Ti</u>meline).**

   The Timeline should appear at the bottom of the Movie Maker window.

2. **Click Record Narration on the Timeline controls.**

   The Record Narration dialog box opens (Figure 6-8).

Figure 6-8:
Use this
dialog box
to record
narration.

3. **If you want the narration to completely replace the audio that was recorded with the video, place a check mark next to "Mute video soundtrack"; otherwise, move the Record level slider back and forth to adjust audio levels between the video track and your narration.**

4. **Click Record to begin recording.**

5. **When you are done recording, click Stop.**

   The Save Windows Media File dialog box appears, allowing you to name and save the file. I suggest that you give it a name that describes the project it is intended for.

The Record Narration feature in Movie Maker includes a bug related to certain types of sound cards. In some cases, if the movie project you are working on already includes audio — be it sound that was part of the video track or something that you inserted into the audio track yourself — you will not be able to record narration. When you click the Record Narration button, you will instead see the warning dialog box shown in Figure 6-9. In this case, you have to use the standard Record dialog box to record your narration as a separate audio clip.

Figure 6-9:
If Movie
Maker
doesn't like
your sound
card, you
may see this
warning
dialog box.

Windows Movie Maker

ⓘ Audio device currently not available for recording. It may be in
use by another application.

OK

Chapter 7

Working with Still Images

*W*hen you think of creating movies with Windows Movie Maker, you probably imagine yourself creating grand, full-motion video productions and then being showered with laurels and praise from all your friends and family members because it was simply the greatest school play video they had ever seen in their lives.

Videos are cool, but sometimes a good, old-fashioned picture is pretty nifty, too. With Movie Maker, you can easily slip still images into your movies, or even create movies that consist entirely of still graphics. In fact, if you're just starting to use Movie Maker and don't have a digital video camera or camcorder yet, a slide show may be the only kind of movie you can make right now.

What Kinds of Graphics Does Movie Maker Support?

Movie Maker can import some of the most common image formats in use today. Supported formats include:

✔ **.BMP:** *Bitmap* graphics files are common in Windows. If you create a graphic in Paint, such as a slide for a movie title, it is saved as a .BMP file.

✔ **.DIB:** These files are called *device independent bitmaps* and are similar to regular bitmaps except in the way color is managed. Graphics with the .DIB extension are rare.

✔ **.GIF:** Short for *graphics interchange format,* this format was originally developed for CompuServe users and is still common on the Internet.

✔ **.JFIF, .JPE, .JPEG, .JPG:** JPEGs (Joint Photographic Experts Group) have become the most common type of image file used on the World Wide Web and may have any one of these four file extensions. Photographs are often distributed in this format.

Any image file that is in one of these formats (its filename extension should match one of the formats listed previously) can be imported into Windows Movie Maker and used in your movies. If the image is in another common format, such as .PNG, .TIFF, .PCX, or one of the many other graphics formats floating around out there, you won't be able to use it in your movies.

Note: You can, of course, convert just about any electronic image into one of the supported formats if you have the right software. Graphics-editing programs such as Microsoft PhotoDraw or Adobe Photoshop can convert virtually any image into something that Movie Maker can use, such as .BMP or .JPEG.

Preparing Your Pictures for Prime Time

You're probably well aware by now that poor video source material produces poor movies in Movie Maker. The same holds true for still images, although a lower level of quality for stills is often acceptable when they are inserted into a video. This is because still graphics tend to have higher clarity and resolution than video images; the poor quality of a video image is obvious when you view a single frame of a video and compare it to a photograph taken with even a mediocre digital still camera. But in spite of this, some preparation is in order *before* you import the stills into Movie Maker.

Making the most of your stills

Relatively few of the problems that typically plague video images also infect stills. For instance, stills tend to be better lit, colors are less likely to be over-saturated, and parallel lines don't cause the same waviness (called *moiré patterns*) that they often do in video. But you should keep some things in mind when you insert a still into your video:

✔ If the picture was too small to begin with, it may look blocky or pixelated in the video. Try to work with graphics that are the same size and shape as the video picture that you plan to eventually output.

✔ Take extra care when transitioning between still clips. Depending on your style preferences, straight cuts are usually acceptable when transitioning from video-to-still and still-to-video, but can seem abrupt when transitioning from still-to-still. In most cases I prefer a cross-fade transition between consecutive stills.

✔ Always carry a still camera with you when you shoot video, and take photographs of some of the key scenes in your video. If your video has narration, a still can be inserted so seamlessly that your viewers won't even know (or care) whether they're looking at a still image or video shot from a tripod.

Editing pictures in a graphics program

If you'll be working with still pictures much, you will need a good photo-editing program. Unfortunately, Windows doesn't come with one. Fortunately, if you have a scanner or digital camera, it probably *did* come with a simple photo editor such as Adobe PhotoDeluxe.

Each photo editor has different options and capabilities, so I won't try to cover them all here. But you will need to use a photo editor for:

✔ Adjusting the size of the pictures

✔ Rotating the picture to the landscape position if you took it while holding the camera in the *portrait* position; doing so will make the picture appear right-side up in your movie

✔ Dealing with image problems such as red eye, pictures that are too dark, and others

✔ Converting noncompatible image formats into a format that Movie Maker can import

Most photo editors let you choose a quality setting when you save the file. Higher quality means bigger files, so you may be in the habit of compromising on quality somewhat when you prepare graphics for use online. But because the quality of a single still has little effect on the size of your movie, I suggest that you save pictures that you plan to use in Movie Maker at the highest-quality setting possible.

Sizing up your pictures

When you insert a still image into a movie, Movie Maker automatically shrinks it down so that the whole picture will fit in the screen. As you know, the size of the movie picture (no matter which quality setting you choose) always has a ratio of 4:3. This means that if you have an image that is 400 pixels wide and 300 pixels high, it will fit perfectly into the video area. But if it is wider — say, 600 pixels wide but still only 300 high — black areas will appear at the top and bottom of the 4:3 video picture area. Consider the image in Figure 7-1:

Figure 7-1: This picture is 600 pixels wide and 300 pixels high.

The 4:3 ratio is the screen size ratio of virtually all television sets. Computer monitors share this ratio because the first personal computers were designed to use a plain-old TV as the monitor. The screens in modern movie theaters generally use a wider width-to-height ratio of 16:9. Movies that are distributed on video in their original 16:9 size are often referred to as *widescreen* or *letterbox.*

The ratio of this 600 x 300 pixel image is 2:1, meaning that it is twice as wide as it is high. If I insert this image into a movie in Movie Maker, it will be shrunk to fit in the 4:3 screen. Although this adjustment may give the movie a sophisticated, "widescreen" feel, it also tends to make the subject unacceptably small in the videos that Movie Maker usually produces.

Pictures taken while holding the camera sideways, portrait style, look even worse. Look at the picture in Figure 7-2.

Figure 7-2: This picture was taken portrait style and doesn't fit in my video screen very well.

Blechh. The black strips at the sides of the picture in Figure 7-2 look very uncouth. You would be better off to resize it in your photo editor so that it conforms to the 4:3 screen ratio, as I have done for Figure 7-3.

Figure 7-3:
The picture has been resized to fit the 4:3 screen ratio.

Of course, resizing a portrait-style picture so that it fits a 4:3 video screen means that you will probably have to crop some picture off the top and bottom. In some cases, you may have to use the trial-and-error method to get your pictures sized just right.

When you resize a portrait-style picture so that it fits the landscape-style screen shape of 4:3, make sure that you change the *canvas* size, not the *image* size. In many photo editors, changing the image size distorts the picture, whereas changing the canvas size simply lops off parts that don't fit anymore.

Although Movie Maker automatically shrinks or expands your stills to just fit the picture in your movie, I have found that if Movie Maker has to change the size of the image very much, it turns out pixelated or blocky looking. I suggest that you first determine what size (in pixels) the picture of your movie will be; then, resize your stills in a photo-editing program such as Adobe Photoshop or Microsoft's PhotoDraw before you import them into Movie Maker.

Reorienting your pictures

Most of us hardly give a second thought to turning a camera sideways to snap portrait-style shots of certain kinds of subjects. Tall, skinny objects such as trees, people, or the Washington Monument look best when photographed this way, but it does create a problem when you try to insert portrait pictures into a movie.

When we talk about pictures, *portrait*-style pictures are taller than they are wide. *Landscape* pictures, on the other hand, are wider than they are tall.

Many digital cameras save all images in landscape format when you download them to your computer. If you import them straight into Movie Maker, portrait pictures will be lying on their sides and will appear sideways if you insert them into a movie. Not good. To avoid this, fire up your trusty photo-editing program (Adobe Photoshop or PhotoDeluxe, Microsoft PhotoDraw, and so on) and look for a command that lets you rotate the picture (Figure 7-4).

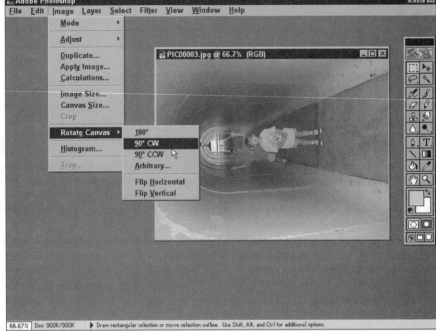

Figure 7-4:
I am using
Adobe
Photoshop
to rotate this
portrait-
style
photograph
90 degrees
clockwise
so that it
appears
upright in
my movie.

4:3 screen sizes

You can use simple arithmetic to figure out the ratio of any image you plan to insert into a movie, but for quick reference, the following list gives various image sizes (in pixels) that conform to the 4:3 screen ratio used by Movie Maker:

- ✓ 1024 x 768
- ✓ 800 x 600
- ✓ 640 x 480
- ✓ 400 x 300

- ✓ 360 x 270
- ✓ 320 x 240
- ✓ 240 x 180
- ✓ 160 x 120

Do the first few sets of numbers look familiar? They should. The 1024 x 768, 800 x 600, and 640 x 480 settings are common ones for your screen area in Windows because your computer's monitor also has a width-to-height ratio of 4:3.

If you use a photo editor to rotate a picture from portrait to landscape, don't forget to resize it so that it still fits in your 4:3 video picture. You will probably have to crop some parts off the top and bottom of the graphic.

Importing Stills As Movie Clips

Windows Movie Maker lets you import many of the most common types of still graphics into the program. When a picture is imported, it becomes a clip just like any sound or video file. To import a still into Movie Maker:

1. **Launch Movie Maker and open the collection where you want the stills to be.**

2. **Choose File⇨Import.**

   The "Select the File to Import" dialog box appears, as shown in Figure 7-5.

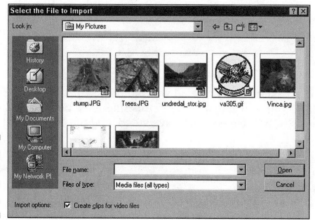

Figure 7-5: Select a still graphic to import.

3. **Navigate to the folder that holds the still or stills you want to import.**

   If you are importing stills from the My Pictures folder in My Documents, the pictures are previewed, as you can see in Figure 7-5. In most other folders, the pictures are simply listed by filename.

4. **Select the still you want to import by clicking it once.**

   If you want to import several stills from the same folder, hold down the Ctrl key on your keyboard as you click once on each photo that you want to import.

5. **When you have selected all the stills you want to import, click Open.**

   Movie Maker takes a few seconds to create clips from the images, after which they appear in your collection, as shown in Figure 7-6.

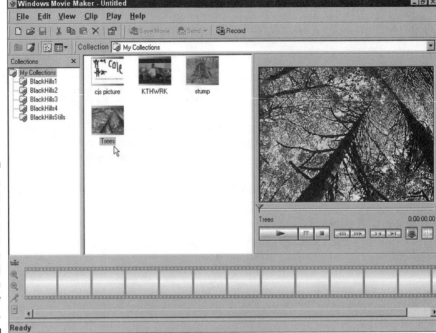

Figure 7-6:
These still clips have been imported into Movie Maker and can now be used in my movies.

You may find it easier to organize all your still clips into a separate collection just for stills. Doing so will help you tell the difference between stills and video more easily, especially if you have video and photographs of the same subject.

Using Stills in Your Movies

Inserting stills into your movies couldn't get much easier. Just drag them to the Movie Maker Timeline (or Storyboard) and voilà! You have added stills to your movie. In fact, if you're too cheap to shell out the big bucks for a presentation program such as Microsoft's PowerPoint, you can use Movie Maker to create slide shows using stills with some music or narration to provide atmosphere. Figure 7-7 shows how I am doing just that: I'm dragging pictures of our new house to the Timeline to create a slideshow "tour" for distant relatives.

Figure 7-7:
Here I am
using Movie
Maker to
create a
slideshow
with stills.
I'll add some
narration
later.

When you drag a still clip to the Timeline, an I-shaped bar appears at the insertion point. You can place stills at the end of a project or insert them anywhere in the middle.

Deciding how long the picture will "play"

When you insert a still clip into a movie, the still displays, or "plays," for a certain length of time. The default play time for stills is five seconds, unless you changed the default in Movie Maker's Options dialog box (View➪ Options). You can customize the play time for any still to make it fit the rest of your movie better.

1. **In Movie Maker, drag a still clip to the Storyboard.**

   The still should appear on the Storyboard where you dropped it.

2. **Click the Timeline button to switch to the Timeline, as shown in Figure 7-8.**

Drag the slider to change the clip's play time.

Figure 7-8:
Use the
Timeline to
change the
length of
time that a
still will be
shown.

3. **Click once on the clip that you want to adjust to select it.**

   Start and End Trim Points should appear.

4. **Hold the mouse pointer over the End Trim point (Figure 7-8) so that it becomes a two-headed arrow.**

5. **Drag the trim point left to shorten the clip's play time, or drag it right to lengthen it.**

   You may find it easier to adjust play time accurately by zooming in on the Timeline. Use the Zoom In (a magnifying glass with a plus sign in it) and Zoom Out (also a magnifying glass, but with a minus sign) buttons on the Timeline controls to control zoom.

6. **When you are done adjusting the play time of a clip, continue inserting additional clips after it.**

You can adjust the play time for still clips in the middle of your Timeline, of course, but unfortunately, all the clips that follow it will not be automatically shifted to compensate. If you change the play time of a clip in the middle of the Timeline, you may have to move the other clips back and forth so that they don't overlap.

How long you display a still image in your movie depends on the still and your needs, but avoid letting it disappear too quickly. If anything, err on the side of showing a still too long rather than not long enough.

Transitioning effectively between stills

Transitions between stills can be handled just like any other transition. In many cases, I like to use a *cross-fade* transition when going from still to still. In a cross-fade transition, one clip fades out as the next one fades in. This is in contrast to a *straight cut*, in which one clip blinks out as the next one immediately appears to replace it. Straight cuts work quite well when transitioning from video to still and vice versa.

A straight-cut transition requires no special effort whatsoever. Simply insert one clip and another on the Storyboard or Timeline, and each clip will cut straight to the next. But to use a cross-fade transition between your stills, do this:

1. **Insert the stills into your movie and switch to the Timeline (if you haven't already) by clicking the Timeline button.**

2. **Click once on the clip that you want to fade into during the transition.**

   The clip is selected and trim points appear at the beginning and end of it.

3. **Hold the mouse pointer over the clip; then, drag it so that it overlaps the adjacent clip, as shown in Figure 7-9.**

Be mindful of the length of time of the transition. Cross-fades can usually happen pretty quickly, especially in the types of movies that you're creating in Movie Maker. Very short cross-fades take the rough edges off each transition without making the transition itself a distraction.

Note: If you aren't sure how effective your transitions will be, preview them by playing the entire Timeline. Right-click any part of the Timeline and choose Play Entire Storyboard/Timeline from the shortcut menu that appears.

Cross-fade transition

Figure 7-9:
Trim points
for each still
have been
dragged to
overlap
adjacent
clips
slightly.

Part III
Cut!

The 5th Wave   By Rich Tennant

"YES, I THINK IT'S AN ERROR MESSAGE."

In this part . . .

*A*fter you have some source material on your computer, it's time to start editing it and turning all those bits and pieces into a movie. In this part, you modify source clips and combine them into movies. You get some help organizing your video clip library, and you see what Windows Movie Maker can (and can't) do to help you improve the quality of poor audio and video. You also record music and narration over your movie projects, and you create and insert title screens into your movies to ensure that all the people who helped on the project receive the credit they deserve.

Chapter 8

The Cutting Room Floor

*I*f every piece of video you filmed was perfect, you wouldn't have much need for Windows Movie Maker, would you? You're good, for sure, but probably not *that* good. Even the pros make a few mistakes here and there, and that's why professional film and video producers shoot multiple takes of most scenes. And it's also why, after all the photography has been done and all the actors have acted, long hours are spent editing the source material into a film or video worth watching.

When you create movies with Movie Maker, you'll go through the same editing process with your audio and video. You have to decide which clips are worth keeping and whether to remove portions of some clips. And finally, you'll possess some clips that you'll want to keep for a long time, so proper clip identification is important.

Choosing What to Cut and What to Keep

What is editing? Basically, when you edit source material — be it video, audio, or whatever — you keep only the good stuff and toss out the bad. Then you assemble the good stuff in an order that makes sense to you. That is editing.

When you shoot your video, keep in mind that you will be able to edit it later. You have Windows Movie Maker, so you may as well take advantage of it, right? A great way to really take advantage of Movie Maker's capabilities is to shoot multiple takes of some important scenes. Oh sure, you won't be able to yell "Cut!" in the middle of your child's school play, but you can shoot several versions of an introductory scene that you film in front of the school. Consider the scene in Figure 8-1.

Figure 8-1:
This was my first attempt to shoot an introduction scene to a family visit to the *Camp Snoopy* amusement park.

I wasn't happy with the way that scene turned out, so I gave a bit of coaching to my "talent" and shot it again (Figure 8-2).

Figure 8-2:
This intro went much better.

It was fortunate that I shot these two versions of the introduction. Now all I have to do is choose the clip I want to use and place it at the beginning of my movie in Movie Maker. Chances are, I will end up deleting the clip shown in Figure 8-1 because I can't imagine ever actually using it.

Evaluate each clip carefully before you delete anything. A clip that seems useless right now may contain valuable source material for future film projects. Consider creating a "Stock Footage" collection for storing some of your miscellaneous but scenic clips.

Previewing Your Clips

When you import a movie into Movie Maker, the program analyzes the movie and automatically creates clips each time a scene cut is identified. The clips are organized into a collection named for the movie that you imported, similar to the collection shown in Figure 8-3.

Movie Maker helps you out by showing a picture from the clip on its icon. In Figure 8-3, each video clip in the "campsnoopy" collection is shown in the collection window in the middle of the Movie Maker screen. Each picture is actually the first frame from that clip. Although the pictures are useful, previewing each clip individually is very important for several reasons:

✔ Anomalies in Movie Maker's clip creation process can leave a "remnant" of one clip at the beginning of the next one.

✔ If the clip is very long, previewing will help you get a better idea of what happens "after" that first frame shown on the icon.

✔ Reviewing clips individually helps you better judge each one on its own merits.

✔ Sound that was recorded with the clip will play when you preview it. A "preview" of the sound will help you decide whether you want to record some narration, add soundtrack music, or simply leave the sound the way it is.

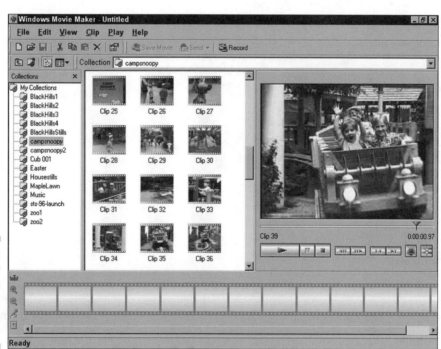

Figure 8-3:
The icon for each clip shows the first frame of the video.

Previewing a clip is easy:

1. **Choose the collection that contains the clip or clips you want to preview.**

   A list of clips should appear.

2. **Click once on the clip you want to preview.**

   The clip is selected and the first frame of it should appear in the preview screen.

   Note: Sometimes the clip doesn't appear in the preview screen right away. This is common, and the clip should appear as soon as you click Play.

3. **Click the Play button.**

   The clip plays in the preview screen and, if there was audio recorded with it, that should play as well.

4. **If you want to pause playback at a certain point, click the Pause button (Figure 8-4).**

   When the video is paused, you can move the slider back and forth to find a specific point.

5. **To cease playback, click Stop.**

Figure 8-4:
Click Pause
to cease
playback at
a given
point.

Experiment a bit with playing the clips and you'll notice that the preview window tends to be kind of sensitive. For instance, if you click the mouse button on almost anything while a clip is playing, playback instantly ceases and the clip disappears from the preview window. In other words, if you want to watch the whole clip, don't touch anything!

Using full-screen preview

If you want to get a really good preview of your clips, free from any distractions, you can preview them in *full-screen* mode. As the name implies, *full screen* means that the playback fills the entire screen of your computer monitor. Previewing a clip in full-screen mode couldn't be much easier:

1. **Select a clip that you want to preview.**

   The first frame of the clip should appear in the preview window.

2. **Click Play.**

   The clip begins playing in the window.

3. **On your keyboard, press Alt+Enter.**

   Your monitor should go black for a moment and then you'll see the clip playing in the entire screen (Figure 8-5).

Figure 8-5:
Press Alt+Enter to view a clip in full-screen mode.

4. **To exit full screen mode, press Alt+Enter again or simply click the mouse button.**

    Movie Maker returns your screen to normal.

If you don't like pressing keys on the keyboard, you can also switch to full-screen mode by choosing Full Screen from the Play menu. Full-screen mode is truly useful only if you have a higher-quality video. If the video size is much smaller than your screen size, the full-screen playback will be blocky looking, like the one shown in Figure 8-5.

Alt+Enter works in Windows Media Player, too. Press it while you are watching a movie in Media Player to make it fill the whole screen.

Previewing frame by frame by frame by. . .

Movies seem like such magical things, but there is really no magic involved in making images move on-screen. A series of images is shown in quick succession to give the illusion of movement. Traditionally, these images have been assembled on a strip of film that runs quickly through a projector, but with video, each image — called a *frame* — is recorded on magnetic tape, a disk, or some other storage device.

Most of the video you see on television and elsewhere is recorded at 30 frames per second (fps). This means that 30 frames are displayed in rapid succession for each second of video that you watch. Movie Maker also records video at 30 fps, but only if the video was recorded using one of the Video for broadband NTSC quality settings. If you use anything but these three highest-quality settings, Movie Maker records at 15 fps.

Even at only 15 fps, that is a lot of video for you to keep track of and edit. Movie Maker lets you review individual frames of a video, an important capability if you want to be able to insert edits and cuts at exactly the right points. To review individual frames of a video clip:

1. **Select a clip that you want to preview.**

    The first frame of the clip probably appears in the preview screen.

2. **Click the Next Frame button on the preview screen.**

    Your clip should move to the next video frame, and you may notice some subtle movement in the subject of the video.

3. **Continue clicking the Next Frame and Previous Frame buttons to review the frames.**

    Figure 8-6 shows that I am viewing the second-to-last frame in Clip 2.

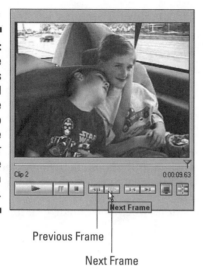

Figure 8-6:
Use the Previous Frame and Next Frame buttons to move forward or back one frame at a time.

Previous Frame

Next Frame

Why is it useful to review a clip frame by frame? Take a look at what happens when I click the Next Frame button again to view the last frame in Clip 2. Figure 8-7 shows that a "remnant" frame from the next clip has been erroneously left here.

Figure 8-7:
This frame is a remnant from the next clip erroneously left here when Movie Maker imported the video.

Obviously, I'll want to edit this clip so that the unwanted frame isn't left at the end of the clip. If I leave it there, transitions in my movies may be kind of rough.

Clip remnants are a common problem in Movie Maker. For this reason, I suggest that you always check the very beginning and very end of each clip that you intend to use in a movie to make sure that unwanted clip remnants aren't fouling things up.

Hacking Up Your Precious Clips

Movie Maker's clip-creation feature is pretty swell, huh? Unfortunately, the clips aren't always created exactly when they should be. The most common problem you will find is "remnants" of adjacent clips at the beginning or end of a clip. The remnant may be a single frame of a scene from the next clip and it can cause some very rough transitions when you create your movies. The solution: Edit your clips!

Deciding where to cut

Before you can cleave any of your clips apart, you need to figure out exactly where you want to cut. Use the previewing techniques described earlier in this chapter in "Previewing Your Clips" to review the clip frame by frame until you find the exact point at which you want to trim the clip. If the "waste" portion of the clip comes at the end, pause the video on the last "good" frame. If you want to get rid of wasted video frames at the beginning of the clip, display the first good frame.

Note: The frame that is displayed before you split a clip will actually become part of both halves of the clip.

Splitting the clips

When you edit a clip in Movie Maker, all you really do is split it into two halves. So, for instance, if you split a clip named "Rushmore," Windows Movie Maker turns it into two clips named "Rushmore" and "Rushmore (1)," respectively. If you split "Rushmore (1)" again, you'll get "Rushmore (1)" and "Rushmore (2)," and so on. You get the idea.

Splitting a clip is easy:

1. **Select the clip you want to edit and locate the point at which you want to split the clip apart.**

   Make sure that the clip is paused.

2. **Click the Split Clip button on the preview screen or choose C͟lip➪Spli͟t.**

   The clip is split into two parts, as shown in Figure 8-8.

3. **If one-half of the clip is garbage, right-click it and choose Delete from the shortcut menu.**

In the example shown in Figure 8-8, the thumbnails for Clip 2 and Clip 2 (1) look similar. However, in this case, I was cutting out the clip remnant shown back in Figure 8-7. Clip 2 (1) consists of only two frames, and I will probably delete it.

Although a split clip looks like two separate clips, those clips are not actually saved as such. Movie Maker simply remembers the trim points in the source video where one clip ends and another begins. The actual source files are unaffected by the splits or any other edits you make.

Figure 8-8:
Clip 2 has been split into two parts.

Adding Descriptions to Your Clips

If you plan to archive any of your clips for future use, you should consider adding a description to them. This is especially useful with longer clips. As you know, when Movie Maker shows you a collection of clips, the thumbnail images show only the first frame of each clip.

I have a clip that was filmed while the camera operator held the camera and did a walk-through tour of a store called *C&A Collectible Toymart*. This one clip is several minutes long and includes views of the storefront, entry, various displays around the store, employees and customers, and the stockroom. Now, you may argue that filming all these things in a single take is not good videographic technique, and you would be right. But the fact is, I have the clip now and it does contain some good source material for a short promotional video I'll be making and putting on *Toymart's* Web site.

So why bother with writing a detailed description for this clip? The clip's thumbnail — taken from the first frame of the clip shown in Figure 8-9 — doesn't tell us about all those other scenes buried inside the clip.

Figure 8-9: This first frame does not tell about the many other scenes in the single-clip walk-through video of the Toymart.

To give the clip a description:

1. **Right-click the clip to which you want to add a description and choose Properties.**

   The clip's Properties dialog box should appears, as shown in Figure 8-10.

Figure 8-10:
The list of
scenes in
this clip's
description
will help me
remember
everything it
contains
later on.

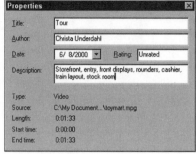

2. **Review the various bits of information about this clip and type your description in the Description box.**

   As you can see in Figure 8-10, I renamed the clip "Tour" and, in the description field, listed the various scenes contained in the clip.

3. **When you are done editing the clip's properties, click the close (X) button to close the Properties dialog box.**

Note: When you record or import a clip into Movie Maker, the program assigns an author's name — usually yours (or whomever the program is registered to) — to the clip. If the clip was photographed by someone else, you should enter that person's name in the Author field of the clip's Properties dialog box. This way, the information will always be with the clip, and you will remember to include the author in the credits of your future film projects.

Chapter 9

Piecing Together All Your Movie Pieces

*N*ow let me get this straight: You say you're using Windows Movie Maker because you want to make really, really, cool movies to share them with your friends and family, right? You want to share only the coolest clips, create some special transition effects, provide a soundtrack, and maybe add a still photo or two, right? Well, combining all your video clips into a movie is one of the most important steps. . .strike that. Combining your clips effectively is *the* most important step in creating your movies. This chapter shows you how to mash your various clips together into a movie worth watching.

Working with Clips

When you import or record some video with Windows Movie Maker, the program splits the video into clips. A new clip is created each time Movie Maker identifies a new scene. When you shoot video with your digital camcorder, you probably start and stop recording several times. Sometimes you stop recording momentarily to reposition the camera, shoot another take, or simply because the interesting stuff that you were filming ended. Each of these video segments becomes a separate clip in Movie Maker. Figure 9-1 shows a collection of clips from some video I shot at Mount Rushmore National Monument.

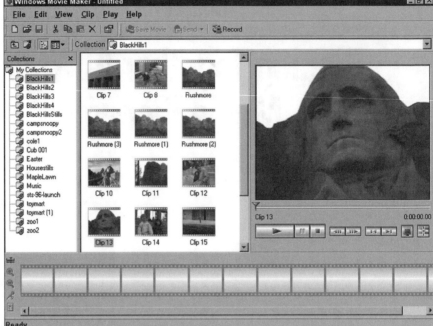

Figure 9-1:
Movie
Maker split
this video
into clips,
making the
task of
editing
much
easier.

Breaking your video into clips makes the video easier to edit in Movie Maker. You can pick and choose among the scenes that you want to include in your movie and decide which ones are destined to be nothing more than "outtakes."

Note: Clips sometimes have undesirable parts in them. One of the most common problems you'll encounter in Movie Maker is that the first or last frame of a clip will actually be from the previous or next clip (respectively). If you have this problem, edit the clips as described in Chapter 8 before you try to assemble them into a movie.

Storyboarding Your Movies

When the pros get ready to make a movie, one of the first things they do is take up pen and paper and draw a series of rudimentary illustrations of each scene in the movie. This series of drawings looks like a comic book and is called a *storyboard,* because it illustrates the story as the producers, directors, and writers envision it taking place. This illustration helps everyone involved with the production better visualize what it is they are trying to create.

Windows Movie Maker includes a tool called a Storyboard, but in this case the Storyboard is something you use *after* all the filming has been done, not before. When you first open the Movie Maker program, the Storyboard is displayed across the bottom of the program window. This is where you assemble all the video clips that you want to use in your movie, in the order that you want to use them. The empty Storyboard looks like Figure 9-2.

Figure 9-2:
Movie Maker's Storyboard provides a workspace in which you can assemble your video clips.

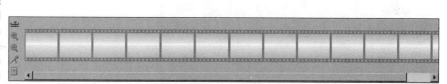

Help! I can't find the Storyboard!

Don't see a Storyboard thingie like the one shown back in Figure 9-2? If you have your Windows screen area set at 640 pixels by 480 pixels, you won't. The Movie Maker program window has a lot of stuff to show — so much stuff that it won't all fit on a 640 x 480 screen. At a minimum, you really need to set your display at 800 x 600 by following these steps:

1. **In Windows, choose Start⇨Settings⇨Control Panel.**

   The Windows Control Panel should appear.

2. **Double-click the Display icon to open the Display dialog box.**

3. **Click the Settings tab to bring it to the front, as shown in Figure 9-3.**

4. **Under Screen Area, move the slider so that your display is set at 800 by 600 pixels or greater.**

5. **Click OK to close the dialog box.**

   Depending on your hardware and Windows setup, you may have to restart the computer to finalize the display changes.

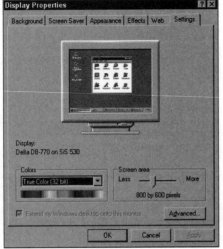

Figure 9-3:
Movie
Maker
requires a
screen area
of 800 x 600
or greater.

Adding clips to the Storyboard

Assembling your clips into amovie is the most basic — and important — step in creating your movies. Fortunately, the process of adding clips to the Movie Maker Storyboard is easy:

1. **Click and hold the left mouse button on a clip that you want to add to the Storyboard.**

2. **Drag the clip down to the Storyboard.**

   When the clip is over the Storyboard, you can see a plus sign next to the mouse pointer.

3. **Release the mouse button over the Storyboard.**

   Your clip is added.

4. **Continue to add clips to the Storyboard using the same procedure.**

   You can add clips from any of your collections to the same Storyboard. As shown in Figure 9-4, I have added clips from two different collections — *BlackHills1* and *BlackHills2* — to the Storyboard.

You can also "drop" clips in between other clips that have already been placed on the Storyboard. Simply drag a clip to the point where you would like to insert it and drop it there. An I-shaped bar appears between the clips you plan to squeeze it in between, as shown in Figure 9-5.

Figure 9-4:
The
Storyboard
now
contains
seven clips
culled from
two
different
collections.

Figure 9-5:
I am about
to insert
a clip
between
two clips
already
on the
Storyboard.

Previewing the Storyboard

Now that you have added a few clips to your Storyboard, how about a little bit of instant gratification? You can quickly get an idea of how your movie project is coming together by previewing the entire Storyboard:

1. **Right-click the Storyboard and choose Play Entire Storyboard/Timeline from the shortcut menu that appears.**

   Movie Maker takes a moment to prepare the movie, and then it begins playing in the preview window.

2. Click Stop in the preview window to cease playback.

As the Storyboard plays, Movie Maker highlights whichever clip is currently playing (Figure 9-6). This can be helpful if you have several adjacent clips that look similar.

You can also preview individual clips from the Storyboard. Click a clip once to select it, and it will appear in the preview window. Click Play to play it just as if you were previewing it from one of your collections.

Removing clips from the Storyboard

You've added a bunch of clips to the Storyboard and you've previewed them. But something isn't right. There was that one scene that just didn't work as well as you thought it would. No big deal; that's what editing is all about. Removing a clip from the Storyboard is easy. Simply right-click the undesired clip on the Storyboard and choose Delete from the shortcut menu. The clip will disappear from the Storyboard but will still be available in the collection you originally found it in.

Preview   Currently playing clip

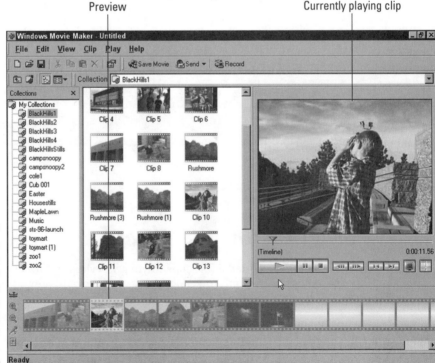

Figure 9-6:
The currently playing clip is highlighted on the Storyboard.

Note: When you right-click a clip on the Storyboard, you may notice that the shortcut menu also includes the commands Copy and Cut. These commands allow you to copy a clip or move (cut) it to a new location. Right-click the clip, choose Copy or Cut, and then right-click a blank area at the end of the Storyboard and choose Paste. You can paste clips only intothe empty parts at the end of the Storyboard.

Reordering clips on the Storyboard

Are you getting the hang of this drag-and-drop thing with your clips? Good! Because you can also change the order of clips on the Storyboard using drag-and-drop:

1. **Click once on a clip that you want to move to select it.**

   When the clip is selected, its border on the Storyboard should turn blue.

2. **After the clip is selected, click-and-hold the left mouse button on it and drag the mouse pointer left or right along the timeline.**

   As you drag the mouse pointer, you can see a bar appear between clips, similar to the one shown back in Figure 9-5.

3. **Release the mouse pointer when you see the bar appear in the spot to which you want to move the clip.**

   After a few seconds, the clip should appear in its new location.

Mastering Time with the Timeline

The editing workspace at the bottom of the Windows Movie Maker screen can toggle back and forth between two modes. The first mode — the one that appears when you first open Movie Maker — is the Storyboard. The Storyboard helps you quickly and easily assemble your clips in the basic order that you want them.

When you have all your clips in the right order, you'll want to start doing some more advanced editing. You will want to control transitions, overlay soundtracks, and change the length of time that some clips play. You do this with the Timeline. The Timeline is the other mode for Movie Maker's workspace, and you can display it by clicking the Timeline button, shown in Figure 9-7.

Figure 9-7:
Click the
Timeline
button to
switch from
the
Storyboard
to the
Timeline.

Click here.

Another way to display the Timeline is to choose View⇨Timeline from Movie Maker's menu bar.

When you switch to Timeline mode, the former Timeline button changes to a Storyboard button. I give you three guesses for what happens when you click the Storyboard button, and the first two don't count.

As you can see in Figure 9-8, the Timeline gives you a bit more information about each clip and also provides access to four new workspace controls. They are as follows:

✔ **Zoom In:** Click to zoom in on the Timeline so that you can work with smaller time increments.

✔ **Zoom Out:** Click to zoom out so that you can see more of your movie at one time.

✔ **Record Narration:** Click to record narration over your movie project.

✔ **Set Audio Levels:** Use this to control the balance between audio recorded with your video and audio clips added later using the Timeline.

Figure 9-8:
The Timeline
lets you
perform
more
advanced
editing on
your movie
projects.

Zoom In

Zoom Out

This clip includes sound.

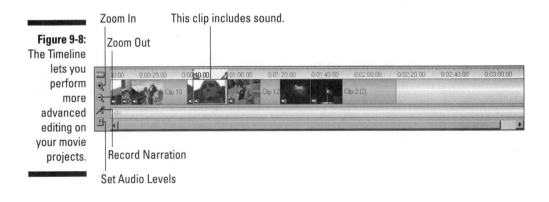

Record Narration

Set Audio Levels

One more thing you should note in the timeline: If a video clip that you insert into a project includes audio (such as the sound recorded by the microphone on your camcorder as you shot the video), it has a little sound icon in the lower-left corner of the clip. This icon is present only in Timeline mode; you don't see it when viewing the Storyboard.

Clipping film with the Timeline

Movie Maker lets you trim your video clips using the Timeline, although I have found that it is usually preferable to trim and edit your clips *before* inserting them into a movie project. Editing clips individually is described in Chapter 8. Still, many times you *will* want to trim clips on the Timeline, and the process is pretty easy. You should realize, however, that some important differences exist between the Start Trim point — the trim point at the beginning of the clip — and the End Trim point. I demonstrate using the Start Trim point first.

Sometimes when you select a really short clip on the Timeline, you won't see any trim points. Does this mean that the clip is too short to trim? No, it just means that you need to zoom in some more. Click the Timeline control Zoom In to expand the view of the Timeline and that clip.

Editing with the Start Trim point

The Start Trim point is at the beginning of a clip and lets you trim content from the beginning of a clip. Edits you make with the Start Trim point can be undone. To trim some content off of the beginning of a clip:

1. **Open a movie project that you have been working on and switch to Timeline mode.**

   You should see your clips arranged on the Timeline.

2. **Click once on a clip you want to edit.**

   The clip you select should have a blue border around it.

3. **Use the Zoom In and Zoom Out Timeline controls to adjust the view of the timeline to a point where you can see the entire clip that you want to trim, but also where you can easily see the time increments on the Timeline.**

4. **Hold the mouse pointer over the Start Trim point at the beginning of the clip.**

   The Start Trim point is a triangle at the beginning edge of the clip, and when you hold the mouse over it, the pointer becomes a double-headed arrow, as shown in Figure 9-9.

Figure 9-9:
Drag the
Start Trim
point to trim
content off
the
beginning of
the clip.

Start Trim point

5. **Click and hold the mouse button and drag the Start Trim point right.**

   Notice that as you drag the trim point into the clip, the slider on the pre-view screen moves, too.

   Note: To help you know exactly where in the clip you will be trimming, the preview screen shows the frame that corresponds to your mouse position, but it may take a few seconds for the preview screen to catch up as you move the mouse back and forth. Keep an eye on this preview as you move the trim points.

6. **When you have moved the trim point to the desired spot in the clip, release the mouse button.**

   Movie Maker adjusts your project so that all the clips transition smoothly even after you have performed your edit.

One really interesting thing about the Timeline is that it maintains a record of the original length of a clip even after you've trimmed it. The original length of a clip is represented by a dark-gray area that remains on the Timeline, as if it were casting a shadow of its former self over the rest of the Timeline (see Figure 9-10).

Figure 9-10:
The dark-gray area
represents
the former
size of this
clip after I
trimmed it.

The clip's former size

As I mention earlier, you can undo edits you make with the Start Trim point. The Timeline allows you to drag the trim point back over that dark-gray area in an effort to restore a clip to its original glory. However, when you drag the

Start Trim point back to the left, it adds the trimmed content back in and overlaps the previous clip. This creates a cross-fade transition, described later in this chapter in "Transitioning Between Clips."

So how do you undo your earlier trimming? It's easy:

1. **Drag the Start Trim point back to the original beginning of the clip.**

   In other words, drag it as far to the left as the Timeline allows and release the mouse button. The clip now overlaps the clip just preceding it.

2. **Move the mouse pointer over the clip and press and hold the mouse button down.**

   Drag the entire clip to the right. You should see a negative image of the clip, similar to that shown in Figure 9-11.

Figure 9-11:
You should see a negative image of the clip as you drag it around the Timeline.

3. **Drag the mouse as far to the right as you can and release the mouse button.**

   The clip should now be back to the way it was before you started messing around with the Start Trim point.

Experiment with the Start Trim point a bit to see how useful it can be.

Editing with the End Trim point

The End Trim point is similar to the Start Trim point, but some subtle differences exist in the way they operate. Like the Start Trim point, edits made with the End Trim point can be undone but a few more steps are involved. Follow these steps to trim a clip using the End Trim point:

1. **Click once on the clip you want to trim in the Timeline to select it.**

   You should see a blue border around the selected clip.

2. **Hold the mouse over the End Trim point on the Timeline so that it becomes a double-headed arrow.**

3. **Click and hold the mouse button and drag the trim point left along the Timeline.**

   Monitor the preview screen to see at which point in the clip you currently have the trim point.

4. **When you are at the desired point, release the mouse button.**

   The clip is trimmed, and all of the other clips that follow it slide over to take up the "slack" left by your trimmed content.

As with the Start Trim point, a dark-gray area on the Timeline represents the original length of the clip. To undo the trimming you have done to the end of a clip:

1. **Select the clip and drag the End Trim point as far right as you can.**

   When you release the mouse button, the clip overlaps the clip that follows it on the Timeline.

2. **To get rid of the overlap, select the next clip on the Timeline (the one that is being overlapped).**

   Click and hold the mouse pointer on it and drag it right as far as you can. When you release the mouse button, your clip end trimming should be undone.

Note: If the overlapped clip is shorter than the amount you originally trimmed from the end of clip just before it, you may not be able to select it because it will be completely overlapped. If you have this problem, you will probably have to move in increments to restore the trimmed clippage.

Trimming still images

Still image clips — such as photographs — have trim points on the Movie Maker Timeline just as video does. The main difference is that with video, the trim points let you only shorten the original source video. With a still photograph, you can drag the Start and End Trim points in either direction, effectively lengthening or shortening the amount of time that the still will play in the movie.

Combining clips

Sometimes you'll have a series of clips that you want to keep together. If the clips were recorded contiguously (in other words, they were recorded next to each other in the original source video), you can combine them into a single clip. Doing so simplifies some editing later on because you can simply put the entire segment into your movie project as a single clip.

You can combine clips in both the Collections list and on the Timeline. To combine two or more clips into one, perform the following:

1. **Click once on the first clip to select it.**

   The first frame of the clip may appear in the preview window.

2. **Hold down the Ctrl key on your keyboard and click once on the next clip and each of the other clips, in succession, that you want to combine.**

   Each clip should be selected.

3. **Right-click one of the selected clips and choose Combine from the shortcut menu that appears.**

   The clips are combined into one by Movie Maker.

Note: Sadly, clips that were not recorded contiguously (one after the other) on the source video cannot be combined in this manner unless you save them as a movie and then re-import that movie back into Movie Maker.

You may have noticed that back in Step 1, I said, "The first frame of the clip *may* appear. . . ." Why doesn't the first frame *always* appear in the preview screen when you select a clip? I don't know. Movie Maker seems to be a little buggy about this. If all you see is a black preview screen after selecting a clip, go ahead and click Play. After the clip has previewed once, the first frame should appear in the preview screen without any problem.

Transitioning Between Clips

Just about every single time you watch some film or video, be it a movie in the theater or a television show, the picture changes frequently from one scene to the next. Sometimes the change happens in an eye-blink as one scene disappears and is instantly replaced by the next. Other times, one scene gradually fades away as another one fades in. The change from one scene to the next is called a *transition*, and Windows Movie Maker lets you use two basic types of transitions from clip to clip in your movies:

- **Straight-cut:** This is the simplest (and default) transition method. One scene ends and is instantly replaced by the next.

- **Cross-fade:** One scene fades out as the next one fades in. Cross-fade transitions are adjustable because you can specify the length of the transition period.

Straight-cut transitions are pretty easy to work with. Just assemble a bunch of clips into a movie using the Storyboard, and voilà! A straight cut transition will be used between each clip.

Cross-fade transitions require a little more (make that *very* little more) effort on your part, and you'll have to use the Timeline. To apply a cross fade transition:

1. **Assemble your clips in the order you want them, using the Storyboard or the Timeline.**

2. **Switch to the Timeline if you aren't there already and decide which clips you want to create a cross-fade transition between.**

3. **Click the Zoom In Timeline control to get a better view of the transition point that you will be working with.**

4. **Create a transition by moving the clip on the right side so that it overlaps the clip on the left; to do this, click and hold the mouse on the clip and drag it left until it overlaps the clip slightly.**

   In the area of overlap, you will see a triangle that approximates the length and content of the transition, as shown in Figure 9-12.

5. **Release the mouse button when you have the desired overlap.**

Transition

Figure 9-12: The overlap area represents the cross-fade transition, and the triangle gives an approximation of the transition's length.

How long is too long for a transition? That depends on the material you are working with and your personal preferences. Experiment a bit; in general, I recommend that you tend toward shorter transitions rather than longer ones. Finally, be mindful of a couple of "rules" you must abide by when using cross-fade transitions in Movie Maker:

- ✔ Only two clips are allowed in a transition. You cannot overlap three or more clips in the same transition area.

- ✔ One clip cannot completely overlap another. If you try to completely overlap another clip, Movie Maker won't let you move the transition past the point at which the clip will be completely overlapped.

Where are all the fancy transition styles?

You may be thinking, "Gee. Only two transition types? Couldn't Microsoft have offered more? Shouldn't there be a whole toolbar full of snazzy, mesmerizing transition styles?"

Many other video-editing programs offer really fancy transitions such as wipes and folds. A scene may slide off the edge of the screen, or fold itself in half and implode on-screen to make way for the next stunning snippet.

These wacky transitions seem cute at first, but after the viewer has seen them a few times, the transitions become such a multimedia spectacle of their own that they detract from the video's actual content. What do you want your viewers to remember about your movie: the really neat stuff you filmed, or that each scene seemed to drool off the edge of the screen as a new one dripped in lava-lamp style from above?

Chapter 10

Maintaining Your Video Clip Library

● ●

In This Chapter

▶ Creating clip collections

▶ Organizing your clips and collections

▶ Viewing your collections

▶ Saving Movie Maker projects

▶ Creating a film archive

● ●

Some people are very organized. They manage their finances meticulously, saving every receipt and categorizing them all in neat, alphabetized manila folders with color-coded labels in a tidy file cabinet. Their sock drawers are models of efficiency, too, each pair perfectly matched, rolled, and stacked rank-in-file like recruits marching to morning muster.

The rest of us still need a little help with our organizational skills. We shove tax receipts, socks, and empty fast food wrappers in sagging plastic "in" baskets, vaguely sure that we'll get back to it all eventually. We look on the task of bringing order to our chaos as if we were trying to herd cats. Oh sure, we have to suffer through the occasional IRS audit, and our foot coverings don't always match, but one thing that we are not lax about is organizing the stuff on our computer. Only once do you have to lose a week's worth of work because you backed up the wrong file before you realize that preserving digital data is not to be taken lightly.

Windows Movie Maker likes organization. The program just works better when you keep things neat and tidy. This chapter describes just how far Movie Maker will go to help you stay organized and on top of your video clips. The chapter also shows what you need to do yourself, because even a program as great as Movie Maker can't read your mind.

Pigeonholing Your Clips

If you've been using Microsoft Windows for a while, you're probably already familiar with folders and windows that have names like "My Documents," "My Network Places," and "My Computer." Movie Maker takes this concept a step further by organizing your movie collections in a folder called "My Collections."

When you import clips into Movie Maker, most will appear in the My Collections folder unless you opened another collection folder before importation. Audio, video, and still clips are all treated a little differently:

- ✔ **Audio Clips:** When you import an audio file, it is shown as a single clip called "Clip 1" in the My Collections folder or whichever collection folder you opened before importing the clip. If you import five audio files, they are all called "Clip 1." That's not terribly helpful, so be sure to name audio clips descriptively as soon as you import them.

- ✔ **Video Clips:** Movie Maker automatically creates a new subfolder in the My Collections folder and gives it the same name as the file you're importing. Imported video files are broken down into clips, and those clips are saved in the new folder that was created by the program. Clips are named "Clip 1," "Clip 2," and so on.

- ✔ **Still Clips:** You can import most kinds of still graphics into Movie Maker and, when you do so, they are dumped into the My Collections folder, just like audio clips. Also just like audio clips, each still is labeled "Clip 1." The icons for stills in Movie Maker have the same camera icon as videos.

Creating a new collection

Think back to the first computer book you ever read. It probably covered something basic like Windows or DOS. At some point, the book described why files on your computer's hard drive are placed inside folders or directories. You probably read some dour explanation about why organizing files in this way is so important, and that explanation was almost certainly accompanied by an analogy that involved file cabinets and large, disorganized piles of paper.

I'll save the lecture for now and assume that you already know why organization is an Official Good Thing. In Movie Maker, the best way to keep your clips organized is to create collections and subcollections, which, by startling coincidence, look and act just like folders on a hard drive. Creating a new collection is easy:

1. **Make sure that the Collections list is shown on the left side of the Movie Maker window.**

   If it isn't, click the Collections button on the Collections toolbar.

2. **Click once on My Collections at the top of the list.**

   If My Collections contains any clips, they will appear to the right of the Collections list.

3. **On the Collections toolbar, click the New Collection button or choose File➪New➪Collection.**

   A new collection should appear.

The new collection appears, as shown in Figure 10-1 and is called (surprise!) New Collection. If you want to create collections within collections, just select the one in which you want to create subcollections and click the New Collection button.

You can also right-click any listing in the Collections list and choose New Collection from the shortcut menu that appears.

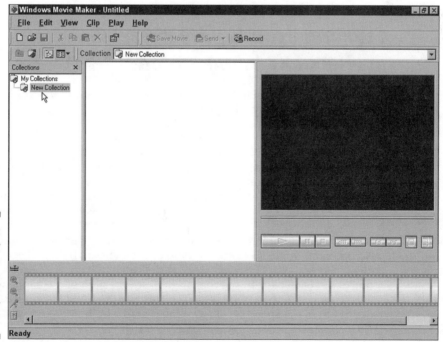

Figure 10-1:
A new
collection
has been
created
under My
Collections.

Renaming a collection

You don't have to create very many new collections called "New Collection" before you realize that the name "New Collection" isn't very useful. Fortunately, Movie Maker lets you assign your own names to collections, and the names have few limitations. Collection names can't be longer than 256 characters, but that's about it. You can go ahead and give them a name that actually means something to you (like "My Blair Witch Spoof") instead of a name that's needlessly cryptic (like "BWspf").

There are basically two ways to rename a collection:

✔ In the Collections list, click the collection name once, wait a few seconds, and then click it once again. Now you should see the cursor blinking. Press the Backspace key on your keyboard and then type a new name.

✔ Right-click a collection in the Collections list and choose Rename from the shortcut menu. Press the Backspace key on your keyboard and then type a new name.

Where, exactly, are these collections being stored?

Looking at clips listed in the "My Collections" window of Movie Maker is not the same as looking at a list of files in My Computer or Windows Explorer. There is no such place on your hard drive called "My Collections," and the clips and subfolders you see are not saved in any one place. The listings are actually just links back to the original files you imported. This means that if you imported the clips from a CD, a DVD, or other removable disk, the clips won't be available after you remove that disk. The same is true if you imported the clip from a computer on your network; if someone turns that computer off or the network goes down, those clips become unavailable.

So you say you don't remember where the file was when you first imported it. No problem! On the Collections toolbar, click Views⇨Details. The view of the clips changes to Details view, which provides much more on-screen information about each clip. To see the original source path of the clip, you may need to scroll to the right a bit in the view window. And if the entire path doesn't fit in the space provided, drag the column border so that the Source Path column is wider, as shown in Figure 10-2.

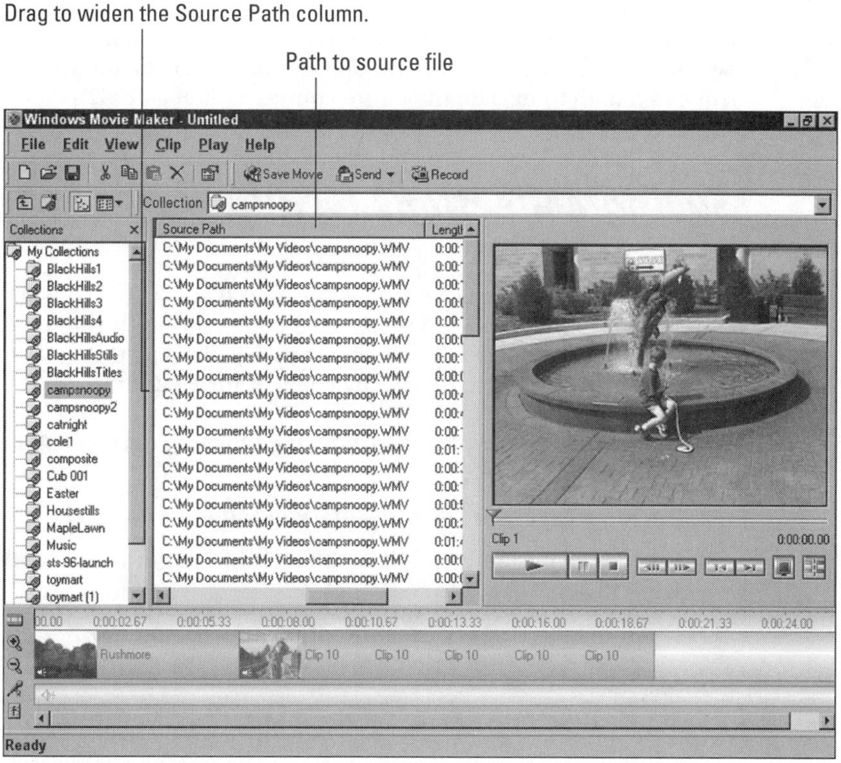

Drag to widen the Source Path column.

Path to source file

Figure 10-2:
Details view
provides
you with the
source path
to your
clips.

The Source Path column shows the actual location of the file from which you imported the clip. If the source says something like this:

```
C:\My Document\My Pictures\xmas.mpg
```

you know that the clip was imported from your local hard drive and you will probably be safe to just leave it there. But if it looks like this:

```
\\Keith\c\My Document\My Pictures\xmas.mpg
```

or this:

```
E:\My Document\My Pictures\xmas.mpg
```

the clip was imported from a source that might not always be reliable. In the example that begins with \\Keith\, the clip was imported from a computer called Keith on your network. In the last example, the clip was imported from a disk drive on your computer that Windows has labeled E:. Is E: a removable disk drive, such as a CD-ROM or Zip drive? If you're not sure, check My Computer.

You can also review the source path of a clip by right-clicking it and choosing Properties. The clip's Properties dialog box lists the source, although it might be truncated to fit in the narrow dialog box. Hover the mouse pointer over a truncated path to expose the entire source path in a ToolTip.

Saving collections locally

Importing clips from a network computer or removable disk can cause problems later on. The best way around these problems is to store all the audio and video files that you plan to use on a hard drive in the computer that you're actually using. Doing so ensures that your clips are always available. To do this, you'll have to leave Movie Maker for a minute:

1. **Open Windows Explorer by clicking Start⇨Programs⇨Accessories⇨ Windows Explorer.**

2. **Decide where you want to store your clips.**

3. **Click once on the location in the left side of the window where you want to store the files.**

   If you're following my example, choose My Computer.

4. **Click File⇨New⇨Folder.**

5. **Type a descriptive name for the folder.**

   Looking at Figure 10-3, you can see that I created a folder called "My Movie Clips" on my D drive.

6. **Now use the left side of the window to navigate through the various folders to the files you plan to use.**

   If the files are located on another computer on your network, click the plus sign next to My Network Places and continue expanding the folder tree until you have found the files.

7. **Select the files and click Copy To.**

   In the Browse for Folder dialog box, locate your new folder and click OK.

Want to select more than one file at a time? Hold down the Ctrl key on your keyboard and click once on each of the files you want to select. Voilà! You have just selected multiple files. You can also select a series of files by selecting the first file, holding down the Shift key, and clicking the last file in the series. Share this knowledge to impress your friends.

If any of the files you moved were previously imported into Movie Maker, you'll have to delete and re-add them in the Movie Maker program. Remember, the clips shown in Movie Maker are only links, so deleting them won't affect the files themselves.

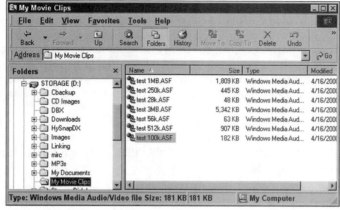

Figure 10-3:
Use
Windows
Explorer to
store your
audio and
video files
on the local
computer.

Another good reason exists to store all your audio and video source files on a local hard drive, and that reason is speed. You're probably well aware that some computers are faster than others. The PC's central processing unit (CPU) is only one part of the puzzle that makes your computer handle data quickly. Data must also pass through the wires and busses that connect your various disk drives to the computer, and the disk drives themselves must be able to handle the data efficiently.

I don't need to get into a long discussion about transfer rates, megabits, and data buffers. Suffice to say that your computer can access files on the hard drives of your computer faster than it can access files on a CD-ROM or DVD-ROM drive, and a storage device connected to your parallel port (such as a parallel-port Zip drive) will be slower still. Your network connection? Yep, it's quite slow, no matter what the guy at the computer store told you.

Do you need speed? If you plan to make a lot of movies, yes. Movie Maker needs to process a lot of data when it records your movies, and every bottleneck created by slow hardware will increase your delays and reduce video quality.

Deleting old collections

The usefulness of old collections, like old soldiers, eventually fades away. Actually, a collection doesn't need to be very old in order to be useless, but you already knew that. Deleting a collection from Movie Maker removes that collection from the program. To get rid of a collection, just select it and click the Delete button on the Standard toolbar. A warning appears, asking you for confirmation that you do, in fact, want to delete the collection and all its contents. When you click Yes, the collection and any clips that were in it disappear.

Collecting Your Clips

If you keep importing clips into the My Collections folder, pretty soon it will be an unbearable mess. You'll be a lot better off if you create your own collections and organize them as you would arrange files and folders on your hard drive. At a minimum, consider creating your own collection folder for:

- **Sound Clips:** Separate all your sound clips from other media. If you really want to get fancy, create subfolders in your Sound Clips collection for narration and music, and within music, create folders for different artists or genres.

- **Family Clips:** If you shoot a lot of video of your family, create a separate collection just for those clips. Create a separate collection for any type of subject that you film on a regular basis.

- **Titles:** Store the picture files you use to add titles and credits to your movies in a single place. See Chapter 13, "Giving Yourself Credit with Titles," to find out more about creating titles.

- **Still Clips:** You'll probably end up using a few still graphics in your movies. Store them here and, if necessary, use subfolders to categorize them.

- **Movie Projects:** Create a separate collection for each project you are working on. This will help you keep the clips you are editing for a specific project separate from your main source files.

Organizing your clips and clip collections

You already know how to create new collections; now it's time to put stuff in them. The easiest way to move clips is to simply drag-and-drop them to a new collection. To do this, you must have the Collection list shown in the Location bar. Drag a clip from the middle pane to the desired collection, as shown in Figure 10-4.

You can also move collections to a new location using the drag-and-drop method.

Renaming a clip

Having forty different clips all named "Clip 1" stinks. It probably won't be very long before you get sick of the name that Movie Maker assigns to many of your clips. Fortunately, it's an easy thing to change.

But are you sure you really want to change the name of every clip? That probably depends on what kind of clip it is. In the case of audio or still clips, yes, you probably want to give them a more descriptive name. But if you have imported a video, Movie Maker probably created many clips from that single file. Movie Maker creates a new clip every time it identifies a new scene or shot in the video. If you import an entire movie from, say, a DVD, Movie Maker may create hundreds or even thousands of clips from that single file. As long as all the clips are in a collection that identifies the movie they are part of, you are probably better off leaving the names as-is for now. If you decide to copy a few clips out of that video and use them elsewhere, *then* you may want to give them a better name.

The fastest way to rename a clip is to right-click it and choose Rename from the shortcut menu. Then type a new name.

Another method for renaming a clip — and, by the way, the method I prefer — is to right-click it and choose Properties. This opens the Properties dialog box for the clip, which should look something like Figure 10-5. This box is handy because it tells you a bit more about the clip, such as the source of the clip and (if it is just one clip from a longer video) the start and end times for the clip. If you look at the Source field shown in Figure 10-5, you'll see that this clip was imported from a file on another computer on my home network.

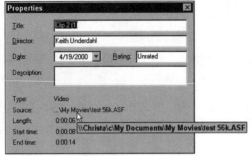

To rename a clip using the Properties dialog box, simply type a new name in the Name field and click Close. The new name should now appear in the Movie Maker window.

Deleting clips

The term "Deleting" sounds so final, but fortunately when it comes to deleting clips in Movie Maker, it really isn't. Remember, the clips you see listed in Movie Maker are merely links back to the source file, and if you decide to delete a clip from Movie Maker, all you're really deleting is that link. The source file is unaffected. To remove a clip from Movie Maker, simply select it and click the Delete button on the standard toolbar.

Changing the View of Your Collections

It's not hard to tell that Microsoft is responsible for developing Movie Maker. The program shares many characteristics with Windows itself, including the way in which clips are displayed. Consider one of the windows in, er, Windows, and the various ways that files can be displayed. You can view the list of files as large icons or small; you can view a simple list of all filenames; or you can choose a view that shows such details as file types, sizes, and the last time each file was modified.

Movie Maker gives you some of the same options for controlling the view of clips. Three view choices are available:

✔ **Thumbnail:** This view shows a thumbnail preview of most clips. Thumbnails cannot be provided for sound files (for obvious reasons).

✔ **List:** A simple list of clips and collections is shown. Small icons indicate whether the clip is audio or video. List view allows you to see the greatest number of clips on-screen without the need to scroll down.

✔ **Details:** The clip name, date it was imported, length of the clip, and source are shown in Details view. You may need to scroll left and right to see all the information that's available.

The default view in Movie Maker is Thumbnail view, shown in Figure 10-6. To change the view, click the Views button on the Collections toolbar and choose a different setting.

You can make a little more room on-screen by holding the mouse pointer over the border between the Collections list and the pane showing your clips. When the mouse pointer turns to a double-headed arrow, click-and-hold the mouse button and drag the windows to a new size.

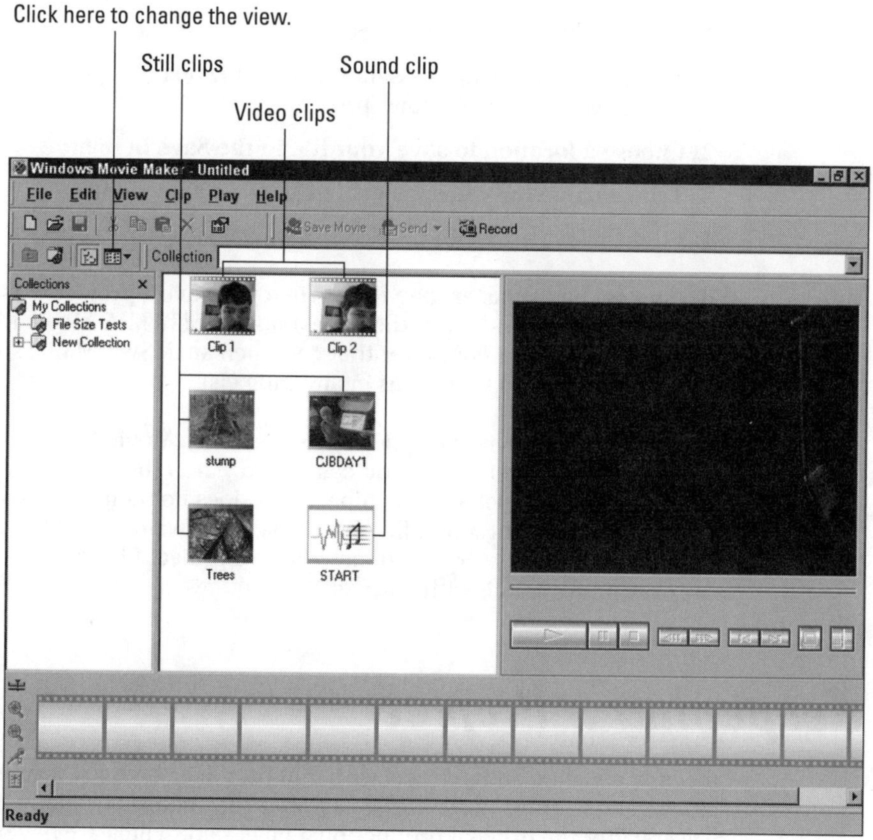

Click here to change the view.

Still clips

Sound clip

Video clips

Figure 10-6:
Movie
Maker's
Thumbnail
view shows
a thumbnail
preview of
movie and
still clips,
but not
sound.

Saving Your Projects

All work you do on a movie is called a *project*. When you save that work so that you can come back to it later, you save it as a project file. Movie Maker project files are pretty small because they don't actually contain all the sound and video that your movie will use. Projects include:

- ✔ The names of clips used
- ✔ Trim points for each clip
- ✔ Play times for each clip
- ✔ The order that the clips are played in
- ✔ Any other customizations you performed in Movie Maker

Saving a project is easy:

1. **In Movie Maker, click File⇨Save Project.**

   This action brings up the same Save dialog box that you've seen in just about every other Windows program.

2. **Choose a location to save your file in the Save in menu.**

3. **Type a name for your project in the File name menu.**

4. **Click Save.**

It doesn't get much easier than that. When you save a project, it is saved in a proprietary format and given the file extension .MSWMM. Movie Maker is the only program on your computer that can open an .MSWMM file, so don't bother trying to open those files in anything else.

When you save a movie (as opposed to a project), Movie Maker outputs a .WMV file. This is the file that you can use to watch the movie in Windows Media Player on almost any machine, but it does not contain the same information that a project (.MSWMM) file does. If you want to be able to go back and edit your movie later on, youmust save a project file or you'll have to start over from scratch with your edits.

Reopening a Project

I recently watched an interview with film producer George Lucas about the 1997 re-release of his epic *Star Wars*. About the changes he made to the film 20 years after the original production, Lucas said, "Films are never completed, they're only abandoned." Surely if George Lucas felt that even a film classic such as *Star Wars* had room for improvement, you should not be surprised when you also decide to revise your own film projects down the road.

Project files don't contain the actual audio and video clips used by your movie, so make sure that the clips are available before you try to work on the project.

If the project you want to edit is one you have worked on recently, open it using the Documents folder in the Windows Start menu. Click Start➪ Documents and, if your project is listed, click it to launch it in Movie Maker.

Of course, if you haven't worked on the project in a while, you can open it by clicking the Open Project button on the Movie Maker toolbar and navigating to the project file in the Ye Olde Open dialog box.

Creating a Film Archive: Because Bad Things Happen to Good Computers

For day-to-day work, the best place to store all your Movie Maker files — sound, video, stills, others — is on a local hard drive. And modern hard drives are reliable, too, but you know how the saying goes: Stuff happens (or something like that). Viruses infect data, misplaced mouse clicks send beloved files to the virtual great beyond, and yes, hard drives sometimes take a dive. You need to back up your data because, as everyone knows, being fully prepared for the worst is the best way to ensure that the worst never actually happens.

You should, of course, back up your whole system on a regular basis, but as far as Movie Maker files go, you should keep backups of:

- All audio, video, and still image files
- Project files (they have the .MSWMM file extension)
- The file `Windows Movie Maker.COL`, located in the folder C:\WINDOWS\ Application Data\Microsoft\Movie Maker\

That last item is a configuration file that contains information about all your clips and collections. Without it, you must re-import every clip after a system crash, and if you don't recreate all your clip and collection names exactly as they were, your project files won't work.

Where are you going to back all these things up? One economical option — if you have the technical know-how or someone from a local computer store who can help you — is to install a second hard drive used just for archiving. Large IDE hard drives are pretty cheap right now, and it is unlikely that you would experience two hard drive failures at the same time.

Another excellent option, and the one I recommend most, is to invest in a CD-R (Compact Disc-Recordable) recorder. Good recorders are available for less than $200, blank CD-Rs can be had for about $2 each (a lot less if you shop around), and each disc holds 650MB of data. A package of ten CD-Rs can store many hours of archived audio and video files. The added benefit of having a CD-R "burner" is that you can put some of your larger movies on CD-Rs and share them with anyone else who has a computer.

Most CD-R devices sold today also let you record on CD-RW (Compact Disc-Recordable/reWritable) discs. Although the ability to "rewrite" CDs is enticing, CD-RW media is usually not as reliable as CD-Rs. You want the most reliable media possible when backing up your files, and high-quality CD-Rs are your best choice. One more thing you should be wary of is Movie Maker's own "backup" feature. The first few times you close Movie Maker, you will see a warning similar to Figure 10-7. Click Yes and a backup file called "Windows Movie Maker Backup.bak" will be created in the My Videos folder. This backup file can be misleading, because the actual video, audio, and still source files are not backed up. Only specific information about clip start and finish points is saved. Thus, you cannot rely on Movie Maker's own backup feature to create backup copies of all of your material.

Figure 10-7:
Movie
Maker asks
whether you
want to
back up.

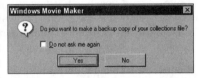

Chapter 11

Dealing with Troubled Video

· ·

· ·

*I*t's a sad fact of movie making: Sometimes every shot is golden, and other times your movies just don't turn out the way you hoped they would. You'll have problems with poor-quality source video, and bad audio will rear its ugly head, too. And just when you think you've recorded awesome audio and video, you may find out that your computer isn't fast enough for all of Movie Maker's features.

This chapter helps you identify some common problems in audio and video and show you what you can (or can't) do about it.

Bad Video? Consider the Source

I'll let you in on a little secret: Professional videographers usually shoot many, many hours of source video in preparation for even relatively short projects. Everyone makes mistakes when they are shooting video, or the lighting isn't just right, or someone forgot to remove a pop can from the scene, or someone walks in front of the camera, or. . . . Well, you get the idea. Stuff happens.

My first recommendation is that you shoot extra video whenever possible. Granted, tapes and other storage media for digital camcorders are expensive, but if you have enough tape to shoot scenes several times, do it. Having multiple copies of a scene to choose from later has several advantages:

✔ You can experiment with lighting and camera angles and choose the best combination later during the editing process.

✔ Mistakes made by actors and other subjects on-scene can be easy to overlook when the pressure is on and the camera rolling. Those mistakes may become apparent only during editing, so it's nice to have more than one shot, or *take,* available to pick from.

> ✔ Hardware glitches can occur, especially if you are working with worn tape or a dirty lens. Obviously, you want to keep your gear in top condition, but if you have a really important shot that will be difficult to reproduce later, shoot two or three takes just to be safe.

And that last point, of course, points once again to the importance of keeping your camera and other gear in top working order. Protect your lens, keep the camera clean and properly maintained, and avoid re-using tape as much as your finances will allow.

When Your Computer Isn't Fast Enough

One of the things that makes Windows Movie Maker so remarkable is the fact that it can produce video files that are extremely small. These small files are much easier to share electronically with other people. Consider my video tour of the Toymart, shown in Figure 11-1. Using Ulead's VideoStudio 4, I created an MPEG video at 320 x 240 pixels, with a frame rate of 30fps. In MPEG format, the one-and-a-half minute video used 10.3MB of disk space. Movie Maker, on the other hand, output the same video at 320 x 240 in the .WMV format using just 4.25MB of space. Still big, but if your audience is faced with downloading the video over a slow Internet connection, the smaller file becomes much more desirable.

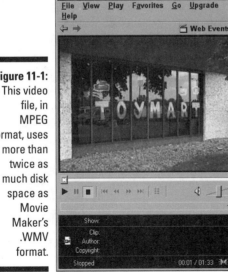

Figure 11-1: This video file, in MPEG format, uses more than twice as much disk space as Movie Maker's .WMV format.

The size of the final movie file output by the program is not the key aspect, however. Before you can even edit the video, you have to import the video into your computer from the storage media in your camcorder. The video-editing program takes charge of this importation, but different programs don't all do it the same. Here's how a conventional video-editor such as VideoStudio 4 does it:

1. Billions of ones and zeros — the digital bits of your video — pass from the camera into the FireWire cable.

2. The bits are sucked through the cable by your IEEE-1394 adapter.

3. The IEEE-1394 adapter sends the bits across the PCI bus that it's plugged into inside your computer.

4. The bits find their way into RAM, along with everything else your computer happens to be working on at the moment.

5. Finally, those ones and zeros are taken from RAM and written to your hard drive via the EIDE or SCSI hard drive bus.

Meanwhile, the video-editing program uses the computer's CPU *(central processing unit)* to command all this digital activity. Reasonably modern CPUs don't have a problem with the series of events I describe in the preceding steps, but there is a problem: After you have imported the video, the file of ones and zeros on your hard drive is huge; remember that one-minute, thirty-three second Toymart video? Ulead's VideoStudio 4 imported it and wrote it to the hard drive as an uncompressed .AVI, devouring 320MB in the process! That is a lot of storage space for such a short video.

The same video, when imported into the computer using Movie Maker, is just 4.25MB. How is this possible? Just as VideoStudio does, Movie Maker uses the FireWire cable, the IEEE-1394 adapter, the PCI bus, and the RAM, but before the video gets written to the hard drive, it is compressed. Guess which component has the responsibility of compressing the video? That's right — the CPU.

The CPU has no problem managing the transfer of large quantities of video from the camcorder to the hard drive. But when you ask the CPU to squeeze the video while it manages that transfer, it is forced to work much, much harder. Remember that scene from *I Love Lucy* in which Lucy tries to box pies on the speeding conveyor belt? That's pretty much what your CPU is going through when you import video using Windows Movie Maker.

Signs that your computer is too slow

If your computer isn't able to keep up with the demands of Movie Maker, you will experience two main symptoms:

✓ **Garbled audio:** Sound seems to be the first thing that suffers when your computer is too slow. The audio becomes garbled or sound as though it is stuttering.

✓ **Dropped frames:** If your CPU can't keep up with the video that is being fed to it by the camcorder and IEEE-1394 adapter, it will begin to drop or lose frames. When you review your video later, it will look like it is playing back in fast motion. How many frames are lost depends on how overtaxed your CPU is, but if it drops every other frame, a two-minute video will play back in just one minute.

If you experience these symptoms in the video you import into Movie Maker, the reason is almost certainly that your CPU isn't fast enough to keep up.

Note: Garbled audio and dropped frames are problems associated primarily with devices (such as digital camcorders) attached to IEEE-1394 adapters. You are less likely to have these problems with video imported from a TV tuner card, USB camera, or another video file that is already on your hard drive.

How fast is fast enough?

If your computer's CPU is fast enough, it will have no problem keeping up with the conveyor belt of pies, er, I mean, digital video. The minimum system requirements that Microsoft recommends for using Movie Maker are as follows:

✓ **CPU:** Pentium II (or equivalent), 300mHz or higher

✓ **RAM:** 64MB (megabytes) or more

✓ **Hard disk space:** 2GB (gigabytes)

✓ **Special equipment:** FireWire (IEEE-1394) adapter and digital camcorder

These requirements are, in my opinion, arbitrary, not altogether accurate, or both. I have, for instance, used Movie Maker on computers with much slower CPUs, but found that if I want to import video from a digital camcorder, I can't do it on anything slower than a Pentium II-500mHz. Fortunately, technology is getting to the point at which even entry-level PCs have fast CPUs, but if you have an older computer with a slower CPU, you're asking for trouble.

RAM? Well, 64MB is barely adequate. Consider 128MB as a baseline amount for efficient digital editing. And as for hard disk space, it is difficult to put a finger on a number and say, "This is what you need," because all you'll use the disk space for is storing video files. The more space you have, the more digital video you can store.

Finally, your FireWire adapter must be OHCI (Open Host Controller Interface) compliant. If not, you may not be able to capture video using your current adapter. Checking your FireWire adapter is easy:

1. **Choose Start⇨Settings⇨Control Panel.**

   The Windows Control Panel launches.

2. **Double-click the System icon to open it.**

3. **Click the Device Manager tab to bring it to the front.**

4. **Click the plus sign next to 1394 Bus Controller.**

   The tree expands and you should see a listing for your FireWire controller, similar to Figure 11-2. The listing should say "OHCI Compliant" somewhere in the name of the controller device.

Figure 11-2:
Use the
System
Properties
dialog box
to ensure
that your
FireWire
(IEEE-1394)
adapter is
OHCI
compliant.

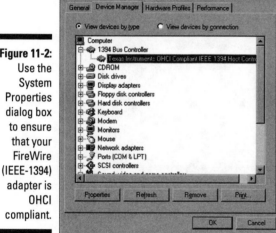

My computer is too slow. Now what?

You have come to terms with the fact that your computer isn't fast enough to import video from your camcorder using Windows Movie Maker. It's good of you to admit that. Fortunately, all hope is not lost. While still using Movie Maker, there are three things you can do to try to improve the quality of the video you import:

✔ **Close all other open programs.** Disable any screen savers or desktop wallpaper you have activated in Windows Me, and if you are using the Active Desktop, deactivate it. If you have a bunch of little icons in the Windows system tray (that's the area next to the clock), close as many of them as possible. Are you running anti-virus software? Temporarily turn it off, too.

✔ **Disable preview while recording.** By default, Movie Maker plays a preview of your video in the Record dialog box as you import video from the camcorder. Disabling this preview frees some resources in your CPU, but you have to use the viewfinder on your camcorder to monitor the progress of the video's playback. Figure 11-3 shows you how to disable the preview.

✔ **Try a higher-quality setting.** You can specify a quality level before you begin importing and recording video, but don't assume that a lower-quality setting will reduce frame dropping and audio garbling. Higher-quality settings actually place slightly less demand on the CPU because they do not require as much compression. If you want a smaller file to output later on, you can always choose a lower quality later when you save the final movie.

Disable preview

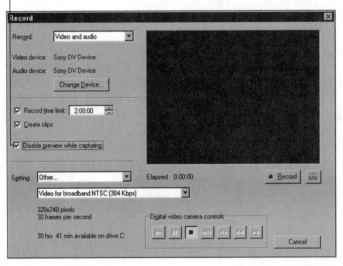

Figure 11-3:
Place a check mark next to "Disable preview while capturing" to reduce some load on your CPU.

If none of those things works, you can always resort to importing the video using another program that does not compress video as it imports it. Chances are that your camcorder or IEEE-1394 adapter came with a program similar in purpose to Movie Maker but does not produce the ultra-small video files that Movie Maker is capable of.

I can't possibly tell you how to capture video using every video-editing program on the market. However, if you are familiar with Movie Maker, you shouldn't have too much trouble figuring out the basics on most other programs. Most video editors share some basic terminology and on-screen elements, such as a Storyboard and Timeline, capture controls, and such. Figure 11-4 shows Ulead's VideoStudio 4, which, although not quite as intuitive as Movie Maker, still provides a relatively simple interface.

I can hear your question before you've even asked it: If you have to use another video editor to import video onto your computer, why bother importing it into Movie Maker at all? Two compelling reasons exist for continuing to use Movie Maker for editing and final movie output, even if you have to use another program to import the video:

✔ Movie Maker's editing interface is simpler than most other video-editing programs. Clip creation, in particular, makes it very easy to pick and choose scenes that you want in your video.

✔ The .WMV file format produced by Movie Maker is more compact, on average, than the .AVI, .MOV, and MPEG formats produced by other video editors. If you share movies online, Movie Maker's small file sizes are hard to beat.

Remember, Movie Maker can also output movies in .ASF format. To use this format, simply add the .ASF extension to the end of the file-name when you save a movie in Movie Maker.

Figure 11-4:
If you can't import video with Movie Maker, try the software that came with your IEEE-1394 adapter or camcorder.

After you have successfully imported some video onto your hard drive using another program, make sure to save it in a format that Movie Maker can use. You'll have to review the program's Output or Save As dialog box to make sure it saves the movie in one of the following formats:

- .ASF
- .AVI
- .M1V
- .MP2
- .MPA
- .MPE
- .MPEG
- .MPG
- .WMV

Also, of course, don't forget where you saved the file. After you've output the file from that program, open Movie Maker and import the video using the File⇨Import command. When Movie Maker imports it, it automatically creates clips to ease your editing. And because it can read from the hard drive much more quickly and easily than from an IEEE-1394 adapter, you are far less likely to experience garbled sound and dropped frames.

Can Movie Maker Fix Poor Video?

You've imported some video into Movie Maker, and it has problems. The color is too saturated, the lighting is off, the camera angle is wrong, and a coffee cup is sitting right in the middle of your otherwise pristine set. What can you do about it?

Sadly, not much if you are using only Movie Maker. Windows Movie Maker excels by being simple, but that means that if you want to do advanced video editing such as retouching, recoloring, or special effects, you'll have to look elsewhere. You can also look to see whether your video capture card (the IEEE-1394 adapter) came with a utility that lets you control some of these factors. Some cards have utilities to help you control color saturation and overall brightness.

Chapter 12

Adding Sound and Music to Your Movies

*W*hen we talk about creating movies, it's easy to overlook the fact that good sound and music is just as important as the video images that will appear. Try to imagine *Star Wars* without laser and explosion sound effects, a PBS documentary about hyenas without any narration, or *The Sound of Music* without music, and you'll get the idea.

If much of your video comes from a digital camcorder, you'll probably tend to favor the audio that was recorded with that video by the microphone on the camera. But in some cases, that audio is merely incidental, and in other cases it is downright distracting. When I took a trip recently to the Black Hills in South Dakota, I shot some video of Mount Rushmore. Much of that video shows the mountain, but most of the audio tracks that were recorded with that video consist of chatting tourists in the background. I may choose to cover some or all of that audio with some marching music, or I may add narration that describes the mountain and discusses the U.S. Presidents depicted on it. Whatever the choice, adding good audio to video in Movie Maker is an important part of the editing process.

Narrating Your Movies with the Movie Maker Timeline

Have you ever tried to narrate some video you were shooting as you shot it? Sure you have. We all do it, yakking away as we hold the camcorder, making snappy comments about the things we are filming. Unfortunately, reviews of the source video later on often reveal that what you thought was witty and timely narration on the scene didn't work out quite as well as you had hoped. The sound quality wavers as you move the camera around, wind fouls the microphone, you forget to mention important details about your film subject, and you stutter a lot.

Narration is better done in "the studio" after you have recorded your video. It gives you greater control over the quality and content of your narration.

Scripting narration (you'll thank yourself later)

I used to teach a two-week course in which I trained other people to conduct their own classes. My students were learning to be teachers themselves, and the most important technique that they had to master was the ability to speak clearly and concisely without the benefit of a script. You can't teach a class by reading a script word-for-word because your audience is in the same room with you and they expect more personal interaction on your part. And you have to be ready to respond to questions and other unforeseen circumstances.

As a movie narrator, you do not have this problem, and there is no real reason that in some situations you can't script every word you plan to say. When composing a script, keep several things in mind:

- ✔ Compose your narration after most or all of your video editing has been completed. If you start moving clips around after you record some narration, you may have to record the narration all over again.

- ✔ Have the video in front of you as you write the narration. It will help inspire your writing and give you quick reference to what will be shown in the movie.

- ✔ Practice reading the narration several times as you play the video that will go with it. Monitor the timing of the narration and video, and adjust your rate of delivery as necessary.

- ✔ If you are recording your narration away from the computer, write down the time you have to fill and keep a timer running as you read the narration.

Of course, scripted narration isn't always exactly what you are hoping for. Sometimes you want the narration to have a more casual, conversational tone. In this case, scripting every single word can be detrimental.

Umm. . . Ahhh. . . Okay. . .

Speaking off-the-cuff is harder than you may think. One of the biggest problems speakers have is that they often fill "empty" spaces in a talk with nonwords such as "umm," "ahhh," or "okay." These meaningless little utterances — called *nonverbal connectors* among professional orators — are pervasive in "formal" speaking situations, such as when you are teaching a class, giving a public speech, or narrating a film.

The truly frustrating thing about nonverbal connectors is that the speaker doesn't even realize that he or she is uttering them. When I was training instructors, one of my evil deeds was to sit in the back of the room and make tick marks on a piece of scratch paper every time a student teacher said, "umm," "ahhh," or "okay" during a practice training session. A tally of 60 or 70 nonverbal connectors in a ten-minute talk was not uncommon, and invariably, the student teachers were flabbergasted when I revealed these totals to them. "I don't remember saying that at all," was a common response.

So we started videotaping the evidence. The video doesn't lie.

When you are recording narration, be on the lookout for nonverbal connectors. They rear their ugly heads during playback and become very distracting as the minutes and "umms" roll by. Fortunately, movie narration can be scripted, and reading directly from a script can help you avoid this problem.

Recording narration over video in Movie Maker

Movie Maker gives youtwo ways to record narration. You can record audio using only Movie Maker's Record dialog box, or you can use the Record Narration tool on the Timeline. This simple tool lets you quickly record narration to accompany the video in your project. The narration will be recorded as a .WAV file and imported into your movie if you follow these steps:

1. **Open the collection where you ultimately want your narration clip to be stored.**

2. **On the Timeline, click Record Narration. The Record Narration dialog box appears, as shown in Figure 12-1.**

3. **If you want your narration to completely cover the audio that is part of the video track you are recording over, place a check mark next to Mute video soundtrack.**

4. **Click Record to begin recording.**

   The video should begin playing in the preview window as you record.

Figure 12-1:
Use this
dialog box
to record
narration
over
existing
video.

5. **Click Stop to cease recording.**

   The Save Windows Media File dialog box appears.

6. **Name and save the file.**

Your narration is saved as a .WAV file and placed in whichever collection you chose back in Step 1. It is also imported directly into your current project.

Note: Depending on your hardware, you may find that the Record Narration feature works only if the video that you insert into a project contains no audio of its own. If you see a warning dialog box claiming that your audio device is not currently available, use Movie Maker's Record tool instead to record your narration.

Adding a Music Score to Your Movies

Narration can be useful and important in many of your film projects, but let's face it: Narration just isn't as exciting and fun as music. Thankfully, music can be added to your movie projects just as easily as any other kind of audio file. You can use a music track in the background of other audio that was recorded with your video, or even overlap and transition audio clips just as you can video clips. The right music can have a major impact on the overall mood and quality of your movies.

Note: Just as with video clips, Movie Maker does not let you completely over-lap audio clips. Thus, if you want to add a continuous soundtrack of music to the background of your movie project, you may have a hard time adding other sound clips in the middle of the movie.

What kind of music can I import?

Windows Movie Maker supports some of the most common formats of audio files used on PCs today. They include:

- ✔ **.WAV:** WAV files are common on computers running Windows. Most of the sounds that Windows makes — including the Microsoft sound that you hear when Windows first starts and the crumpled paper sound that the Recycle Bin makes — are recorded in .WAV format. Files recorded with Windows Sound Recorder use this format as well.

- ✔ **.AIF, .AIFC, .AIFF:** Audio files recorded using the *Audio Interchange File Format* (AIFF) are common among Macintosh users. This format can be thought of as the Macintosh equivalent of .WAV.

- ✔ **.AU, .SND:** If AIFF is the Mac equivalent of PC .WAV files, .AU files serve the same purpose on UNIX platforms. Some newer audio applications designed for computers running Linux (a UNIX variant) also produce .SND files.

- ✔ **.MP3:** MP3 files provide near CD-quality sound but at a much smaller file size. MP3 has become a popular format for sharing music over the Internet. A few MP3 recorders are available (see Chapter 6).

- ✔ **.WMA:** These files are designed specifically for Windows Media Applications such as Windows Media Player and Windows Movie Maker.

If you have some audio that is not in one of these formats, you won't be able to import it directly into Movie Maker. The most common type of audio that you can't import directly is CD Audio (.CDA), the format that is used on music CDs like those you listen to in the CD players in your home and car stereos. Chapter 6 describes how to convert .CDA audio into a file that you can use, such as .WMA.

Importing sound files

If you have some sound files that you want to use in your movie project, they need to be imported into Movie Maker before you can use them:

1. **Launch Movie Maker, if it isn't open already, and open the collection where you want to store the audio you plan to import.**

   You may want to create a new collection specifically for storing audio files.

2. **On the menu bar, choose File⇨Import.**

   The Select the File to Import dialog appears, as shown in Figure 12-2.

3. **Navigate to the file you want to import and select it.**

Click to choose a different folder or disk.

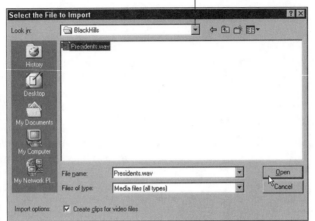

Figure 12-2:
Locate and
select the
audio file
that you
want to
import.

4. Click Open.

The file is imported and will appear in the collection you chose back in Step 1. Figure 12-3 shows a collection full of audio files that have been imported into Movie Maker.

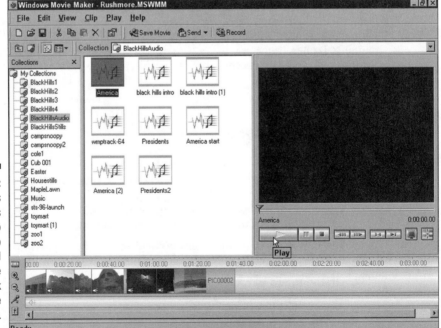

Figure 12-3:
This
collection is
used to
store audio
files that I
plan to use
in my Black
Hills movie
projects.

Adding Audio Files to Your Projects

Movie Maker's Timeline makes adding audio files to your projects easy. Open a project that you've been working on and want to add an audio file to. Then follow these steps:

1. **Switch to Timeline mode.**

   You cannot add audio clips to the Storyboard.

2. **Open the collection that contains the audio clip you want to add.**

3. **Click and hold the left mouse button on the audio clip and drag it to the approximate location on the Timeline where you want to add it.**

4. **Release the mouse button.**

   The clip appears on the audio track portion of the Timeline, as shown in Figure 12-4.

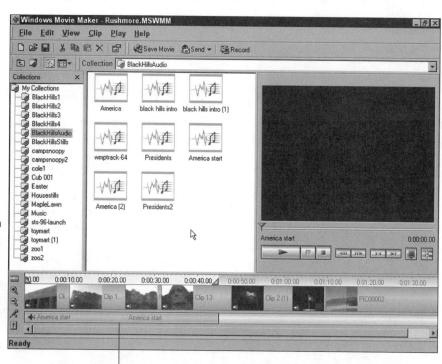

Figure 12-4: An audio clip has been added to the beginning of this project.

Audio clip

You can follow these steps to add additional audio clips to your project. One of the key ways in which audio clips differ from video clips is that they can have space in between them. Long periods with no audio track can elapse in your movie, or the movie may just have the audio track that was recorded with your video.

Audio clips on the soundtrack of your movies can also be moved easily. Simply click and hold the mouse pointer on the audio clip and slide it left or right along the Timeline. As you move the clip, you see an outline of it, as shown in Figure 12-5.

Figure 12-5:
Adjust an audio clip by sliding it left or right along the Timeline.

Working with audio clips on the Timeline

Just as with video clips, sometimes you will want to trim your audio clips a bit to better fit the overall project. This is especially true if you are working with long audio clips such as songs. In my Mount Rushmore film project, I use portions of the Neil Diamond song "America" in the soundtrack. But that song is more than four minutes long, and my entire movie project lasts less than half that time. If I simply insert the entire song as an audio clip (as Figure 12-6 shows that I have), it will continue playing to a black screen for almost two and a half minutes after the actual video in my movie has ended. Clearly, some trimming is in order.

Figure 12-6:
The audio clip "America" is obviously too long for this video.

End of video

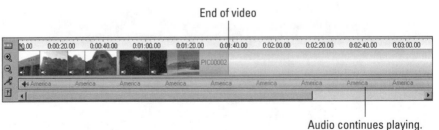

Audio continues playing.

Splitting an audio clip

Before inserting a song or doing any trimming, you need to decide exactly which portions of the clip you want to use and where. In my Mount Rushmore project, I use the first part of the song in the beginning of my movie, followed by some narration clips; finally, I close the movie with the end of the song.

The best way to implement this is to first split the song clip into several portions. Because I'm basically using two parts of the song "America," I split it into three parts: The beginning, the middle (which I don't plan to use), and the end. To split an audio clip:

1. **Click once on the clip in the collection to select it; then, right-click the clip and choose Copy.**

2. **Right-click a blank area of the collection and choose Paste.**

   A copy of the clip is pasted into the collection.

   Note: Copying the clip allows you to make as many changes as you want while preserving an unmodified version for future use.

3. **Select the clip copy and click Play in the preview screen.**

   The clip should begin playing.

4. **When the song reaches the point at which you want to split it, click Pause.**

   It may take some practice and several tries to get the song paused at exactly the point at which you want to split it.

5. **On the preview controls, click Split Clip (or choose Clip⇨Split on the menu bar).**

   Movie Maker splits the clip into two parts.

6. **Repeat these steps to split the clips into even smaller portions as needed.**

Now you can insert the smaller, more manageable clips into your movie project. As Figure 12-7 shows, I have placed four audio clips into the current project, with the "America start" and "America end" clips acting as bookends for the whole soundtrack.

Figure 12-7:
Four audio clips have been added to this project.

Trimming audio clips

The first audio clip in my Mount Rushmore project, "America start," is still too long. It needs to be trimmed so that it fits the project better. Trimming an audio clip is easy:

1. **Click once on the clip you want to trim to select it.**

   Trim points should appear on the Timeline at the start and end of the clip.

2. **Click and hold the mouse pointer on one of the trim points and drag it left or right to shorten the clip.**

   Movie Maker does not automatically reposition the clips, so you may have to do some repositioning manually after you have performed your trimming (see Figure 12-8).

Figure 12-8:
"America start" has been trimmed, and now all the audio clips need to be repositioned.

3. **Click Play on the preview screen to listen to the audio clip.**

   Make sure that you haven't clipped off something really important.

Transitioning between audio clips

Audio clips can be overlapped just as video clips can. And, as with video clips, one audio clip cannot completely cover up another audio clip. Overlapping can be handy if, for instance, you want to hear both narration and music simultaneously. Figure 12-9 shows several audio clips overlapped on the soundtrack.

When you overlap video clips, Movie Maker automatically incorporates a cross-fade transition. Unfortunately, Movie Maker cannot transition audio clips in this same manner. That means that if you have trimmed an audio clip of a song and the music now ends rather abruptly, the transition in the movie will be abrupt as well. The only way around this is to edit sound clips with another program so that they fade in or out at the transition points.

Figure 12-9:
Audio clips
can overlap
each other,
but one
cannot
completely
cover up
another.

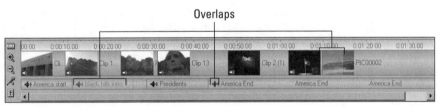

Overlaps

Many other video-editing programs allow two or more audio tracks. This feature allows you to overlap multiple audio tracks, such as narration and background music. If you have another program that allows multiple audio tracks, try using it to produce an audio file with the exact characteristics you want.

Adjusting audio levels

Sometimes, the audio tracks you add are meant to augment the audio already recorded with your video. Other times, you'll want to completely replace that audio with a soundtrack of your own. Movie Maker lets you adjust the over all audio level for each movie project, letting you specify whether the project's audio track or the video's audio track should be predominant. To adjust the audio level, click Set audio levels on the Timeline or choose Edit⇨Audio levels from the menu bar. You should see a dialog box similar to Figure 12-10.

Figure 12-10:
Adjust audio
levels to
give
preference
to the audio
that you
inserted in
the Timeline
or the audio
that came
with the
video.

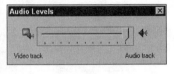

If you placed a song in the audio track that you want to play softly in the background, move the slider left toward "Video track." But if you prefer your own soundtrack to the one that was recorded with the video, move the slider right toward "Audio track." As Figure 12-10 shows, I have moved the slider all the way to the right so that the audio recorded with the video is completely silenced in favor of my audio track.

Can you set different audio levels for different parts of a single movie? No, unfortunately, you can't. Maybe if we all whine loudly enough about this oversight, Microsoft will include it in the next version.

Creating Video-less Movies

Movie Maker was designed to help you make movies; no big surprises here. But that doesn't mean that you can use it only for editing videos. You can also use this program for creating slide shows using nothing more than a few still photos and some audio clips. You may find this capability especially useful if you want to share some photographs but also want to be able to provide a verbal description of each picture.

Figure 12-11 shows a movie I created using only still photographs and a narration clip.

Video-less movies such as this let you get really creative. Try setting some of your favorite digital photos to music and see how it turns out!

Figure 12-11:
This home tour "movie" was made up entirely of still photographs and a narration track.

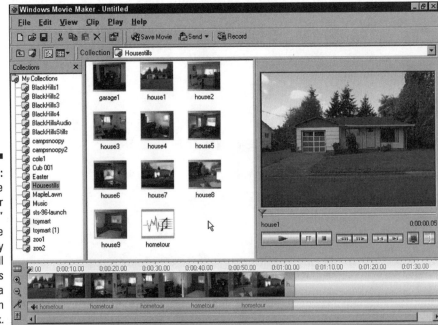

Chapter 13

Giving Yourself Credit with Titles

*H*ow many chapters in this book begin with some sort of witty analogy that mentions *Star Wars* at least once? Most of them. I'll save some time for now and pretend that I've already said something about the opening scenes of *Star Wars* — I probably would have said something about the famous screen that begins the story with, "A long time ago, in a galaxy far, far away. . ." — and that you fully understand the importance of scenes in a movie that contain printed words.

I will also make believe that I made a heartfelt plea to give credit where credit is due, and you now feel compelled to finish every movie with a series of title screens that list everyone involved in the filming and production of your desktop movie masterpiece. Okay? Time to get on with it, then.

Go Ahead, Pat Yourself on the Back

You worked hard on your movie. You know it. Most of the people you are sharing it with know it. But does everyone know about the hours and hours of retakes you forced your children to stand through? Are they aware that your kid brother Larry spent that entire amount of time holding a 30-pound microphone boom, or that your spouse refreshed the entire film crew with a hearty lunch? Do they even know the names of all the people who appear in your movie?

Heartfelt gratitude is in order, and one of the best ways you can show your appreciation for all the tireless effort that everyone put into your movie is to give each one credit in a title screen at the beginning or end (or both) of your movie, like the credit shown in Figure 13-1. Besides, it's a lot cheaper than a *real* gift, so what have you got to lose?

Figure 13-1:
A title
screen can
be a great
way of
giving credit
to your
helpers and
is cheaper
than
treating
them to
dinner.

Giving credit to people who worked on your movies isn't the only use for title screens. Other uses can include:

- ✔ Provide some introductory text that gives a background of the movie's story. "It is a dark time for the rebellion. . . ."

- ✔ In a movie that consists of still photographs, use title slides between the pictures to explain each one.

- ✔ Find some piano music, dub it over the entire video, and use title slides to provide dialog, silent-movie style.

Of course, you really, *really* should make a title slide that gives credit to everyone involved for every movie project you do. If nothing else, doing so will help you remember who worked on it when the movie file turns up years later on a disk at the bottom of your desk drawer. And don't forget to identify yourself in there somewhere! When your movie becomes a cult favorite on the Internet, you'll want the millions of viewers to know who the genius is who produced it. Unless, of course, anonymity better suits the type of movie you are producing.

Creating Title Slides

It is time to start creating some title slides, but before you fire up Movie Maker, I should warn you that Movie Maker is incapable of creating such slides. You're going to have to use another program that can create title slides that can then be imported into Movie Maker. Microsoft recommends that you use Windows Paint, and so do I, because if you have Windows Me, you have Windows Paint. Paint is a graphics editor, but you can use it to create bitmap (.BMP) images containing words. Bitmaps can be easily imported into Movie Maker and then inserted into a project.

To launch Paint, choose Start➪Programs➪Accessories➪Paint. The Paint program appears, as shown in Figure 13-2.

Drawing tools

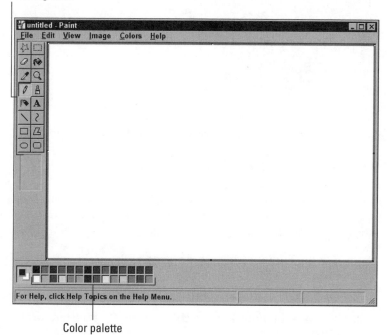

Figure 13-2:
Use
Windows
Paint to
create title
slides for
your movies.

Color palette

Creating title screens

Your first step in creating a title screen in Paint should be to make the shape of your image the same as the shape of Movie Maker's video screen. The video screen has a width-to-height ratio of 4:3, and because the largest size video that Movie Maker can produce is 320 by 240 pixels, that is a good size to work with in Paint as well. Adjusting the size of the screen is easy:

1. **In Paint, choose Image➪Attributes from the menu bar.**

   The Attributes dialog box appears, as shown in Figure 13-3.

2. **Change the Width to 320 and the Height to 240.**

3. **Click OK to close the Attributes dialog box.**

   The size of the image area is probably smaller than it was.

Figure 13-3:
Change the
size of your
image to 320
by 240
pixels.

Now you are ready to begin creating your actual title slides.

Creating a plain black slide

One of the handiest slides you can use in a movie project is also one of the simplest to create. You should create a plain black slide that you can use as a placeholder or break between various scenes in your movies. Follow these steps:

1. **Click the Fill tool from the drawing tools on the left side of the Paint window.**

   The Fill tool looks like a bottle of spilling ink.

2. **Make sure that black is the color currently selected for the left mouse button.**

   The two squares in the bottom-left corner of the screen show you which colors are currently selected for the left mouse button (top) and right mouse button (underneath).

3. **Click once with the left mouse button in the image area.**

   The entire area should fill with black, as shown in Figure 13-4.

4. **Choose File➪Save from the menu bar.**

   In the Save As dialog box, givethe picture a simple name (such as "Black") and save the file. Make a note of where you are saving it!

A plain black slide will come in handy many times as you create and edit movie projects. It can also serve as a good background for other title slides.

Creating a basic title slide

Paint includes a Text tool to let you type text onto a graphic. This is the tool that you will use to create your titles but it takes a bit of practice to truly master. Text is difficult to line up properly, it often ends up too big or too small for the screen, and the text tool itself is sensitive to imprecise mouse clicks.

Fill tool

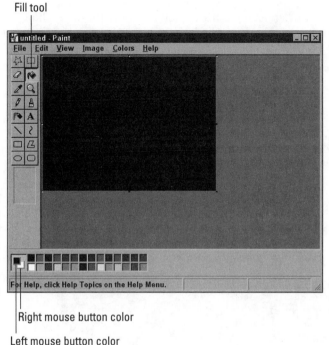

Figure 13-4:
Use the Fill
tool to turn
the entire
image black.

Right mouse button color

Left mouse button color

But using the Text tool is still worth the trouble. To enter some text onto a graphic:

1. **Format the graphic so that it measures 320 by 240 pixels, and color the entire background black as described earlier in this chapter in "Creating a Plain Black Slide."**

2. **Click the color white in the color palate with the left mouse button to change the left mouse button color to white.**

   If you are working over a black background, black text usually doesn't show up very well. Text that you type using the text tool will be in whichever color you choose for the left mouse button.

   Note: Actually, you don't have to choose white; just choose something that will contrast well with black. Experiment a bit to get a color that looks right to you.

3. **Click the Text tool (it has the letter "A" on it) to select it.**

4. **Locate the two pictures directly under the drawing tools and choose the bottom one, as shown in Figure 13-5.**

The upper picture shows a green square in an area with a white background, whereas the bottom picture shows the same thing with a clear background. Choosing the bottom picture makes the background of the text box transparent.

5. Move the mouse pointer over the image area.

The pointer should become a cross-hair.

6. Use the mouse pointer to draw a box in the image area approximately where you want the text to appear.

To draw a box, click and hold the mouse button and drag the pointer to draw a box.

Select this.

Text tool

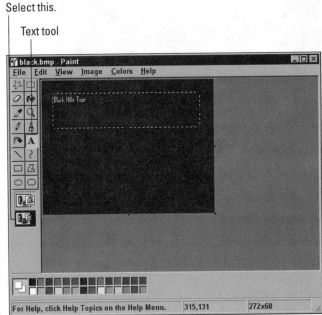

Figure 13-5:
Type text in the text box, remembering that the text color is based on the left mouse button color.

6. Release the mouse pointer when the box is the size you want it.

If anything, make the box a bit bigger than you think it should be. Also, try to center the box on the slide as much as possible.

7. Type some text.

Chances are good that you won't be happy with the formatting of the text, and I show you how to fix that next. As you can see in Figure 13-5, the text I typed is currently too small and the font is ugly.

8. **On the Paint menu bar, choose <u>V</u>iew⇨Text Toolbar.**

   The Fonts toolbar (why isn't it called "Text"? I don't know, either) appears, as shown in Figure 13-6. Move it out of the way of your text if necessary.

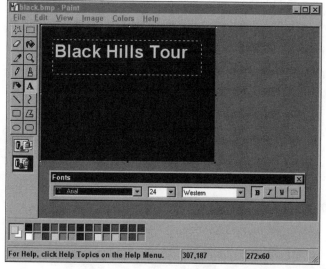

Figure 13-6:
The Fonts toolbar lets you modify the characteristics of your text.

9. **On the Fonts toolbar, choose a different font, font size, or font style (if applicable) from the various drop-down menus.**

   You can also click buttons to make the text boldfaced, italicized, or underlined. Looking at Figure 13-6, you can see that I have changed my title to boldfaced 24-point Arial. Simple yet effective.

10. **If you want to center the text, do what they always tell you not to do in word processing books: Place the cursor in front of the text and press the spacebar a few times until the words are sufficiently centered.**

11. **When you are done typing and modifying the text in this text box, click somewhere outside the text box.**

    Clicking outside the text box chisels the text into the stone of your picture, and after the text box is closed, no way exists for you to go back and edit it.

12. **If you want to add more text to the slide, repeat the steps to create more text boxes, but keep in mind that your audience won't have much time to read each slide.**

13. **When you are done creating the slide, choose <u>F</u>ile⇨Save <u>A</u>s; then, name the file descriptively (and remember where you are saving it) and click Save to save the slide.**

Paint offers a huge variety of fonts (depending on your Windows installation), and some of them are pretty fancy. But keep in mind that your title screens will probably display for short periods of time, so maximum readability should be one of your main concerns when you choose a font. In most cases, I suggest something simple such as Arial or Times New Roman.

Using still images for your background

Besides creating basic little bitmap files for title slides, you can also use Paint to perform basic editing of JPEG and GIF images. JPEGs and GIFs are the two most common picture formats used on the Internet and thus have become popular for digital images in the entire PC world.

Why does this matter to you? You can use Paint to add some text to a picture or even modify a picture that you plan to import into Movie Maker. Because this book is not called *Windows Paint For Dummies*, I stick to describing how to add text to a picture:

1. **In Paint, choose File⇨Open.**

   The Open dialog box appears, as shown in Figure 13-7.

Figure 13-7: You can open some of the most common picture types in Paint.

Choose All Picture Files.

2. **In the "Files of type" box at the bottom of the dialog box, choose "All Picture Files" from the drop-down menu.**

3. **Navigate to the folder that contains the picture you want to use, select the picture, and click Open to open it.**

   The picture opens in Paint. Resize or crop it to 320 x 240 pixels as necessary.

4. **Click the Text tool to enable it.**

   Under the drawing tools, make sure that you choose the option to create a text box with an invisible background.

5. **Choose an appropriate color from the color palette.**

   Color choice can be tricky, especially if you want to place text over a really colorful area.

6. **Draw your text box and type your text.**

   If you want to change the text's formatting, choose View⇨Text Toolbar. As Figure 13-8 shows, I drew my text box over the roadway in the photograph because it was easy to contrast with and unimportant enough to cover with words.

7. **When you are done, choose File⇨Save As and save the picture.**

Figure 13-8:
Paint lets you enter text on pictures, such as this .JPEG image.

I strongly urge you to save the picture with a unique filename. That way, the original copy of the picture remains text free for use another time.

Importing Title Screens into Movie Maker

Creating title screens with Paint makes a lot of sense because they can be easily imported into Movie Maker when you're ready to use them. You import the title screens just the same as any other still graphic:

1. **Select the collection in Movie Maker where you want to save them.**

2. **Choose File⇨Import and then locate the files you want to import.**

As usual, I recommend that you create a special collection just for collecting title screens.

Positioning Title Screens in Your Movies

Many of the titles you plan to use will probably be right up front at the beginning of your movie, but of course, you can insert them anywhere you want. Inserting a title screen into a movie project is a lot like inserting any other still clip:

1. **Open the project that you want to add the title screens to.**

2. **Select the first title screen clip and drag it to the workspace (Storyboard or Timeline, it really doesn't matter).**

3. **For effect, place a plain black clip directly after the title clip you just inserted.**

   Placing this clip makes the transition from one title clip to the next smoother.

   Note: Don't have a plain black clip? See "Creating a Plain Black Slide," earlier in this chapter.

4. **Continue adding title clips, remembering to put a plain black clip between each title clip.**

   The result may look similar to Figure 13-9. Also place a black clip between the last title clip and the first video clip.

Figure 13-9:
Place a
plain black
slide
between
each title
slide you
insert.

Control how long title screens display

Chances are that you still have Movie Maker set up so that still images play
for five seconds each in a video. Five seconds is probably too long for most
title screens, especially the black ones that you put between each title clip.
You should adjust the play time for each clip individually using the Timeline:

1. **Switch to Timeline mode if you haven't done so already.**

   If necessary, zoom in on the Timeline to get a better view.

2. **Select a title clip and use the trim points at the beginning and end of it
   to adjust the length of time it displays for.**

   Generally speaking, the black slides between each title should play for a
   very short time, usually not more than a second. Your Timeline will
   probably end up looking a lot like the one in Figure 13-10.

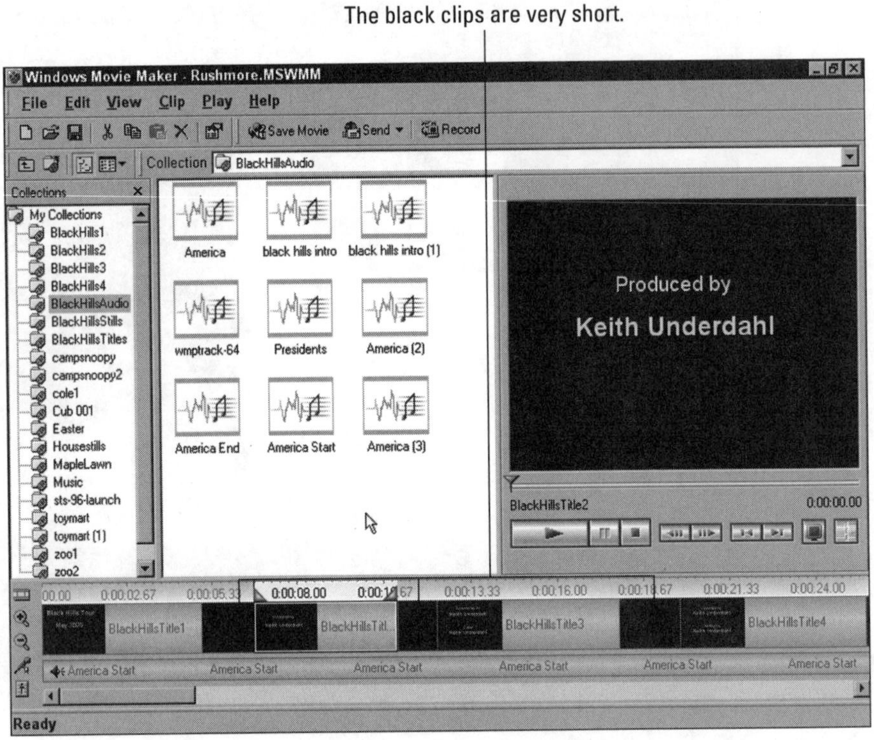

The black clips are very short.

Figure 13-10:
The title
clips on this
Timeline
vary in
length. The
length of
each one
was
dictated by
the music
that accom-
panies it on
the audio
track.

The whole process will probably require some trial-and-error editing, especially if you are trying to synchronize the titles with some music. As a general
rule, try to set the play time for title screens so that you can read it twice
before it disappears again.

Clean up those transitions!

The main reason I suggest that you place plain black clips between title
screens is that they tend to smooth the transitions between clips nicely. You
may decide after some experimentation that you prefer to leave the black
clips out, and that's fine. But they can also come in handy, especially if the
background of each title screen is also black. If you create a cross-fade transition between a plain black clip and a title clip with a black background, it
makes the words look as though they are fading in or out, as opposed to
"blinking" in or out with a straight-cut transition. Depending on the type of
sequence you are looking for, you may want the words to blink in and fade
out, fade in and blink out, or even fade in *and* fade out. Again, each movie
project is a little different, so you should experiment to get just the right
effect each time.

As with video clips, you can create a cross-fade transition by dragging a trim point from one clip over an adjacent clip so that they overlap slightly. Figure 13-11 shows that I have created cross-fade transitions at the beginning and end of each title clip. The preview screen shows one of the title clips fading into view.

Just as with video clips, you control the length of cross-fades by increasing or decreasing the overlap. The greater the overlap of clips, the slower the words appear to fade in or out.

If you have already synchronized your title clips to some music and now you want to add some cross-fade transitions, move only the End Trim points for each respective clip, including the black clips. Each clip will begin to appear at the same point it did before if you leave the Start Trim points alone.

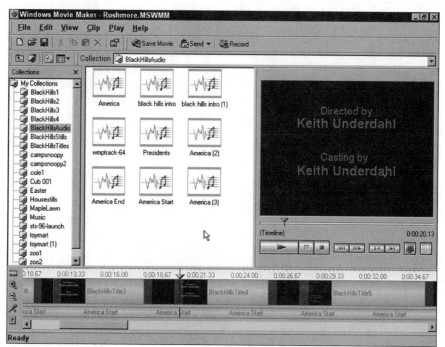

Figure 13-11: The clip BlackHills Title4 is just fading in.

Part IV
And the Award
Goes to . . .

The 5th Wave   By Rich Tennant

@RICHTENNANT

"Of course graphics are important to your
project, Eddy, but I think it would've been better
to scan a _picture_ of your worm collection."

In this part . . .

*1*t's time to put the finishing touches on your movie projects and distribute them to your friends and loved
ones. In this part, you master Windows Media Player, the
program used to view the movies you create in Windows
Movie Maker. You also create a simple Web page to serve
as an online screening room for your movies and e-mail
movies to people as well. In case you want to distribute
your movies on CD or videotape, the last chapter of this
part guides you through that process.

Chapter 14

The Director's Cut

*I*f you want to make good movies — and I mean *really* good movies — you'll have to spend a lot of time reviewing and re-editing your project. Careful review may show you that the soundtrack isn't synchronized just right, or that a certain clip doesn't show long enough, or that you forgot to identify someone in the credits. Review may even reveal that whole new scenes need to be added.

In this chapter, I look at ways to more efficiently review your movie projects, and you see how, when you have everything *just right,* to save the finalized movie. Finally, you create a short version of a longer film project for promotional purposes or those poor souls with slow Internet connections.

Previewing Your Movie

I probably don't have to tell you how important previewing your movie is before you start sharing it with other people. But do you know the best way to preview it? While you are still editing it in Movie Maker, you have a couple of ways to preview. The simplest method is to simply preview the entire project from start to finish:

1. **Open the project you want to preview.**

2. **Right-click the Timeline (or Storyboard) and choose Play Entire Storyboard/Timeline, as shown in Figure 14-1.**

   You can also choose Play⇨Play Entire Storyboard/Timeline from the Movie Maker menu bar.

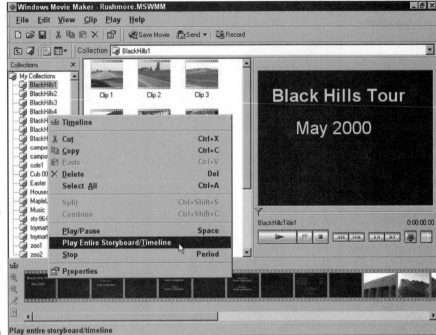

Figure 14-1: Choose Play Entire Storyboard/ Timeline to preview your project.

3. Wait a few seconds.

The preview screen should eventually start playing your project, complete with sound and video.

As the movie plays, the Timeline or Storyboard (whichever is shown) shows some progression during the playback. In Figure 14-2, you can see that the current clip is shown on the Storyboard. Also, the preview screen identifies the current playback as "Timeline" instead of naming a specific clip.

4. Click Pause under the preview screen to pause playback at any time.

If you click Stop, the entire playback will stop.

Of course, previewing your movie in Movie Maker tells you only one thing: The movie works well in Movie Maker. To be really, really sure that everything is okay, you need to save the movie and preview it in Windows Media Player as well. You should do this after you've made most of the edits you want to make, by the way. And don't forget to save your project before closing Movie Maker! This will make future edits much easier.

Current playback point   Make sure it says "Timeline" here.

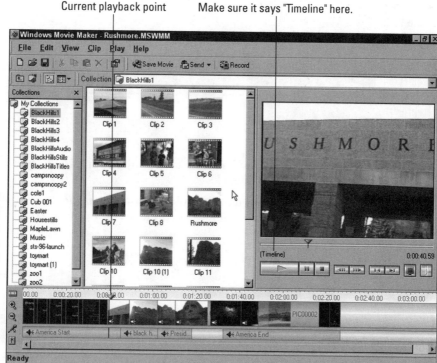

Figure 14-2:
As the movie project plays, the Timeline indicates the current point in the movie.

Beginning playback in the middle of the Timeline

Sometimes you don't want to preview the entire movie; you just want to start playback at a certain point somewhere in the middle. This can be done in Timeline mode by following these steps:

1. **Switch your project to Timeline mode if you haven't already.**

2. **Click in a gray area of the Timeline, as shown in Figure 14-3.**

   The entire Timeline should turn to a solid color (see Figure 14-4). Also, you should see the word *Timeline* under the preview screen.

Click here.

Figure 14-3:
Click a gray
area of the
timeline to
select the
entire
project.

3. **Click in the yellow Timeline area on the approximate spot where you want to begin playback.**

   The Play Indicator moves to that spot, and you should see the frame corresponding to the indicator in the preview window, similar to Figure 14-4.

Play Indicator

Entire timeline is yellow.

Figure 14-4:
Click the
yellow
Timeline to
move the
Play
Indicator.

4. **Click Play to begin playback from this point.**

When you want to stop playback, click Pause or Stop as appropriate.

If you need to move the Play Indicator to a very specific spot in the timeline, pause playback as close to that point as possible and use the Previous Frame and Next Frame buttons to get to the exact spot you want.

Deciding what to cut and what to keep

Proofreading a writing project is a difficult and challenging task. Whether you are proof reading a memo to your co-workers, a research paper for a class, or a ...*For Dummies* book, you probably change something every time you read through. This makes the whole process of proofreading difficult because you never actually read through the whole thing, start to finish, as your readers will. Without an uninterrupted read through, it can be difficult to get a good feel for what the readers will think after *they* read it.

You may find that previewing a movie project works the same way. You start previewing, but then you see something you want to adjust, so you pause playback and make some more edits. You could spend hours editing a ten-minute movie without ever actually watching it as your audience will, *start to finish*. So it may take some special effort, but do try to review your complete movie, from beginning to end, a few times before releasing it.

During review, a few things to watch for include:

- ✔ Clips that run too long
- ✔ Straight-cut transitions that would work better as cross-fades, and vice versa
- ✔ Cross-fades that happen too fast (or take too long)
- ✔ Clips that enhance the overall movie experience a lot less than you thought they would

One of the things I observed when I was previewing my Mount Rushmore movie was how abruptly the title slide at the end came and went. As Figure 14-5 shows, I added a plain black slide to the very end of the movie and created a cross-fade transition into it. Now, as the last of the music on the soundtrack trails off, the screen slowly fades to black.

Figure 14-5:
The black
clip at the
end of this
project was
added after
the preview
showed that
the movie
ended too
abruptly.

Saving Your Film

You've gone to all the trouble of creating your own movie masterpiece. You probably did all this work because you want to share the movie with other people, right? Windows Movie Maker helps you share your movies in many ways, including easing the process of e-mailing movies or placing them on Web servers.

But sometimes, all you really need is a file. Saving a movie project as a file is easy:

1. **When you are done editing your project in Movie Maker, save the project by choosing File⇨Save Project.**

   The project file is saved.

2. **After you have saved the project, click Save Movie on the Project toolbar (or choose File⇨Save Movie from the menu bar).**

   The Save Movie dialog box appears, as shown in Figure 14-6.

3. **Choose a quality level for the movie you plan to save from the Setting menu.**

   If you don't like the basic Low, Medium, and High settings, choose Other for a greater variety of choices. Notice that as you change the quality setting, the dialog box gives you an estimate of the file size and download times at various Internet connection speeds. If you plan to share the movie only on disk, save it at the highest-quality setting possible.

   Note: The download times listed in the Save Movie dialog box are more for the benefit of your audience than for you. Remember that many (perhaps most?) of the people you plan to share your movie with have fairly slow Internet connections, and if your movie is too big, they will not be able to view it.

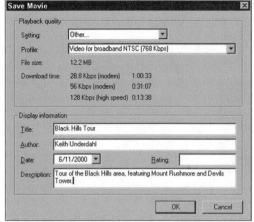

Figure 14-6:
Choose a
quality level
and enter
other
information
about your
movie here.

4. **Enter additional information about the movie such as the Title, Author, rating, and a description.**

   This information appears in the Windows Media Player display as the viewer watches the movie.

5. **Click OK.**

   The Save As dialog box appears, as shown in Figure 14-7.

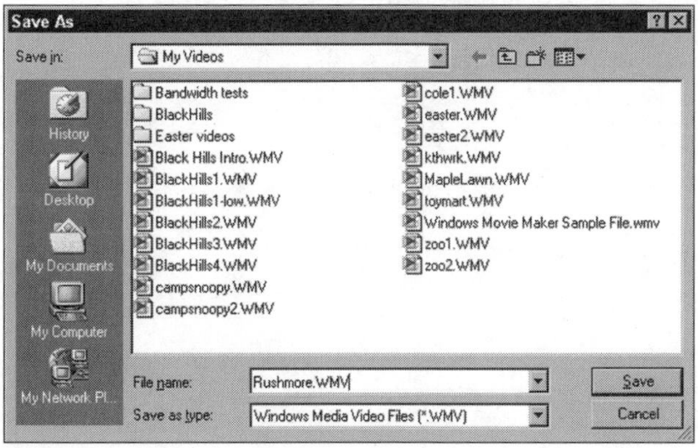

Figure 14-7:
Give your
movie a
name and
make a note
of the
location
where you
are saving it.

6. **Give the file a name and click Save.**

   Movie Maker creates the movie and saves it to your hard drive. The movie-creation process may take a few minutes, depending on the length of your movie, during which time you'll see the Creating Movie dialog box, as shown in Figure 14-8.

7. **After the movie is created, a dialog box asks whether you want to watch it; click Yes to open Windows Media Player and have the movie begin to play.**

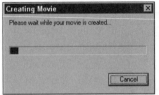

Saving your movie as an .ASF file

When you save a movie in Movie Maker, the program saves it as a Windows Media Video (.WMV) file. .WMV is similar to — but not exactly the same as — .ASF video files. A little-known secret of Windows Movie Maker is that you can save movies as .ASF files rather than .WMV simply by putting the .ASF extension on the end of the movie's filename when you save it. Figure 14-9 shows that I am saving my Mount Rushmore movie as an .ASF rather than a .WMV movie.

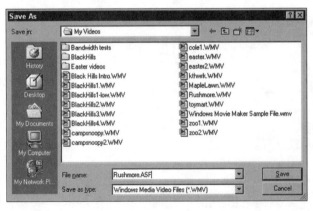

Why bother saving a movie as an .ASF file? In rare cases, some Web servers will not accept .WMV files because they do not recognize the format. If you are trying to upload a .WMV movie to a server that for some reason won't accept it, try saving the movie as an .ASF file instead.

Furthermore, some older versions of Windows Media Player cannot play .WMV files, but they are able to play .ASF files without any problem. If you have viewers who complain about this problem, you should probably first suggest that they download a newer version of Media Player. But if they are very stubborn about it and you really want them to see the movie, saving it as .ASF may help.

You saved your movie; where is it?

In a fit of excitement, you created and saved your movie, but now you can't remember where you saved it. If you picked a different folder in the Save As dialog box and now you can't remember which one you picked, I can't help you a whole lot. But if all you did was name it and click Save, it is probably in the folder C:\My Documents\My Videos. That is the default location for saving movies in Movie Maker.

As a last resort, you could, of course, search for it in Windows. Choose Start➪Search➪For Files or Folders. The Windows search window appears, and you can search all the disk drives on your computer for the filename. You *do* remember what you named the file, right?

If you can't remember a filename, try using the asterisk (*) as a wildcard in your search and look for all movie files. To do this, enter ***.WMV** or ***.ASF** in the search field.

Creating Short Versions of Your Films

In theory, no limit is placed on the length of movies you can make with Windows Movie Maker. But in practice, most of your movies will be fairly short, especially the ones you plan to share online. As movies get longer, their file sizes increase, to the point at which most movies that are longer than about ten minutes are simply too big to be shared online, especially if you want to maintain some level of acceptable quality.

For instance, I created a 25-minute movie. Using Movie Maker's very lowest-quality setting — Video for Web servers (28.8Kbps) — the file is still 3.1MB. Saved at a quality level that I would consider marginally acceptable — Video for single-channel ISDN (64Kbps) — that 25-minute film is more than 8MB. At the highest setting, this movie is about 125MB, small enough to fit on a CD-ROM but too big for almost anything else.

When you have longer movies, you may want to create shorter versions of them for several reasons:

- ✔ Shorter versions of a film will let people with slower Internet connections view some highlights without your having to reduce video quality.
- ✔ If you offer really long movies on CD, place a short, promotional version on your Web site.
- ✔ If the movie depicts an event or other news, some viewers may want to see the entire video whereas others prefer just the highlights.

If you decide to create a short version of one of your longer movies, use a narration track or song over the entire video and set the audio levels so that audio from the video track is obscured.

Don't forget to save your short video as a separate project in Movie Maker! If you simply shorten an existing project and click Save, much of your work from the longer project may be lost.

Chapter 15

Playing Your Movies with Windows Media Player

*Y*ou've spent a lot of time perfecting your videos in Movie Maker. But all your effort is for naught if you can't share your movies with friends and family. If you don't mind me asking, how exactly were you planning to accomplish this? Were you planning to put them on a disk or e-mail them as electronic .WMV (Windows Media Video) or .ASF (Advanced Streaming Format) files? Or were you simply going to record them onto a VHS videocassette tape?

Whatever method you decide on for "distributing" your movies, you need to make sure that you do it in a format that your intended audience can use. For instance, if you record .WMV movie files onto CDs, they won't be of much use to people who don't have computers. And even those people who *do* have computers won't be able to watch the movies if they don't have a program that can play .WMV files.

Windows Media Player — abbreviated here as WiMP — is the main program for playing .WMV files. Are you sure that your audience has WiMP? Do they know how to use it? Do you? This chapter shows you how to use WiMP and helps you teach others to use it. But first you need to figure out whether your audience can view your movies at all.

Determining Who Can (And Can't) Watch Your Movies

If you can record movies from your computer onto videocassette tapes, anyone with a VCR can view them. Just about everyone you know has a TV and VCR, so videotapes should ensure the widest possible audience.

Fewer people have computers, and fewer still have computers that can play the .WMV files produced by Windows Movie Maker. When you tell Movie Maker to "Save Movie," it saves it in the .WMV format, a format that only Microsoft seems to support. Windows Media Player is the most widely available program for playing .WMV files, and it is available for Windows 3.1 and higher, as well as Macintoshes running System 7.6.1 and higher.

Before sending electronic movie files to people, make sure that they have the ability to view them. You can determine this by asking them the following questions:

- ✔ **"What kind of computer do you have?"** If they have a Macintosh or are running Windows, they will probably be able to view your movies. If they have Windows 98 or higher, they should already have Windows Media Player installed.

- ✔ **"How fast is your Internet connection?"** Check this before you e-mail a movie to anyone. If someone's Internet connection is 56Kbps (Kilobytes per second) or slower, avoid sending movies larger than a couple hundred kilobytes.

- ✔ **"Do you have a CD-ROM drive?"** Don't assume that everyone does. If you are going to send your movie on CD, make sure your recipients know that it's meant to be used in their computer, not in a home DVD player or some other kind of player.

- ✔ **"Does your computer have sound, and does it work?"** You would be amazed how many people haven't figured out how to make the sound work in their PCs, or who have dead batteries in their speakers. Many business-use computers don't have any sound capability at all.

- ✔ **"Can your computer display 256 colors or better?"** This will be tougher to check if your audience is filled with novices. Windows users should be able to check this in the Display icon in their Control Panel, and Macintosh users can check the "Monitors & Sound" Control Panel item.

- ✔ **"Do you have Windows Media Player installed?"** If they don't have it installed already, direct them to the Microsoft Web site, where they can download it. Just tell them to visit www.microsoft.com and look for "Windows Media Player" in the "Downloads" section.

If you've asked all these questions, you're still not sure whether sending the person a copy of your movie is worthwhile. Videos require a lot of system power and memory when you play them on a computer, and if the viewer's system isn't up to the task, the movie will not play properly. Microsoft has stated some minimum requirements for using WiMP, but for playing movies, those requirements are not good enough. Instead, your viewers' computers should meet the requirements recommended listed in Table 15-1.

Table 15-1	WiMP Minimum System Recommendations	
Windows 3.1	*Windows 95+*	*Macintosh*
Pentium 90	Pentium 120	PowerPC 180MHz
16MB RAM	32MB RAM	32MB RAM, 10MB free for WiMP
16-bit sound card	16-bit sound card	MacOS 8
256-color video card	256-color video card	16-bit display adapter
Video for Windows		

A growing number of people use the Linux operating system rather than Windows or a Macintosh. No .ASF player is currently available for Linux, but the innovative nature of the Linux community means that one may appear in the near future. If anyone in your audience has Linux, that person probably has a better idea of what programs are available for it than you do.

Are other players available?

No, not really. Well, actually, one program is available for Windows 95 and higher. It's called FMV — Full Motion Video — and is available from Slipstream Systems at www.f-m-v.com. It supports all multimedia formats from Microsoft, including .ASF. FMV also supports Apple-specific formats such as .MOV that are not supported by WiMP.

How does FMV get away with this? FMV doesn't actually play the .ASF files. It simply controls Media Player, which actually plays the file but remains hidden. The program also controls Apple QuickTime, providing you with a single interface from which to play just about every video format that is available. Because FMV controls WiMP, you must have Media Player 6.02 or later installed on your computer. Apple QuickTime 4.0 is also required.

If you're looking for an alternative player that allows you to save space by foregoing Windows Media Player, this isn't it. But if you want to be able to play Microsoft and Apple multimedia files using a single interface, FMV is a good choice.

Who Are You Calling a WiMP?

Windows Me comes with Windows Media Player, or "WiMP" for short. WiMP can play many different kinds of multimedia files, including the .ASF files that are produced by Movie Maker. And if you like to listen to music on your PC, WiMP can be used as a sort of virtual jukebox to play MP3 files or audio CDs that you insert in your CD-ROM drive. You can even use WiMP to listen to radio stations over the Internet!

Windows Me comes with Version 7 of Media Player, but Version 6 can play .ASF files, too. Version 6 came with Windows 98 and 2000 and can be downloaded for free from Microsoft. WiMP 7 supports many popular file formats, as shown Table 15-2.

Table 15-2	WiMP 7 Multimedia Formats
File Extension	*Format*
.CDA	CD Audio
.IVF	Intel Video Technology
.AIF, .AIFF, .AIFC	Macintosh AIFF resources
.ASF, .ASX, .AVI, .WAV, .WAX, .WMA, .WMV, .WVX	Microsoft multimedia formats
.MPEG, .MPG, .M1V, .MP2, .MP3, .MPA, .MPE, .MPV2, .MP2V, .M3U, .PLS	MPEG (Moving Picture Experts Group) multimedia formats
.MID, .MIDI, .RMI	MIDI (Musical Instrument Digital Interface) files
.AU, .SND	UNIX multimedia formats

The only major multimedia file formats that WiMP does not support are those exclusive to Apple's QuickTime Player. But then, QuickTime can't play .ASF files, so I suppose that makes it even. It would be nice if everyone would just settle on one standard, but that isn't going to happen anytime in the near future. Thus, having the right player for your movies is important, and for movies created by Movie Maker, the "right player" is Windows Media Player.

Launching Media Player

Before you can use Windows Media Player, you need to open it. In Windows Me, click Start⇨Programs⇨Accessories⇨Entertainment⇨Windows Media

Player. Depending on your Windows installation, you might have a shortcut for Windows Media Player on your desktop, too. WiMP 7 looks similar to Figure 15-1.

Figure 15-1:
Windows Media Player 7 is open and ready to entertain.

If you are working with an older version of Windows or on another system on which Windows Media Player 6 is installed, the program will be a lot simpler. Figure 15-2 shows WiMP 6 playing a streaming movie from the NASA Web site.

Figure 15-2:
Windows Media Player 6 has a much simpler interface.

Although you can use WiMP to play movies and music on your own computer, many of the program's features require you to be connected to the Internet. I've found that Windows Media Player 7 works more efficiently if an Internet connection is established before opening the program. And, of course, most online media such as movies and music require the highest connection speed you can obtain.

Customizing the WiMP display

Microsoft has done a pretty good job of redesigning Windows Media Player for Version 7. One of the best things about this latest version is the fact that you can change the way the display looks depending on what you want to use it for. You need different controls and different information displayed depending on whether you're watching movies, listening to the radio, listening to a CD, or "channel surfing" the Web.

WiMP 7 has seven buttons on the left side of the window that take you to different screens in the program:

- **Now Playing:** Click this to view whatever media happens to be playing at the moment. If you're just playing music, a graphic appears so that you have something colorful to look at. The graphic is a 3D visualization of whatever sound is playing and can be changed by clicking arrow keys at the bottom of the display.

- **Media Guide:** Microsoft has an online media guide, which you can view by clicking here.

- **CD Audio:** Use this screen to play audio CDs with the CD-ROM drive in your computer. You can also record music from CDs onto your hard drive. The music is recorded in .WMA format, which uses only about one megabyte of storage space per minute of music.

- **Media Library:** Use the WiMP Media Library to organize the multimedia files stored on your computer, including movies.

- **Radio Tuner:** Locate and listen to radio broadcasts on the Internet. You can program preset stations if you wish.

- **Portable Device:** Manage the music on your portable player, such as an MP3 player. You can drag-and-drop music to and from the player when it is connected to your PC.

- **Skin Chooser:** Don't like the way Windows Media Player looks? Choose a different appearance, or "skin," here.

A smaller WiMP

When you are using Windows Media Player to play music or small-screen movies, you may want it to take up less of your computer's display. WiMP has two basic view modes: *Full mode* and *Compact mode.* Full mode is the mode you see when you first open the program. There you should find a button in the lower-right corner for switching to Compact mode. Click it and WiMP switches to a smaller window similar to that shown in Figure 15-3.

As you can see, WiMP actually becomes two small windows in Compact mode. If you click the button in the middle of the small square window, you see a menu with a few basic program controls.

As with almost any Windows program, you can maximize, minimize, or restore the WiMP screen when you are in Full mode, using the controls in the program's title bar. You can also stretch or shrink the window by dragging the borders with the mouse.

Click to change the audio visualization.

Click to view your playlist.

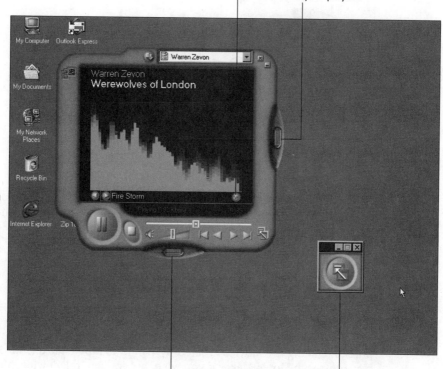

Figure 15-3:
Compact
mode hides
everything
but the
basic
controls
needed for
playback.

Access basic program controls here.

Click to view audio equalizer controls.

There's more than one way to skin WiMP

You've seen the standard appearance of Windows Media Player, but you can choose three other "skins" to make the Compact mode a bit more, ahem, colorful. To change the current skin, switch to Full Mode and click the Skin Chooser button. You can choose one of thirteen skins:

- ✓ **Default Media Player:** This is the boring old skin you've already seen.

- ✓ **Classic:** If you think the Default Media Player skin is boring, try the Classic skin. This skin mimics the display of WiMP 6. Yawn.

- ✓ **Miniplayer:** The most compact skin. Use this if you just want basic playback controls using the least amount of screen space.

- ✓ **All the others:** Want Media Player to look like a big green head, a rusty control panel, a heart, or an abstract painting? Try one of the ten custom skins offered by Media Player (Figure 15-4 shows one of them).

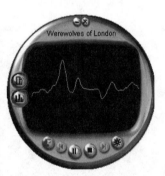

Figure 15-4: The Roundlet skin gives Media Player a round custom look.

From time to time, Microsoft develops more skins for Media Player. You can usually download them for free from the Microsoft Web site by switching to the Skin Chooser screen and clicking "More Skins" at the top of the window.

Playing Movies with Media Player

The strength of Windows Media Player is its versatility. You can use WiMP to play almost any kind of multimedia file you're likely to have on your computer, including the movies created by Windows Movie Maker. Sure, you can play movies in Movie Maker if you wish, but for general viewing, Movie Maker's interface isn't too friendly.

Playing a movie with WiMP is easy:

1. **Open WiMP if it isn't already by clicking Start⇨Programs⇨ Accessories⇨Entertainment⇨Windows Media Player.**

2. **Click File⇔Open.**

   The Open dialog box appears.

3. **In the Open dialog box, navigate to the folder or disk that has the movie you want to watch.**

   You probably want to look in "My Videos" in your My Documents folder, or a desktop movie archive if you have one.

4. **When you find the movie you want, select it and click Open.**

   The Now Playing screen should appear and your movie begins to play.

Controlling playback

Windows Media Player is pretty easy to control. It has controls similar to a CD player or VCR, with Play, Pause, Stop, Rewind, Fast Forward, and buttons to move to the next or previous track.

When you are playing videos, you will also want to take advantage of the special video settings that you can adjust. To view the settings, open the View menu and choose Now Playing Tools⇔Video Settings. Video settings should appear along the bottom of the playback window, as shown in Figure 15-5.

Figure 15-5: Adjust the appearance of your video with these settings.

If you don't like the way the video looks, you can move the sliders to adjust the image brightness, color contrast, hue, and saturation. If you make too many changes, just click Reset to quickly move all the sliders back to the middle. You should also find some left and right arrows underneath the controls. Click them. You'll find controls for several other items:

- ✔ **Media Information:** If you're viewing online content, you may find some information about it shown here.
- ✔ **Captions:** If the video has captions, this tab will show them.
- ✔ **Graphic Equalizer:** Want to customize the levels or left/right balance for the audio playback? WiMP offers a graphic equalizer that allows you to accomplish this.

Viewing movies in Full Screen mode

You spent a lot of money on your computer and video equipment. Why are you watching your videos on a tiny three-inch window on your PC? Wouldn't it be nice if the video playback could fill the entire screen, as it does on a television set?

Windows Media Player has a Full Screen mode that lets you do just that. When a movie is playing, open the View menu and choose Full Screen. Poof! The rest of your screen elements disappear and your super-expensive computer monitor becomes a TV.

Now that you can't see any of the controls on your screen, you're probably wondering how to switch back to what we professionals like to call "Not Full Screen" mode." Because nothing is available to click on, you have to use the keyboard. Press Alt+Enter (that means hold down the Alt key and press the Enter key).Clicking a mouse button also returns you to "Not Full Screen" mode.

Note: You can use Alt+Enter to toggle back and forth between Full Screen and Not Full Screen modes for any video playing in Media Player, but if the quality of the video can't handle Full Screen, the program will automatically snap back to a smaller display.

Of course, some videos have better quality than others. Low-quality video files will have jerky or blocky playback in Full Screen mode, so some experimentation may be called for.

Using Media Player to Download Online Content

One of the things that Microsoft would really like you to use Windows Media Player for is downloading and enjoying online multimedia content. This hasn't been very practical in the recent past, but with so many people getting high-speed Internet connections, it is becoming more practical to watch video and listen to rich audio over the Web. WiMP 7 is supposed to be your gateway to the online world of multimedia.

Okay, I'm putting aside the hype for a moment to show you how to actually download something. Try this:

1. **Launch WiMP, if it isn't already open, and make sure that an Internet connection has been established for your computer.**

2. **Click the Media Guide button on the left side of the window.**

   The program takes a minute to download some stuff from Microsoft, after which you'll see a window that looks something like Figure 15-6.

Figure 15-6:
Microsoft provides this gateway to online media.

Note: If all you see is a useless screen telling you how great the Media Guide is if only you can access it, it means you probably didn't connect to the Internet and the program didn't do it for you. No problem: Just establish your connection and then go back to the Media Guide window and press F5 on your keyboard. This should refresh the Media Guide and — with any luck — guide you to some media.

3. **Click an item to download it.**

   Pay attention to bandwidth requirements. If you have a choice between downloading, say, a 100k (kilobyte) video or 300k video and you have a 56Kbps Internet connection, the smaller video should play more efficiently on your system.

4. **If the playback is jerky or cuts out occasionally, click Stop and try to download a lower bandwidth version.**

My testing showed that if your Internet connection speed is slower than about 50Kbps (kilobytes per second), most online content available for WiMP will be useless.

Listening to the Radio

Why bother listening to your favorite talk radio show on a $15 transistor radio when you can use your $1,500 PC? You want to get your money's worth out of the thing, right? Many radio stations and networks now offer live audio feeds over the Internet, and guess which program that comes with Windows Me is designed to handle these broadcasts?

If you guessed "Minesweeper," you are incorrect. But if you guessed Windows Media Player 7, congratulations! Treat yourself to something nice this evening. Go ahead, you deserve it.

WiMP gives you several ways to find radio broadcasts online:

- In the Media Guide, click the Radio tab. This takes you to a selection of 32Kbps radio broadcasts.

- Click the Radio Tuner button on the left side of the Media Player window. This takes you to a search page, where you can locate various broadcasts.

- In the Media Library, click Radio Tuner Presets to view radio stations that have been preset in Media Player (Figure 15-7). Double-click a radio station to listen to it.

- Locate a "streaming" audio broadcast on a Web site and click the link for the "Windows Media Player" link.

Figure 15-7:
Double-click
a radio
station
preset to
listen to it.

The last option may be the one you use most, especially if you're a talk-radio addict. Many popular radio shows, including *Coast-to-Coast AM, The Rush Limbaugh Show,* and *All Things Considered,* all offer live broadcasts of their radio shows over the Internet.

If you find a radio station you want to listen to regularly, add it to your selection of presets:

1. **Open the broadcast in Windows Media Player.**

2. **While it is playing, choose File⇨Add to Library⇨Add Currently Playing Track.**

   The track is added to your Media Library.

3. **Click the Media Library button and then click the "All Audio" listing to find the audio track you just added; double-click it to play it again.**

Many radio shows that offer live broadcasts on the Internet ask that you use the online broadcast only if you are unable to listen via a conventional radio. This helps lessen the load on their server so that people who couldn't otherwise listen can enjoy the show.

Teaching Your Audience to Use Windows Media Player

You're a Windows Media Expert, but that fact doesn't do you a lot of good if the intended audience for your movies can't figure out how to use the program. To ensure that they get the most out of their viewing experiences, I suggest that you buy a copy of *Microsoft Windows Movie Maker For Dummies* for each and every person you ever intend to share a movie with.

Barring that, and assuming that we all still have our feet grounded firmly on the planet Reality, you may have to provide a brief tutorial to some of your audience members. What instructions you give them will probably depend on which version of Windows Media Player they have and, for that matter, what kind of computer they're using. To watch your movie, your audience members need to:

- ✔ **Find the file.** Did you e-mail the movie or send it on a disk? Tell them to save the file on their hard drive as soon as they receive it. Then they can locate it using My Computer (Windows 95 and up), Finder (Macintosh), or File Manager (Windows 3.1).

- ✔ **Make sure that they have the right program.** No matter what kind of computer they have, your audience members need to have Windows Media Player 6 or higher installed to view your movie.

- ✔ **Open the file.** If they've found the file, usually all they have to do is double-click it to open it. Macintosh and Windows 3.1 users may have to open WiMP and use File⇨Open to open the movie.

- ✔ **Play the file.** Click Play. It's that easy.

Chapter 16

Creating an Online Screening Room

*O*ne of the really great things about Windows Movie Maker is the fact that it is a complete package. The program doesn't just allow you to record and edit video on your computer; it also helps you distribute those movies. With just a few mouse clicks, you can send your movies to friends via e-mail or publish them to a Web server.

Of course, before you can publish a movie to a Web server, you must have access to a Web server and some storage space available to you. And most important, that server space needs to be something that your intended audience can easily access. Do you know what that means? That means you're going to have to create a Web page. Ahhh!!!

A Crash Course in Simple Web Page Design

Creating a Web page is a lot easier than you might think. Creating one that is worth looking at . . . well, that's a bit more challenging. Lots of people create their own Web pages, but many of them are ugly, if not downright annoying. You know what I'm talking about — those Web pages on which you can't read the words because a big picture is in the background, or the color of the background and the words don't contrast sufficiently. Blechh.

The very best Web pages — whether they are designed by an individual hobby-ist or a professional Web designer — are simple. Visit Yahoo! (www.yahoo.com) to see a prime example of good, simple Web design. Yahoo! is one of the most visited Web sites in the world, yet it gets by without such complexities as frames, colorful backgrounds, or Java applets. If Yahoo! doesn't need all that stuff, you probably don't, either.

Want to see a prime example of Web design gone totally awry? Just visit the Web site of any automobile manufacturer. Car makers' sites are universal in their efforts to amaze and astound you with the very latest in Web design technology, but in most cases, they end up as a bunch of error-filled pages that take forever to download.

The first step in designing a Web page is to determine a goal for the page. What do you want the viewer to use your page for? Go ahead and write your goal down. It might look something like this:

I want to give my friends access to my movies.

Excellent. A simple goal demands a simple Web page if you want people to have a pleasant experience when they visit. If you want to create a sort of online screening room for your movies, you don't need to create anything too terribly complex. Simpler pages are less likely to cause errors in the Web browsers of your audience, and they are usually easier to read, too.

Creating a five-minute Web page with Notepad

Web pages are createdusing a simple programming language that tells the Web browser how to display a page. This language is called *HTML (HyperText Markup Language)* and is fairly simple to learn and use. HTML works by giving instructions to a Web browsing program, such as Internet Explorer, Netscape, or Opera, on how to display the page. HTML can be created with any text-editing program, including Notepad, which comes with Windows. To launch Notepad, choose Start⇨Programs⇨Accessories⇨Notepad.

"Real" programmers like to point out that "HTML is not a programming lan-guage!" They say this because HTML files don't actually create programs. Instead, they serve as documents that give instructions to a Web browser. Whatever. If it looks like a fish and smells like a fish, then it's fishy enough for our purposes here.

A crash course in HTML

HTML gives instructions to the Web browser using tags, which are enclosed in brackets. Some tags, such as those that tell the browser to insert a picture, stand by themselves. Other tags have an opening part and a closing part. Consider this paragraph of text on an HTML page:

```
<p>My favorite book ever is <i>Windows Movie Maker For
         Dummies</i> from IDG Books. The cover looks like
         this:</p>
<p align=center><img src="cover.jpg"></p>
<p><a href="http://www.dummies.com/">Click here to visit the
         Dummies.com Web site.</a></p>
```

This is raw HTML. If you open an HTML document in a text-editing program such as Notepad, this is what it would look like. But if you open it in a Web browser, the brackets and everything inside them would be invisible.

Look more closely at the sample HTML. A <p> tag denotes the beginning of a paragraph, whereas the end of the paragraph is indicated by </p>. You can see that the italics tag (<i>) also has a closing tag (</i>). If you view the preceding HTML document in a Web browser, you'll see the words "Windows Movie Maker For Dummies" italicized.

The second paragraph has something added to the <p> tag. The align=center command tells the Web browser to center that paragraph on the screen. You'll also notice that the second paragraph doesn't have any words in it. Instead, it contains only an image (img), whose filename is cover.jpg (src="cover.jpg").

The third paragraph in this HTML sample contains a hyperlink to the IDG Books Web site. All the text between <a href="http://www.dummies.com/"> and </a> will automatically be blue and underlined, and when viewers click on those words, they will jump to the IDG Web site.

Why a Web page?

You're probably wondering right now why a book about making and editing movies is telling you to create a Web page. And you are right to wonder. Wouldn't it just be easier to e-mail my movies to people?

In the short term, yes, e-mailing a movie is easier. But what if you decide to e-mail the same movie to another person later on? Movie files can get pretty big, so sending a single movie out many times via e-mail can hog a lot of your Internet connection time. Furthermore, if you're not absolutely certain that the recipients want you to e-mail them that 5MB movie, you could end up angering them and causing problems on their mail server.

If you put your movies on a Web server and create a simple Web page that allows people to access them, you have to upload the movie to the server only once. And your viewers can download the movies whenever it is convenient for them, without clogging up their e-mail account.

Typing your own HTML

An HTML document has two main sections: the <head> and the <body> (don't ask me what happened to the <arms> and <legs> because I don't know). The <head> section contains information that doesn't actually appear on the Web page but is important nonetheless. Bits of <head> information can include:

- The title of the Web page
- Keywords and phrases to help Internet search engines find the page
- Meta tags, Cascading Style Sheets, and some other really technical stuff that you don't need to worry about right now

The <body> of your HTML document contains:

- Everything else

To create your very own Web page, open Notepad and type a few lines of HTML that look like this:

```
<HTML>
<HEAD>
<TITLE>Keith's Online Movie Theater</TITLE>
</HEAD>
<BODY>
<H1>Keith's Online Movie Theater</H1>
<P>Click one of the movie titles below to view the film.</P>
<UL>
<LI><P><A HREF="easter.wmv">Easter Egg Hunt</A></P>
<LI><P><A HREF="cycles.wmv">Motorcycle Racing</A></P>
<LI><P><A HREF="bkhills.wmv">Road Trip: The Black
            Hills</A></P>
</UL>
</BODY>
</HTML>
```

This HTML, with your own movie names, filenames, and other text in place of my own, will give you a basic Web page on which to present your movie projects. When you are done typing, don't forget to save your work as an HTML file:

1. **In Notepad, click File⇨Save to open the Save As dialog box.**

2. **Move to the My Documents folder (if you're not there already) and click the Create New Folder button, as shown in Figure 16-1.**

   A new folder appears with the name "New Folder." Type a new name, such as "Online Theater," and press Enter.

3. **Double-click that new folder you just created so that it opens.**

   It should be empty.

Click to create a new folder.

Give your new folder a name.

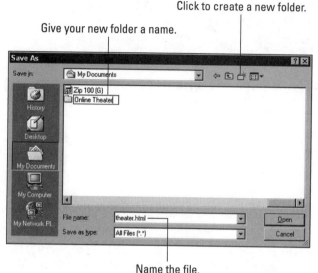

Figure 16-1:
Create a
new folder
for all your
Web files.

Name the file.

4. Type a name for your HTML file in the File Name box.

The filename must be eight characters or fewer if you plan to put it online. Add the extension **.html** to the filename. As you can see in Figure 16-1, my file is named theater.html.

5. Click Save to save the file.

Now that you've saved your new HTML file, you should test it. Open your Web browser (probably Internet Explorer or Netscape). You don't have to be connected to the Internet for this test, but it won't hurt, either. Now, select File⇨Open in the browser and navigate to the HTML file that you just created. Open it. If you typed the HTML exactly as described in the sample on the previous page, it should look like Figure 16-2.

You'll notice that sometimes I show HTML code in uppercase letters and other times in all lowercase. The case of letters used in HTML tags doesn't matter, so you can use whichever is easier for you.

Cracking the code

A lot of new HTML code is in that sample that you just typed. I break it down bit by bit here so that you can better understand what you're looking at. First, take a look at the ⟨head⟩ portion of the document:

```
<HTML>
<HEAD>
<TITLE>Keith's Online Movie Theater</TITLE>
</HEAD>
```

Figure 16-2:
This is the
Web page
generated
by the HTML
you typed
earlier.

The first tag (<HTML>) is necessary at the beginning of every HTML file. It tells the Web browser that this is indeed an HTML document. After you have opened the document with that <HTML> tag, you need to open the head with <HEAD>. My head is simple, with only a title for the page. The <TITLE> element tells the Web browser what to show in the title bar. Turn back to Figure 16-2 and you'll see that, indeed, "Keith's Online Movie Theater" appears in the title bar of Internet Explorer. Swell.

After you have closed the head (</HEAD>), it's time to work on the body of page. This is the meat of every good HTML document. Begin by opening the body:

```
<BODY>
```

As does the head, the body of the HTML document has opening and closing tags. Everything that will actually appear on your Web page must appear between the <BODY> and </BODY> tags. Next you find a heading:

```
<H1>Keith's Online Movie Theater</H1>
```

<H1> is a canned style of heading that every Web browser knows how to interpret. It indicates a first-level heading. <H1> headings have the largest font size of all the heading styles and work best as an overall title for the Web page. Other, lesser heading styles are available if you care to use them, from <H2> all the way down to <H6>. Don't overuse these.

Next you put in a short paragraph of text:

```
<P>Click one of the movie titles below to view the film.</P>
```

Simple enough. Yes? Good. Moving on to the list of movie titles:

```
<UL>
<LI><P><A HREF="easter.wmv">Easter Egg Hunt</A></P>
<LI><P><A HREF="cycles.wmv">Motorcycle Racing</A></P>
<LI><P><A HREF="bkhills.wmv">Road Trip: The Black
          Hills</A></P>
</UL>
```

Lists occur frequently in Web documents. And as with headings, they come in some canned styles. Here I have created an unordered list with the tag <UL>, known in some circles as a *bulleted list*. If you want to create a numbered list, use the <NL> tag instead.

Each list item is denoted with the tag <LI>. The <LI> tag does not need a closing tag, but you should use paragraph tags (<P> and </P>) after each <LI>. When you're done with the list, close it with </UL>.

Finally, don't forget to close the HTML document at the end:

```
</BODY>
```

Here a link, there a link

The HTML code for hyperlinks looks kind of tricky, but it's a lot simpler than you might think. Hyperlinks are usually used to link to other Web pages, but they can be used to link to files as well. When you are creating an online screening room for your movies, you will use hyperlinks to link to the movie files.

Consider this hyperlink:

```
<A HREF="easter.wmv">Easter Egg Hunt</A>
```

I made a movie of my kids participating in an Easter egg hunt. When I saved the movie in Windows Movie Maker, I called is easter.wmv. It is important to keep the filename under eight characters (plus the .WMV extension) for any Web documents, so you may need to rename some of your movie files.

The preceding hyperlink assumes that the file easter.wmv is in the same directory (a.k.a. *folder*) as your HTML file. But if you store movies in a subdirectory called *movies*, the link would need to look like this:

```
<A HREF="movies/easter.wmv">Easter Egg Hunt</A>
```

The folder name comes first, followed by the actual filename. Piece of cake, right? But what if you store the movies on a different Web server altogether? In that case, you might have to put in the entire address, or *URL (Uniform Resource Locator)*, of the file. For instance, if you were linking to a file stored on the IDG Books Web site, it might look like:

```
<A HREF="http://www.idgbooks.com/movies/
    easter.wmv">Easter Egg Hunt</A>
```

In the example shown here, the file I am linking to is located on the IDG Books Worldwide Web server. If the file is actually there, I can link to it, even if the actual HTML file is located on another server entirely. This means that I can put my Web pages on my local ISP server — the one that all my friends and family know the address for — but store the large movie files somewhere else.

Many Web servers are case sensitive when it comes to filenames, so if the file-name was actually Easter.wmv, the link shown here may not work. Check with the people who run the Web server to find out whether filenames are case sensitive. If they are running a UNIX-based server, the files probably are case sensitive.

Linking to the Windows Media Web site

If you put your Web page and movies on the Web, just about anyone with Internet access should be able to find them. But if they don't have Windows Media Player, they won't be able to watch the movies you created with Movie Maker. Why not help out your audience by reminding them of this fact? Good idea! And while you're at it, provide a link to the Microsoft Web site so that they can quickly download the appropriate version of Media Player for their own computer.

Microsoft provides a neat little logo that you may use on your own Web site specifically for the purpose of linking to the Media Player download page. It says "Get Windows Media Player," making its purpose clear to your audience. You can learn more about this logo, including Microsoft's guidelines for using it, at http://www.microsoft.com/windows/windowsmedia/en/create/logo.asp. The address of the Windows Media Player download page is http://microsoft.com/windows/mediaplayer/download/default.asp. To add this logo and link to your Web site, follow these steps:

1. **Open Internet Explorer and visit** http://www.microsoft.com/windows/windowsmedia/en/create/logo.asp.

   Find the link that says "Get Windows Media Player logo and guidelines" and click it.

2. **Read all instructions on the screen, including the logo usage guide-lines.**

3. **Locate copies of the "Get Windows Media Player" logo on this Web page.**

   You will probably find one with a white background, another with a black background.

4. **Decide which logo you want to use (or just get both now and decide which one to use later); then, right-click the desired logo and choose Save Picture As from the shortcut menu.**

5. **Navigate to the folder where you store your Web page files and write down the exact filename on some scratch paper, using the correct case.**

   When I downloaded it, the filenames were GetPlayerW.gif (white logo) and GetPlayerB.gif (black logo).

6. **Click Save.**

   The file will be saved to the folder.

7. **Open the HTML file for your Web page in Notepad and add the following lines of HTML to the code, at the point where you want the logo to appear:**

```
<P>These movies require Windows Media Player. Click
    below to download this program.</P>
<P><A HREF="http://www.microsoft.com/windows/
    mediaplayer/en/download/default.asp">
<IMG SRC="GetPlayerW.gif"></A>
</CENTER></P>
```

   Note: The instruction to insert the image (`<IMG SRC="GetPlayerW.gif">`) assumes that you are using the white logo. If you are using the black logo, change the filename to `GetPlayerB.gif`.

8. **Save your HTML file and close Notepad.**

Notice that the image is located inside the hyperlink. This means that the image itself will be the hyperlink, and when your viewers click it, they will be transported instantly to the download site. When you are done adding this code, open the HTML file in your Web browser to see what it looks like. It should look similar to Figure 16-3.

Although you have already created a good, basic Web page, you may want to try building something a bit more advanced later on. If so, check out *Creating Web Pages For Dummies,* by Bud Smith and Arthur Bebak, published by IDG Books Worldwide, Inc.

Visitors can click here to download Windows Media Player.

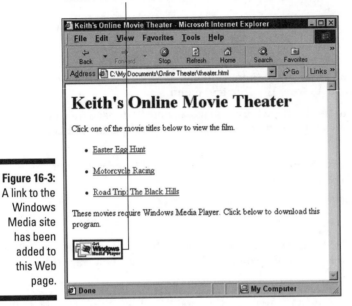

Figure 16-3:
A link to the
Windows
Media site
has been
added to
this Web
page.

Locating an Online Home for Your Movies

A Web page that serves as an online theater or screening room for your movies won't do your audience much good if it isn't actually online. People on the Internet can't easily access the files on your hard drive, meaning that you're going to have to publish your Web page and movies to a Web server.

Using your ISP's Web server

Many Internet service providers (ISPs) provide free Web server space to their members. This is a nice benefit because it allows you to simply and quickly publish some of your movies online. If you're already paying for it, you may as well take advantage of it. You do need to check some important things if you plan to use the ISP's Web server:

- **How much disk space does it provide?** Most ISPs provide only five or ten megabytes of disk space at the basic level, although you can usually pay extra for more space.

- **Is the server case sensitive?** If it is, be extra careful with the filenames in your HTML documents.

✔ **What will your URL be?** You need to know the address of your Web site. It will usually be some permutation of the ISP's Web address and your user name, but double-check with the service provider to be sure.

✔ **What is the procedure for uploading files?** You will probably use an FTP server for uploading your Web page files to the ISP. You can obtain the address for this server, as well as any passwords, required software, or other special information from the ISP.

Armed with this information, you should be able to take advantage of the Web server at your ISP. Your main limitation may be space. If you don't get enough space for all your movies, or if extra disk space from your ISP costs too much, consider some of the free options that are available in the online world.

To accurately measure the size of the files you plan to upload to the server, place them together in a folder on your local hard drive. Then open Windows Explorer or My Computer and see how much data (in megabytes) is stored in that folder.

Finding free Web space

Contrary to popular opinion, you can still get some really, really good things in life for free. One of those things is Web server space. That's right, Web servers are just itching to host your Web documents — including those huge movies you created in Movie Maker — for free! All they ask is that you let them display some advertisements at the edges of your pages.

Numerous free servers are available. You can do a search for them with your favorite Internet search engine, or try one of the services listed in Table 16-1. Some of them are truly huge, with free space ranging as high as 500 megabytes!

Table 16-1	Free Web Servers	
Server	*URL*	*Maximum Free Space Provided*
50MEGS.COM	`http://www.50megs.com/`	50MB
AcmeCity	`http://www.acmecity.com/`	20MB
Angelfire	`http://angelfire.lycos.com/`	30MB
Fortune City	`http://www.fortunecity.com/`	100MB
Freeservers.com	`http://www.freeservers.com/`	20MB
Homestead	`http://www.homestead.com/`	16MB

(continued)

Table 16-1 *(continued)*

Server	URL	Maximum Free Space Provided
MSN Home Pages	`http://msnhomepages.talkcity.com/`	30MB
POPcast	`http://www.popcast.com/`	10MB
TripodWeb sites:	`http://www.tripod.lycos.com/`	11MB
XOOM.COM	`http://xoom.com/`	500MB
Yahoo! GeoCities	`http://geocities.yahoo.com/`	15MB

Each free Web service offers a different package of goodies to try to attract you to its site. Some have wizards to help you create your Web site, and some even allow you to forgo the on-screen advertisements for a small fee. Four of these services — AcmeCity, Fortune City, POPcast, and XOOM.COM — can be accessed directly from Movie Maker. Just click the Sign Me Up. . . button in the Web server configuration dialog box to find out how.

Check each service out to find the best value for you. When you do decide on one, make sure to get all the necessary instructions for uploading files!

The Final Step: Putting Your Files Online

Now you need to transfer your movie files to the Web server. The easiest way to do this is with the Send To. . . feature in Windows Movie Maker, but it's not the only way.

Using Movie Maker to put files on the Web server

Windows Movie Maker tries to make it as easy as possible for you to upload your movies to a Web server. When you're done editing your movie, do this:

1. **In Movie Maker, choose File⇨Send Movie To⇨Web Server.**

2. **Choose an output quality, keeping in mind how long it will take your audience to download the movie.**

3. **Click OK.**

4. **In the next dialog box, name the movie and click OK.**

Make sure that you give the movie a name that is eight characters or fewer. Movie Maker now creates your movie, which can take a few minutes depending on how long it is and the quality you selected. When the movie is created, the Send To Web dialog box appears, as shown in Figure 16-4.

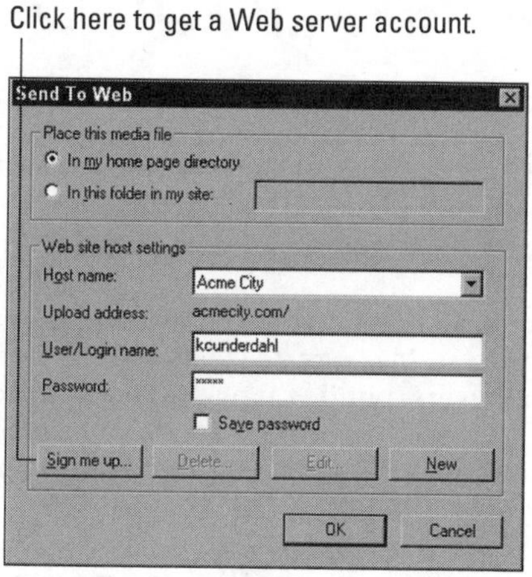

Click here to get a Web server account.

Figure 16-4:
Enter the information for your Web server here.

5. **Select a name for your host in the Host Name box and enter your user name and password.**

   If you don't have a server account, click Sign me up. . . to get an account.

6. **Click OK.**

   A progress window appears. If you see the word *Uploading* followed by your filename, as shown in Figure 16-5, everything is working properly.

Figure 16-5:
The file is being uploaded to the server.

7. **When you see the Upload Succeeded dialog box, click Close.**

   You can also click Visit Site Now to visit the site and make sure that everything uploaded properly.

You can define your own Web host in Movie Maker as well. To do so, click New in the Send to Web dialog box and enter the information requested in the Create Web Host Settings dialog. Most of the information in that dialog box — such as the FTP address, Web address for uploaded movies, and advanced settings — should be provided by the Web host.

The backup plan: Using an FTP client

Movie Maker helps you upload only movies to a Web server; it doesn't take care of uploading other files — such as any HTML files or other graphics that you plan to use — to a Web server. Nor can it delete old files that you no longer want on the server. For this you need a program called an FTP client. FTP, which stands for *File Transfer Protocol*, is a method for sending files over the Internet.

Many excellent FTP clients are available for you to download from the Internet and use for little or no cost. My favorite is WS_FTP LE from Ipswitch. This program is free for private users, but if you plan to use it in conjunction with a commercial operation, you will have to pay for it. You can learn more about the terms of use and download the program directly from Ipswitch at www.ipswitch.com.

Note: WS_FTP LE is just one of many excellent FTP programs you can choose from. For a more comprehensive list of FTP clients, visit one of the big software download sites such as Tucows (www.tucows.com).

A dedicated FTP client such as WS_FTP LE is handy because it allows you greater flexibility in how and what you upload to a Web server. But don't take my word for it; give the program a try:

1. **Visit** www.ipswitch.com **and download WS_FTP LE for Windows.**

   Follow the instructions provided by Ipswitch for installing the program.

2. **Launch the program by choosing Start➪Programs➪WS_FTP LE➪ WS_FTP LE.**

   The program opens to the Session Properties screen, shown in Figure 16-6.

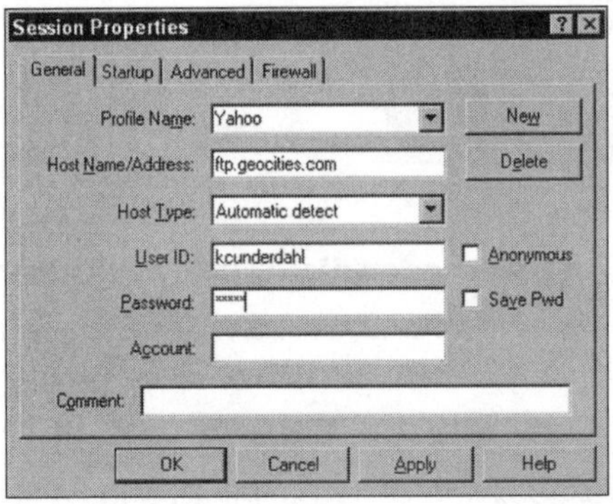

Figure 16-6:
Enter the information required for accessing your Web server.

3. **Click New and enter all required information for logging on to your Web server.**

   At a minimum, you should provide the Host Name/Address, User ID, and Password. To save this "profile" so that you can use it again later, type a Profile Name in as well.

4. **Click OK.**

   The program takes a few seconds to log on, after which you see the main WS_FTP LE program window, shown in Figure 16-7.

   The left side of the window shows the contents of your computer and the right side shows your directory on the Web server.

5. **On the left side of the window, navigate to the local folder that has the files for your Web site.**

   You can double-click the up arrow at the top of the file list to move up; double-click folder names to open them.

6. **When you find a file you want to upload, select it once on the left side and click the transfer arrow in the middle of the window.**

   Some stuff happens, the program makes some strange noises, and the file appears on the right side of the screen.

7. **Click Close when you are done to log off the Web server.**

8. **Don't forget to test your movie before sending the URL to all your friends!**

Double-click to move up in your computer's folder tree.

Your computer

The Web server

Click to transfer a file.

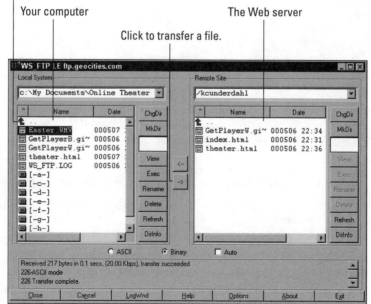

Figure 16-7: Use this window to transfer files between your computer and the Web server.

Dealing with Web servers that don't accept .WMV files

On rare occasions, you may find that the Web server to which you are trying to upload a movie does not accept .WMV files. This problem is relatively simple to deal with but requires you to re-open Movie Maker and save your movie as an .ASF file instead. Virtually all Web servers accept .ASF files. The .ASF and .WMV formats are closely related and both can be played using Windows Media Player.

To save your movie in .ASF format, follow these steps:

1. **Re-open the project file for the movie you are trying to upload.**

   You did save the movie's project file, didn't you?

2. **Click Save Movie on the Project toolbar.**

   The Save Movie dialog box appears.

3. **Choose a quality setting, provide a title, and click OK.**

4. **In the Save As dialog box, choose "All Files" in the Save as type menu, as shown in Figure 16-8.**

Figure 16-8: If your Web server won't accept .WMV files, save your movie as an .ASF file instead.

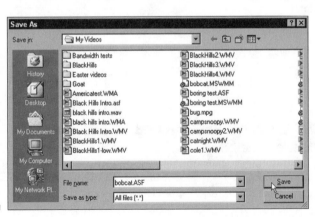

5. **Remove "WMV" from the end of the filename and add "ASF".**

   Figure 16-8 shows a properly renamed movie that I am about to save in .ASF format.

Chapter 17

E-Mailing Movies to a Few Dozen Close Friends

● ●

● ●

*M*icrosoft would like you to think of Windows Movie Maker as your own personal movie studio. But can it really do everything that a big, powerful Hollywood studio can do? Well, movie studios do more than just make movies, and so does Movie Maker. Among other things, this amazing program helps you distribute your movies. And one of the easiest distribution methods is via e-mail. With Movie Maker, you can instantly send a movie to one person or a whole list of people.

Is E-Mail the Best Way to Share Videos?

When you e-mail a movie to someone, it is sent as an attachment in a standard e-mail message. Because you can specify the recipients of your e-mailed movies, this method is much more private than simply placing your movies on a Web server. And it's also generally a lot quicker than preparing and mailing movies on a CD or videotape. Click Send, and zap! The movie is on its way. No HTML to create, no FTP servers to get lost in . . . it's simply the simplest way to send a movie.

But — and there is always a *but,* isn't there? — some limitations on what you can and cannot send via e-mail do exist. The biggest problem you face is file size. A five-minute .ASF or .WMV movie saved at medium-high quality can be more than 7MB. With all of the hullabaloo over high-speed Internet connections, you may easily assume that most people can handle a file this large with ease, but the fact is that many still cannot. Table 17-1 lists some of the "dos and don'ts" of e-mailing movies.

Table 17-1	E-Mail Dos and Don'ts
Do. . .	*DON'T. . . !*
Warn the recipient before you send the movie.	Sporadically send out movies whenever the whim strikes you.
Advise the recipient of the size of the file you plan to send.	Assume that the recipient's Internet connection is just as fast as yours.
Make sure that recipient's e-mail account can receive attached files.	Send movies to Internet mailing lists.
Describe the attached movie in the body of the message.	Open a movie that was sent to you by someone else without warning.

I say it elsewhere, but I would like to reiterate the fact that when you send a movie via e-mail, you are sending it as a file attachment. Computer viruses often spread through innocent-looking attachments (remember *Melissa* and *I LOVE YOU?*), so make sure that you advise your recipients *before* you send the movie. Not only will this prevent aggravations regarding the size of the file you send, but also your recipients are less likely to simply discard the attachment as a suspected virus.

A majority of e-mail servers still have a 5MB limit on the size of a user's inbox. This means that any file you send that exceeds the mailbox's capacity will be bounced back to you. If you routinely e-mail movies larger than 5MB, brace yourself for trouble.

How Fast Is My Connection?

It's pretty important to know how fast your Internet connection is and how fast the connection is of the people you are sending movies to. If you have a "56K" modem, does that mean you are receiving data at 56 Kbps (kilobits per second)? No.

Most people still connect to the Internet using a modem connected to their telephone line. Generally speaking, the fastest connection you will ever get over a conventional phone line is about 50 Kbps, but most people actually get quite a bit less. If you live in an outlying area where your phone line is routed through an extra set of phone company switching equipment, you'll be lucky to get even 28.8 Kbps. Thus, no matter how fast your modem (or, for that matter, your whole computer), it still must drink through the same tiny straw.

A growing number of people are seeking out higher-speed connections in the form of cable modems, a digital subscriber line (DSL), an integrated services digital network (ISDN), or some other strange acronyms that all mean "fast." But still, the *actual* connection speed is important. To determine the speed of a dial-up connection in Windows, connect to the Internet and then double-click the connection icon (it looks like two little computers next to the clock). You should see a dialog box similar to Figure 17-1.

Figure 17-1:
I live on the outskirts of town, so I get only a 28.8 Kbps connection.

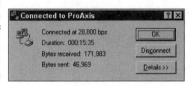

Note: If the dialog box reads "115,200 Kbps," I can almost guarantee that it is not reading accurately. This problem is usually caused by the modem's driver software not being installed properly. Check the documentation for your modem and reinstall the driver in accordance with the provided instructions.

Setting Up E-Mail Options in Movie Maker

By default, Movie Maker is set up to use your default e-mail program for sending movies. If you have more than one e-mail program, you can easily change the default setting to something else by following these steps:

1. **Open the View menu and choose Options.**

   The Options dialog box appears.

2. **In the Options dialog box, click Email Options to display the E-mail Movies dialog box, shown in Figure 17-2.**

   If you have more than one e-mail program installed on your computer, most if not all of them should be displayed here.

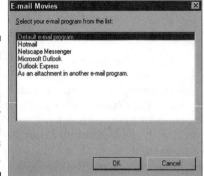

Figure 17-2:
Choose a
specific
e-mail
program for
sending
movies
here.

3. **Click the program you want to use for sending movies.**

4. **Click OK twice.**

This should return you to the main Movie Maker window.

E-Mailing a Movie

Sending a movie to a friend via e-mail is easy. It can also be dangerous, because if you send your friend a huge file that she is not expecting or is ill-prepared to receive, she may not be your friend anymore. See Table 17-1, earlier in this chapter, for some tips on things to do *before* you e-mail a movie.

To e-mail a movie that you just finished creating, try this:

1. **Click Send on the Project toolbar and choose E-mail.**

The Send Movie Via E-mail dialog box appears, as shown in Figure 17-3.

2. **Choose a Playback quality setting.**

Keep the connection speed of your recipient in mind when making this choice. In Figure 17-3, my wife and I are sending Grandpa a five-minute movie of our kids hunting for Easter eggs. But if he connects to the Internet at 28.8Kbps (close to average), it will take more than 15 minutes for him to download it!

3. **Enter any other display information you wish, such as the author's name, movie title, rating, and a brief description.**

This information is displayed outside the playback area by Windows Media Player.

These times are only estimates.

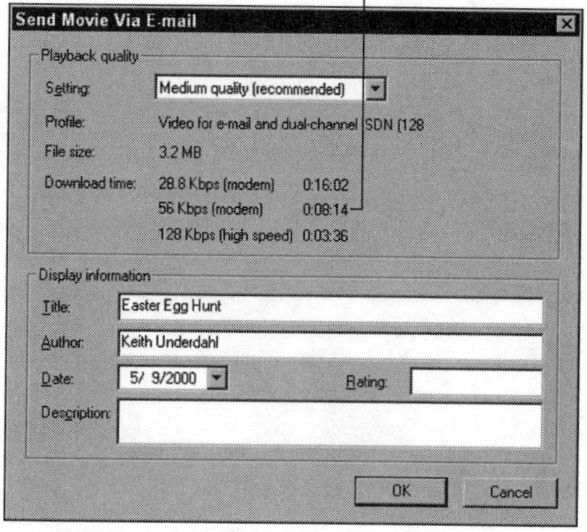

Figure 17-3:
When
choosing a
playback
quality,
consider
carefully the
connection
speed of
your
recipient.

4. Click OK.

A dialog box similar to Figure 17-4 appears, asking you to provide a file-name for the movie. Just to be on the safe side, try to give it a name that is fewer than eight characters long. Longer filenames can be a problem, especially if the recipient is using Windows 3.1.

Figure 17-4:
Try to keep
filenames
under eight
characters.

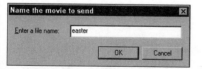

5. Click OK again.

Movie Maker shows a dialog box indicating that your movie is being created.

When the movie is created (it takes a while), you see a dialog box asking you to confirm which e-mail program you wish to use to send the movie.

6. Choose a program (or just leave "Default e-mail program" selected) and click OK.

The e-mail program you choose launches and a new message appears with your movie inserted as an attachment. As Figure 17-5 shows, the message body includes some instructions for the recipient.

The movie is included as an attached file.

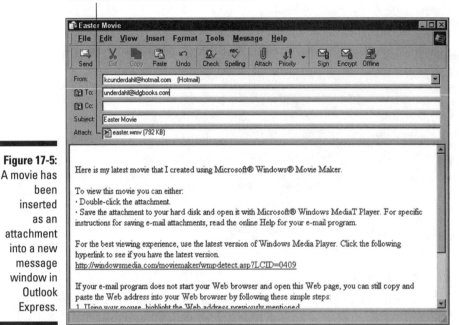

Figure 17-5:
A movie has been inserted as an attachment into a new message window in Outlook Express.

7. **Enter the e-mail address of the person you want to send the movie to; also enter a subject and any additional text.**

8. **Click Send.**

    The message is sent.

About Movie Maker's time estimates

When you prepare to send a movie via e-mail, Movie Maker estimates how long downloading will take at various connection speeds. For instance, Figure 17-3 shows sending a five-minute movie saved at medium quality. Movie Maker estimated that with a 28.8Kbps connection, that five-minute movie would take about 16 minutes to download. If the recipient has a 56Kbps connection, the time would be about half that amount.

Unfortunately, Movie Maker's estimates are really "best case" times. Many variables can affect the speed at which someone downloads a file. Even though people may be connected to their ISP's server at 56 Kbps, if Internet traffic is high, the actual download time can be much longer.

Sending the movie to more than one person

If you can send a movie to one person, you can send it to the whole world. Well, maybe not the *whole* world, but a fairly significant portion of the people you know, anyway. E-mailing a movie to several people at one time makes a lot of sense, especially when you consider how long it takes Movie Maker to create a movie and prepare it for e-mailing. If you already have a list of people you want to send the movie to, you have to prepare the movie only once if you send it to all of them simultaneously.

But before you do send the movie to more than one person, you have a few things to consider:

- ✔ **Know the bandwidth capabilities of each recipient.** If your uncle has a fast DSL connection to the Internet but the rest of your family is lucky to connect at 33.6 Kbps, you may want to send him a separate, higher-quality copy of the movie.

- ✔ **Avoid distribution lists.** Do you have a list of people set up in your e-mail program to whom you regularly send jokes, virus warnings, and other very important messages? Some of those people probably don't appreciate your mailings much, and nothing identifies who those ingrates are better than sending a large movie to the list. If you do this, stand by for a lot of negative responses.

- ✔ **Make sure to use a good e-mail address for each person.** Some people have more than one e-mail address. Some of those addresses can receive file attachments and some can't. Double-check with the people ahead of time to make sure that their mail account can handle your movie.

To send a movie to multiple recipients, simply follow the procedure for e-mailing a movie once. When the message composition window appears, enter multiple e-mail addresses in the To: and Cc: fields. In most e-mail programs, you can separate multiple e-mail addresses with a semicolon (;).

If you send a movie that is larger than 5MB and many of the mailboxes you send it to can't receive files this big, the movie will be returned to your own mail account in full every time it is rejected. At best, this means that you'll have to wait several eternities as all the bounced messages are sent back to you. At worst, if your own mailbox has a 5MB limit, it can cause a feedback loop that can crash mail servers and make legions of people very, very mad at you.

What if my e-mail program isn't supported?

Movie Maker supports the most popular e-mail clients used on PCs today, but you may conceivably prefer a program that is not supported. If this is the case — or if you simply don't like having Movie Maker and your e-mail program work together — you can still use the program to help get you started e-mailing a movie.

Follow the steps to e-mail a movie in Movie Maker. When you are asked which e-mail program you would like to use, choose the last option, "As an attachment in another e-mail program," and click OK. You will see a dialog box containing instructions similar to Figure 17-6.

Make a note of this filename and location.

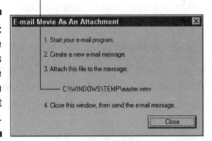

Figure 17-6:
Follow these
instructions
to send the
movie as an
attachment
later.

The instructions include the location and name of the movie file. This is extremely important because, without this bit of information, you may have a hard time locating it later on. Carefully write it down on some scratch paper just to be sure that you don't lose it; then, click Close.

When you want to send it, open your e-mail program, begin composing a new message, and attach the movie to the message before you send it. Most e-mail programs have an attachment button that looks like a paper clip.

Note: Some e-mail programs — such as older versions of Eudora Light — don't support sending file attachments with e-mail messages. If your e-mail program doesn't support attachments, you won't be able to send movies with it.

Will My Recipients Be Able to Watch the Movie?

You have been very careful to notify your recipients *before* you e-mail them the movie. Good job. They received it just fine, but now do they know how to play the movie? Do they even have the right software to view it with?

The canned instructions that Movie Maker automatically inserts into the body of the outgoing message tell recipients exactly what they need to do. But chances are that many of the people you send movies to will ignore these instructions and call you instead.

> *"I'm so excited to see your movie but I don't know how. Help!"*

Calm your friend down and explain that to watch the movie, he needs to have a program called Windows Media Player. It is available for Windows and Macintoshes. If your friend does not have this program, tell him to visit microsoft.com/windows/mediaplayer/download/default.asp.

Although it should almost go without saying, you may need to remind your friend to save the movie to the hard drive. Usually, he can double-click it, drag-and-drop it, or right-click it to save it somewhere safe.

Chapter 18

Recording Movies on Tape and CD

• •

In This Chapter

▶ Choosing a media for recording your movies

▶ Working with recordable CDs

▶ Finding DVD players to play your movies

▶ Recording onto videotapes

▶ Packaging your movies

• •

*W*indows Movie Maker makes a lot of assumptions about you. For instance, the program largely assumes that you plan to distribute your movies over the Internet, either by putting them on a Web server or sending them in an e-mail. Indeed, Movie Maker is best suited for this type of distribution because, frankly, the quality of video produced by Movie Maker is not up to the same standard most people have come to expect from videotapes and DVDs.

Still, you may sometimes want to distribute "hard copies" of your movies. For instance, I have many friends and relatives with computers, but few of them have an Internet connection that is fast enough to take advantage of Movie Maker's higher-quality video settings. For those people, I prefer to record the movies onto a CD. And then there are those people living in the dark ages who don't even have a computer at all. For them, a videotape may be the only option.

Which Media Is Best?

You are likely to use two main types of media when distributing hard copies of your movies: VHS videocassettes and recordable CDs (CD-Rs). Table 18-1 lists some of the advantages and disadvantages of each.

Table 18-1	VHS Tapes vs. CD-Rs	
Media	*Advantages*	*Disadvantages*
VHS Tape	Anyone can use them; you probably already have all the equipment you need to use them	Can be expensive; more costly to mail, quality degrades after a while
CD-R	Blank discs are cheap if you buy in bulk; easy to mail; discs can hold other types of data as well	You have to buy a special CD recorder; only computer owners can use them; some brands of CD-Rs are not very reliable

The main deciding factors in choosing videotapes or CD-Rs will probably be your budget and the needs of your audience.

Finding top-quality discs

Prices for recordable CDs (CD-Rs) vary widely. If you buy them individually or in small quantities at your local department store, they can cost four or five dollars apiece. Not surprisingly, the more you buy at one time, the more money you save. The best deals can usually be found when you buy a spindle of CD-Rs. A *spindle* is a stack of CD-Rs and usually comes in quantities of 50. I have seen spindles of 50 CD-Rs offered for less than $30, which works out to considerably less than $1 per disc.

If you buy a spindle, keep in mind that it does not come with the plastic jewel cases that CDs are usually stored in. Jewel cases can be purchased separately and are usually pretty cheap. You can save even more money by simply buying some paper or cardboard CD sleeves, but these offer less protection if you plan to put the disc in the mail.

Not all CD-Rs are created equal. I have had spindles in which more than half the discs were bad, making them not much of a bargain at all. Ask around to find out which brands people have better luck with. Adaptec's CD-R mailing list (www.cdrcentral.com/community.html) discusses this topic frequently, so you may want to join it for a while.

As with any purchase, you need to shop around. After you decide which brand of CD-Rs to buy, check prices at your local electronics stores and on the Internet to find the best deal.

Not all videotapes are created equal

The great thing about videotapes is that you can find them anywhere and they're relatively cheap. Plus, just about everyone in North America has a player for videotapes, meaning that movies you record onto tape can be viewed by just about everyone. If you plan to use VHS videotapes to distribute your movies, consider a few important points:

- ✔ **Use new tapes.** Videotapes lose a considerable amount of playback quality when you record on them more than once.

- ✔ **Buy in bulk.** As with CD-Rs, videotapes are cheaper if you buy larger quantities.

- ✔ **Don't spend too much money on higher-grade tapes.** Enhanced quality videotapes are available, but the quality of video created by Movie Maker doesn't justify the expense.

What about Super VHS (S-VHS) ? S-VHS recorders and tapes offer superior recording and playback quality to regular VHS, but again, movies created in Movie Maker can't take advantage of the higher resolution that S-VHS players can provide. But if you decide later on to move up to more advanced digital video-editing software and equipment, an S-VHS recorder may come in handy for mastering high-quality videotapes.

Other media?

Two other types of storage media deserve mention here. Floppy disks (3.5") can be used to exchange small movies (1.4MB or smaller) and are so cheap as to be basically disposable. But they are small and they deteriorate over time.

You can also use Zip disks from Iomega, and quite a few people have Zip drives nowadays. Disks are available in 100MB and 250MB sizes, so they can store much bigger files than floppies. But if your audience members have parallel-port Zip drives, the drive may not be fast enough to play back the movie efficiently. IDE or SCSI Zip drives are better. And, of course, Zip disks are extremely expensive, costing nearly $10 each for a 100MB disk.

Using CD-R Devices

Good CD recorders can be purchased for less than $200 and have many uses beyond simply letting you record movies onto compact discs. You can use CD-Rs to make backups of the data on your computer, store seldom-used files, exchange large files with other people, and more. A CD-R can typically hold up to 650MB of data.

CD recorders are available as both *internal* and *external* devices. Internal CD recorders are designed to fit inside your computer's case and look just like a CD-ROM drive. Internal CD-R drives usually require an IDE bus, the same type of bus used by your hard drives. If you have never installed a CD-ROM drive or hard drive in your computer, you may want to hire a professional to perform this operation.

Your motherboard probably has two IDE channels. Usually, your hard drive is connected to one IDE channel and your CD-ROM drive is connected to the other. Depending on the computer, you can usually "daisy-chain" two IDE devices on a single channel. You should avoid daisy-chaining a CD-ROM or CD-R drive on the same IDE channel as a hard drive, but it is okay to connect both your CD-ROM and CD-R drives to the same channel.

External CD-R drives usually connect to a SCSI adapter. Many PCs don't have SCSI adapters, so double-check that you have an available connection before you spend the money on a SCSI drive. If you decide to buy a SCSI adapter, it can be installed in much the same way as a FireWire (IEEE-1394) adapter. See Appendix A to learn more about installing an adapter card in your computer.

CD-R drives can be used as CD-ROM drives when you aren't recording a CD, so you may be tempted to replace your CD-ROM drive with the CD-R. Don't do this if you can avoid it! Computer parts wear out after a while. CD-R drives are not designed for the same intensive use as CD-ROM drives and they are a lot more expensive to replace if they fail.

What about CD-RW drives?

CD-Rs are kind of like stone tablets in that after you've recorded the disc, you can't erase or change it. But many CD-R drives can now use a special kind of rewritable disc called a CD-RW (Compact Disc-ReWritable). CD-RW discs cost more than CD-Rs but can conceivably save you money because they can be re-used many times.

In spite of the potential savings, I recommend against using CD-RW discs for recording movies from Movie Maker for two very important reasons:

- ✔ **CD-RW discs are not very reliable.** Many CD-RW users have found that the discs typically fail after four or five re-writes.

- ✔ **Many CD-ROM drives cannot read CD-RW discs.** The only drives that can reliably play CD-RW discs are (surprise) CD-RW drives.

If you are using a CD-RW drive for recording CDs, record at a slower speed, such as 2X or 4X. A faster recording speed (such as 8X) may save you time, but I have found that recording sessions become much less reliableas recording speeds increase.

Choosing good CD-R software

CD-R drives always come with software to help you record discs. Most of them have an intuitive interface similar to Windows Explorer or another such file-management program, and you can use drag-and-drop to copy files from your hard drive into the CD layout. Some programs are better than others.

To get the most out of your CD-R drive, I suggest that you upgrade to better CD-R software. Upgraded CD-R software usually contains added capabilities, such as:

- ✔ Creating labels and jewel case inserts
- ✔ Copying or recording audio CDs
- ✔ Converting MP3 files into CD audio files that can be played in any CD player
- ✔ Audio track editing
- ✔ Creating and editing video

I use and recommend Adaptec's Easy CD Creator 4 Deluxe. As of this writing, it costs $99, but its wealth of features makes the price worthwhile. You can learn more about this program online at www.adaptec.com. Other good CD-R programs include:

- ✔ Golden Hawk CDRWin (www.goldenhawk.com)
- ✔ NewTech Infosystems CD-Maker (www.ntius.com)
- ✔ Cequadrat WinOnCD (www.cequadrat.com)

Formatting the disc

CD-ROM discs have to be formatted, as do any other kind of disks you may use with your computer. CD-ROMs usually use one of two file systems: Joliet or ISO9660. Either one will work with your PC, but they have some important differences that you need to be aware of.

Any CD-R program worth its weight in electrons gives you the option to control which file system you use. Where you find the setting depends on the program you are using, but you can usually find it in a dialog box that controls the CD layout's properties. Figure 18-1 shows where to change the file system in Adaptec's Easy CD Creator 4.

Choose ISO9660 or Joliet.

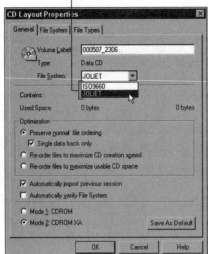

Figure 18-1:
Most CD-R
software
lets you
choose the
file system
for the disc.

A third type of file system that you are likely to encounter is the CD-Audio system. This is the system used on all audio compact discs since they were introduced twenty years ago. You can't record movie files — or any data files — onto a CD-Audio disc.

ISO9660

ISO9660 is the older of the two file systems and resembles the file system used on ancient computers running DOS or Windows 3.1. Filenames can have only eight characters plus a three-digit file extension. If you place a file with a name longer than eight characters on an ISO9660 disc, the name is truncated. So, a file with a name like this:

```
Easter Egg Hunt.WMV
```

is truncated thus:

```
EASTER~1.WMV
```

This is less than desirable and I suggest that, in general, you avoid using the ISO9660 file system on CDs you burn. But a few, rare circumstances may exist in which you need to use this system. Some music and DVD players are now emerging that play computer-based multimedia files such as MP3 music, MPEG movies, and more. If you have a DVD player that claims to be capable of playing the .WMV files like those created by Movie Maker, you should read the player's documentation carefully to make sure that it doesn't specify ISO9660 discs. You may also not be able to use folders to organize your movies. This need is rare but is something to watch for nonetheless.

Joliet

Joliet is the file system that you should use for your CD-Rs most of the time. In fact, it is usually the default setting in your CD-R software. Joliet not only allows greater flexibility in file naming (a filename can be up to 64 characters long and use capitalization) but also ensures compatibility with most other modern operating systems.

Can Macintosh users use my discs?

Probably. Yes, some of your audience members may use a Macintosh rather than a PC running Windows. And yes, most of them should be able to use the CD-R discs you create.

But first, make sure that they have a program that can view .WMV files. Microsoft offers a version of Windows Media Player for Macs, so you should point your Mac audience in the direction of www.microsoft.com. Some of the Mac users won't like the idea of having a Microsoft product on their system, but if they want to watch your brilliant films, they're going to have to, er, get with the program.

Now all you need to worry about are the discs themselves. If users' Macintosh's are running Mac System 7 or higher, they have a tool called PC File Exchange that allows them to access Joliet discs created on your PC. You can even create folders and subfolders on the disc; the Mac can open them just fine.

If the CD will be used on a Macintosh, keep the filenames shorter than 27 characters. Filenames that are longer than this will probably be truncated by the Mac, and they look silly, anyway.

The problem with Macs

There is just one problem. It's a minor problem and it doesn't apply to users of MacOS-X or higher, but it is one you should be aware of. When the Mac user inserts your CD into the CD-ROM drive, the disc "mounts" and an icon for it automatically appears on the desktop. The user can double-click this icon to open the CD, but he or she will be faced with a bunch of PC icons. This is an ugly thing on a Mac.

A PC icon indicates that the Macintosh operating system doesn't know what kind of file it is, and if the user double-clicks it, an error will occur. So, to watch one of your movies, the Mac user must follow these steps:

1. **Launch the Windows Media Player program.**

2. **Open the File menu and choose Open.**

3. **Navigate to the CD (it can be found on the Desktop) and select the desired movie.**

4. **Click Open.**

Your Mac-using friends must follow these steps closely or the movie won't play properly. Then they'll laugh at you and make jokes about you and your part in the Great Wintel Conspiracy. Save yourself the t earache and pass these instructions along *ahead* of time.

Why is the Mac operating system so confounded by your movie files? In the Macintosh file system, files and folders have two distinct parts: a data fork and a resource fork. The *data fork* is the meat of the file, whereas the *resource fork* is a little thingie that tells the operating system what program created it, what program should open it, what kind of icon it should have, which sign of the zodiac it was born under, and so on. Files saved on a PC running Windows are missing the resource fork.

Recording your discs

Recording CDs on a PC is easy, especially if you have a well-designed CD-R program. The exact steps for recording varies depend on the software you're using, but you should always watch for the following basic things:

- ✔ Make sure that you are creating a data CD, not an audio CD.

- ✔ Select the file system (ISO9660 or Joliet) *before* you begin adding files to the layout.

- ✔ Be mindful of the 650 megabyte capacity of the CD-R.

- ✔ Don't be afraid to use folders to organize your movies, especially if the disc contains many small movies. Give the folders descriptive names.

- ✔ Consider writing a short text file in Notepad called Readme.txt that contains some basic instructions on how to use the movies. Place this file at the root level of the CD (that is, don't hide it in a folder).

If you plan to make many copies of the CD, consider saving the CD Layout. Most CD-R software allows you to save the layout so that you can quickly re-open it later and continue burning CDs without having to redo all your work in setting it up.

DVD Players in a Perfect World

DVDs are the hot new medium for home video entertainment today. Some people claim that DVD stands for *Digital Video Disc*, whereas others insist that it is actually *Digital Versatile Disc*. I don't really care. All I know is that DVDs provide premium digital video playback, no matter how many times you use them. They don't deteriorate over time like videotape does and they aren't filled with moving parts that break easily. DVDs are good.

You don't have to study a DVD for very long before you notice, "Hey, this thing looks just like a compact disc." Yes, they are the same size, shape, and color, and most DVD players can also play audio CDs. Can they also play the movies you create with Movie Maker? No.

Well, not yet, at least. DVD players are now emerging that can play MPEG files and MP3 music CDs, and it's not hard to imagine that soon devices will be available that can play your movies, too. But until then, you're stuck with VCRs and CD-ROM drives.

Something else that you'll see coming down the pike soon are DVD recorders for PCs. DVD-ROM drives are already offered on many new, high-end PCs. Adaptec is already developing mastering software to run DVD recorders, and for file storage on a computer, this medium represents the next logical step. Through a complicated laying process, a single DVD can theoretically hold up to 17 gigabytes of data, although DVD-R devices will probably be able to write only about half that amount. Still, with eight and a half gigs of storage space, you can put an awful lot of .WMV movies on a single disc.

Recording onto Videotapes

If you plan to record your Movie Maker movies onto VHS videotapes, you have two options. One is complicated but cheap; the other is simpler but may require you to buy more stuff.

The first option is to record the finished movie back onto the storage device in your digital camcorder. If the camcorder connects to your computer through a FireWire adapter, the adapter card may have come with some software that allows you to do this. Unfortunately, neither Windows Movie Maker nor Windows Media Player has the capability to play its signal back out through the FireWire adapter. You will have to use the capture software that came with the adapter to facilitate this. If you are able to record back onto the camcorder, you can then take the camcorder over to your VCR, connect it using standard RCA jacks, and record from the camcorder onto the VHS tape in the VCR. As I said, it's complicated.

The second option is to buy and install a video capture or TV tuner card that has video output connections. Most do not offer video output, so check carefully before you buy. If the card has video output, you can connect it directly to your VCR and record onto the tapes right from your PC.

Several capture cards that do offer video output include:

✔ ATI All-in-Wonder 128 and All-in-Wonder Pro (www.atitech.ca)

✔ Hauppauge Win/TV-CinemaPro (www.hauppauge.com)

✔ Matrox Marvel G200-TV (www.matrox.com)

Make sure that the video capture card you plan to buy is supported by Windows Movie Maker! Even though the device may be supported by Windows Me, it may not work with Movie Maker. Check the Movie Maker help system for a list of supported devices.

Packaging Is Everything: Making Labels and Jewel Cases

The very simplest way to label your outgoing CDs and tapes is with a permanent marker. But I'm guessing that if you're the kind of person who goes to the trouble of producing entertaining and heartwarming videos for your loved ones, you place a high value on presentation. And a few words scribbled on a disc in black marker is not the most sophisticated way to "present" your movies. You worked so hard, doesn't the media deserve better?

Printing your labels

Pre-cut and sized labels are widely available both for videotapes and CDs. Such labels are usually identified by an *Avery number:* numbers assigned to certain standard label and envelope sizes by the Avery Dennison Corporation (www.avery.com). Although these numbers were developed as product numbers for Avery, they have become industry standards and are used by other companies as well for ease of identification. The Avery number should be identified on the package when you buy labels at your local office-supply store.

Popular word processors such as Microsoft Word and Corel WordPerfect have document templates that make printing labels easier. For instance, if you want to print a sheet of videotape labels (Avery # 5199) in Microsoft Word, do this:

1. **Open Word.**

2. **Open the Tools menu and choose Envelopes and Labels.**

   The Envelopes and Labels dialog box appears.

3. **Click the Labels tab to bring it to the front.**

4. **Click Options.**

   The Label Options dialog box appears, as shown in Figure 18-2.

Figure 18-2:
Choose one
of the
standard
Avery label
sizes to set
up your
document.

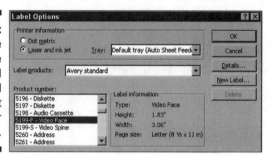

5. **Select the desired label type from the Product Number menu.**

   The correct number should be found on the packaging for the labels you bought.

   Note: Notice that videotape labels — *Avery 5199* — have separate numbers for the cassette tape's face (5199-F) and spine (5199-S). When you bought the labels, the package should have contained an equal number of each.

6. **Click OK to close the Label Options and then click New Document in the Envelopes and Labels dialog box.**

   A new document appears with grid lines to indicate the edges of each label.

7. **In the first label, type in any logos and titles you want, but don't try to cram too much information into the small space.**

   When you have a label you are happy with, copy it to the rest of the labels.

8. **Print a sample of the labels on a regular piece of paper.**

   Hold it up to a light to make sure that the printout lines up with the labels. Double-check to ensure that your text doesn't run across the hole in the middle or off the edge of the label. Follow the instructions that came with the labels for loading them into your printer.

This procedure is the same for printing CD-R labels (5824), although they are a bit trickier because of the hole in the middle of the disc. For a fancier look, try using some of Word's WordArt to curve text along the curve of the CD. Just make sure that you test them carefully before printing on actual labels.

If you need only one label, it may be tempting to run the sheet through your printer for just that one label and save the rest for later. Unfortunately, some label paper can severely damage your printer if you feed it through more than once. The paper gets curled slightly as it passes over the rollers in the printer. If these slightly curled labels pass through the printer again, they can get peeled off inside and ruin the print head.

Graphic design and the jewel case

If you want to get really fancy, consider designing a custom jewel case insert for the movies you distribute on CD-R. For instance, you may want to put a title for the CD and identify yourself on the front, and have a list of movies and other files on the inside.

Many CD-R programs come with tools to help you design and produce jewel-case inserts. Figure 18-3 shows the Jewel Case Creator that comes with Adaptec's Easy CD Creator 4 Deluxe.

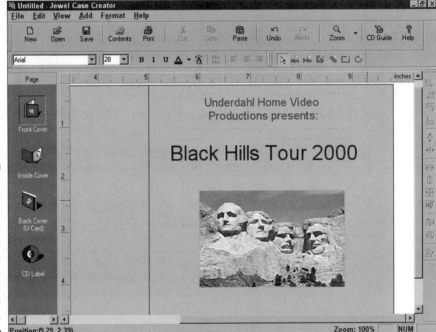

Figure 18-3: This program from Adaptec helps me create nice-looking jewel-case inserts.

Even if you don't have a special program for creating jewel-case inserts, you can create your own in any word processing or publishing program. Just set up the page with the correct measurements. The front-cover insert of a jewel case is a square that measures 4.75" x 4.75" (that's 12cm x 12cm, for you metric folks). If you want to create a cover that folds in half so that it has information printed on both sides, simply double the width.

Part V
The Part of Tens

The 5th Wave   By Rich Tennant

ROOM 101

"I failed her in Algebra but was impressed with the way she animated her equations to dance across the screen, scream like hyenas and then dissolve into a clip art image of the La Brea Tar Pits."

In this part . . .

Everyone loves a good "Top Ten" list, and that's why this is one of the most popular parts of every ...*For Dummies* book. I begin by giving you ten movie project ideas. Then, pro videographer Billy O'Drobinak provides ten tips for shooting better video. You find out how to create (almost) ten special effects, visit ten great online movie resources, and see which ten software tools your PC movie studio can't do without.

Chapter 19

Ten Movie Maker Film Projects

"*I*s that all there is?" you wonder after filming your twentieth school play or music program. "I just spent an entire semester's worth of college tuition on this fancy digital video equipment, but now what am I supposed to film?"

The possibilities are limited only by your imagination. It's easy to get stuck in the rut of filming the same old school plays, family picnics, and trips to the amusement park. And although those types of movies are important, you can have a lot of fun and improve your movie-making skills by trying some creative new film projects. This chapter suggests a few projects that you might want to try.

1. Your Own "Making of. . ." Documentary

Soon after you begin sharing movies that you make with Windows Movie Maker, all your friends and family members will be beating down your door to ask, "How did you do that?!" It is inevitable, so consider yourself warned.

Try to anticipate this desire on the part of your audience and consider creating a short film that shows how you filmed the video, got the video into your computer, and then edited it with Movie Maker. Some things you may want to include are the following:

- Photographs taken by someone else of you holding the camcorder
- A brief instructional video on installing a FireWire adapter
- "Backstage interviews" with some of the movie's cast members
- A film clip or two of you working in front of the computer
- "Screen shots" of Windows Movie Maker in action

Screen shots are pretty easy to get in Windows. Get the Movie Maker window set up the way you want it; then press the Print Screen button on your keyboard. A picture of the Windows screen area will be sent to the Clipboard. Open a graphics editor such as Paint and choose Edit⇨Paste to paste the screen shot into the program. Save the screen shot as a bitmap file so that it can be imported into Movie Maker.

Note: Don't bother trying to show the Windows desktop by filming your monitor with the camcorder. The monitor's image will flicker and be difficult to read when you view it with the camcorder.

Finally, don't forget to include some witty narration and social commentary in your "Making of . . ." video. Good narration and documentaries go together like toast and jam.

2. Home Inventory

For years, insurance companies have been telling you to videotape your home so that you have a good record of your belongings should a catastrophe occur. And they say to keep the videotape in a safe place, but where is a safe place? If the tape is stored anywhere in your home, you may as well not even bother making it. Imagine this post-fire conversation with your insurance agent:

You:	We lost everything. The Monet, the Tiffany lamp, the antique hutch, the cash in the mattress; it's all gone! *(sob)*
Insurance Agent:	There, there. *D,C&H Indemnity* will take care of everything. Now . . . about the painting and the lamp; do you have some kind of evidence? I wouldn't ask, you see, but my boss just got his bolts tightened and insists that I get graphic evidence of these things. Did you make that video like I told you?

You:	Yes, but . . .
Agent:	Excellent! Where is it?
You:	It was in the antique hutch . . . *WAAHHH!!!*

This kind of thing shouldn't happen, but it does. Why? Well, let's face it. Videotapes don't always squeeze into your safe deposit box very well. Instead, record the Monet, the Tiffany lamp, the antique hutch, and the cash in the mattress with your digital camcorder; then, capture and edit the movie with Windows Movie Maker. While you're at it, film yourself in the mirror while holding that expensive digital camcorder. Now — and here's the really cool part — record the movie onto a recordable CD! A CD easily fits into your safe deposit box, or even in your file folder at your insurance agent's office!

When you are making your "home-inventory" video, include clips of any safety equipment that may be in your home, such as smoke detectors, fire extinguishers, alarm systems, and storm shutters. This can help settle disputes with your insurance company later on.

Don't upload a "home inventory" to your Web server, because if you do, every person on the Internet will have access to a complete grocery list of everything you own.

Actually, disputes with insurance companies are rare. But if nothing else, a home-inventory video will help you remember what you owned after a disaster has occurred. Insurance agents often list simple forgetfulness on the part of the homeowner as one of the leading problems when it comes to settling claims.

3. Computer Animation Spectacular

Some of the most spectacular films of the last decade or so have featured digital animation. Films such as *Jurassic Park*, *Forrest Gump*, and *The Phantom Menace* made use of computer-generated graphics in many scenes, and some movies — such as *Toy Story* and *A Bug's Life* — were created entirely by digital artists hacking away in front of computer screens.

Those movies were created using computer equipment and software costing in the hundreds of thousands of dollars. But that doesn't mean that computer animation is out of reach for you. If you're very patient, you can create a simple animated feature using nothing but Windows Me and the tools that come with it.

The basic concept behind animation is simple. Each frame of the animation is a called a *cell*, and these cells are shown in fast sequence to give the illusion of movement.

Creating your own computer animation is a two-step process:

1. **Create each cell in Paint.**

   When you save each cell as a bitmap file, make the filename a number and number each cell sequentially so that you will remember what order they should go in later on.

2. **Use Movie Maker to assemble the cells into a movie.**

Sounds simple, right? Well, those two simple steps will take a mind-numbingly long time to complete. First, you have to decide how long each cell will be displayed. Normal video displays at 30 frames per second (fps), but for your animation project, you can probably get away with much less. A movie made with 5 or 10 fps will look a bit jerky to the viewer but will still provide an acceptable sensation of movement.

Suppose that you've decided to show your animation at 10 fps. That means you have to create 10 cells for each *second* of video. If you want to create a 10-second video, you need to create 100 individual cells! It's a long process, but with a bit of creativity and a lot of elbow grease, you can have some fun with this.

When you assemble the cells in Movie Maker, you do so by inserting each cell into the storyboard as a still. You need to modify the length of time that each still plays by following these steps:

1. **Drag a still image to the storyboard.**

   It should appear where you drop in the file.

2. **Click the Timeline button to display the Timeline.**

   You should see a trim point at the beginning and end of the still clip.

3. **Drag and end point left to reduce the length of play time.**

   You'll have to make each still pretty short to provide decent animation.

If you have a hard time squeezing the stills small enough on the Timeline, zoom in a bit for a better view.

4. Indianapolis Warlock Project

As inevitable as school plays and weddings, your digital camcorder will almost certainly get used at least once to create a *Blair Witch* spoof. It has become a tad cliché, perhaps, but you know you want to do it anyway, so you may as well get it over with.

Your first step, of course, is to get some good source video. Just remember one thing: As real as the characters in the original *Blair Witch Project* may have seemed, they were carefully scripted and brilliantly acted to appear that way. If you're like me, you'll probably try to ad-lib your first few scenes, and they won't turn out nearly as well as you hoped. So, to make a really, really good *Blair Witch*, spoof, you must:

✔ Write a script

✔ Rehearse your actors

✔ Film multiple takes of most scenes

Oh, and you'll need to get a good close up of your own nostrils, as I did (see Figure 19-1). The nose shot is a quintessential element of any *Blair Witch* spoof worth its weight in magnetic tape.

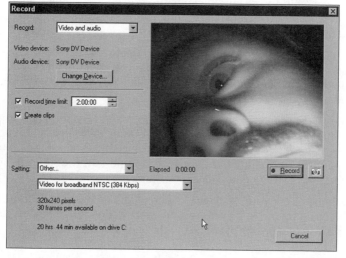

Figure 19-1:
This is the signature scene of every good *Blair Witch* spoof.

Because the *Blair Witch Project* was marketed mainly via the Internet, why should you expect to market your spoof any differently? After you've edited your spoof, use Movie Maker to save it at several different quality settings. This will help your audience choose the best version that they have the bandwidth for.

Note: If you plan to do much filming in dark settings (such as a haunted forest at night), try to get a camcorder with a built-in light. Some Sony digital camcorders have an infrared light that allows for filming in total darkness. Figure 19-1, which appeared previously, shows that I am using a Sony with this feature.

5. Crunchy Devils of the Asphalt

"Extreme" sports are all the rage today. They're so popular that even ultra-active participants and extreme sports fanatics find time to buy extreme sports videos and sit down with them in front of the tube. In many cases, ultimate production quality takes a back seat to creativity and craziness.

Do you have a sport or activity that you participate in and would like to document on film? Now's your chance! Shoot some source video of you and your hobby in action and then use Movie Maker to cut out your most painful injuries and dub over some heavy metal music. Here are some tips:

- ✔ Be careful. Murphy's Law tells us that the likelihood that something will go terribly wrong and someone will get hurt increases exponentially when the camera is turned on.

- ✔ Convertibles, vans, and pickups provide good moving-camera platforms, but without an expensive-camera leveling system (usually kept level using gyroscopes), the film might be unacceptably bumpy.

- ✔ Practice with your camcorder's zoom feature so that you can effectively zoom in as objects move farther away and zoom out as object get closer. If you are skilled enough with the zoom control, the viewer may be unaware that you are zooming at all.

- ✔ Special shots may require special equipment. For instance, if you are filming an activity that involves bicycles or motorcycles, companies such as Saeng/TA (www.saeng.com) sell camera mounts that fit on a standard 7/8" handlebar. Just keep in mind that the ride will be bumpy and your camera could easily be damaged.

- ✔ When editing your "extreme" video in Movie Maker, use short clips that focus on the action. Compressing more action into less film space like this will make your movie seem that much more exciting.

These techniques aren't limited to "extreme sports" wackiness. Many of the same techniques can be used when filming almost any event that involves action and activity, such as your kids' soccer game.

6. Kids These Days

If you have kids, chances are good that you will use your camcorder to film events involving them more than anything else. And that means you'll be using Movie Maker to edit those films so that you can share them with friends and relatives.

Grandparents and other well-meaning people always say that they are just happy to see the grandkids and don't care about a few quality glitches in your film. But you do care, and soon you will learn that filming events involving children are more challenging than they might appear.

One of the biggest problems centers around the fact that your kids are probably shorter than you are. If you simply hold the camera in your hand, you will always be looking down on the kids and see nothing but them and the ground. Consider Figure 19-2. This was shot in front of the Devils Tower monument in Wyoming, but unfortunately, all you see here is a lawn in front of that strange monument.

Figure 19-2:
Kids are
filmed from
this higher
perspective
all too often.

When filming children, do everything you can to get the camera lower. Sit or kneel if you have to. Almost any subject looks best if the camera must look up at it slightly, because it makes the subject look bigger and more important. As shown in Figure 19-3, I've knelt down to interview my son at the base of Mount Rushmore, and the result works out much better for him.

Figure 19-3:
Holding the
camera
slightly
lower than
your subject
works out
more
favorably for
children.

Of course, one problem with getting the camera lower is that someone is more likely to walk in front of it while you are filming (especially those unruly kids!). Use an assistant and instruct your assistant to keep the filming area clear with silent signals and instructions.

7. Don't Touch That Dial

If you are a business owner, you already know both the value and the expense of advertising. With a good camcorder and Windows Movie Maker, you can quickly produce video advertisements for your business at minimal cost. Although it's true that the movies you create with Movie Maker don't have the kind of video quality needed for television broadcast, that can prove to be a significant enhancement to your online presence.

This is not to say that you should make a movie just because you can (although if you really, really want to, I won't stop you). For instance, if your business is, say, telemarketing, a video may not be of much use to your customers. But if you do something that the customers would appreciate seeing in action, such as day care or crop dusting, a video can help a lot.

You can also create a movie that is fun for your Web site visitors. If you own a title insurance company, customers may not care to see your employees recording deed transfers at the county courthouse, but maybe they would enjoy seeing your company's parade float in the recent Veteran's Day Parade. Just keep a few things in mind:

✔ Make sure that the file size of each movie you put online is clearly identified and, if possible, provide a time estimate for download at various connection speeds. You should also consider providing higher-quality movies for customers with more bandwidth, and smaller, lower-quality videos for those who have slower Internet connections.

✔ Do not include movies in any unsolicited advertisements you send out via e-mail. Movies are simply too big for something like this and will create almost universal ill-will toward your business.

✔ Simplify the movie-watching process as much as possible. Provide a link to download Windows Media Player, provide simple instructions for downloading and viewing the movie, and clearly identify what each one is.

8. Here Comes the Bride

Weddings are perhaps the second most popular home movie projects, just behind school plays. And there's a good chance that you want to share a movie of the joyous occasion with some of your online friends. You're in luck, because Windows Movie does weddings!

Filming a wedding can be a bit challenging, especially if it's your own. Chances are that you'll end up pleading with your Uncle Fred, giving him your camcorder, and showing him which way to point it. While you're at it, tell Uncle Fred these things, too:

✔ Remember that everything you say while the camera is recording will be on tape, and I'll hear it later.

✔ Please don't film the back of my head.

✔ Get a picture of the cake *before* we smear it on each others' faces.

✔ Here is a copy of *Windows Movie Maker For Dummies* from IDG Books Worldwide, Inc. If you have a moment, please read Chapter 20 real quickly to find out a thing or two about shooting video.

✔ Speak to the person "in charge" and get permission to be in the best spots for filming at important moments.

✔ Don't be afraid to move around a bit and shoot from several positions.

✔ I want you to get a good shot of The Kiss. It will happen almost immediately after we recite our vows.

✔ Thank you. You know that you have always been my favorite uncle.

Don't be too picky. At least you have Movie Maker to help you edit the video before you share it with your family and friends!

9. Music of the Spheres

German philosopher Friedrich Nietzsche once wrote, "Without music, life would be a mistake." Have truer words ever been committed to paper? For many of us, music is the pulse that keeps our blood flowing through times both good and bad. Through music, we express the sorrows, joys, tragedies, and triumphs of this thing we call life. Some of us are blessed with the ability to create music, whereas the rest are content to enjoy it.

If you like using Movie Maker, you probably won't be content until you have set some video to some of your favorite music. Creating your own music videos can give you a new creative outlet and provide you with some truly enjoyable video. And in a more practical sense, music can also be effective in covering up poor sound on an otherwise useful video. Follow these basic steps:

1. **Assemble the clips you want to use in the video on the storyboard.**

2. **Import the music track you want to use into Movie Maker.**

3. **Drag the music track to the audio track portion of the Movie Maker Timeline.**

4. **Click the Set Audio Levels button on the timeline controls to open the dialog box shown in Figure 19-4.**

Figure 19-4:
Adjust the audio levels so that the audio track dominates the video.

5. **Move the slider right so that the audio track dominates the video.**

    As Figure 19-4 shows, I have set Movie Maker so that the audio that was recorded with the original video track is completely obscured by the song.

6. **Adjust the length of clips as necessary to better match the music.**

Of course, you shouldn't try to sell your new music video, and if you used music created by another artist, your distribution of it is limited by copyright laws. For instance, I recently assembled a video of clips from our road trip across the northwestern part of the United States and synchronized it to Neil Diamond's "America." Obviously, it would be unfair (and illegal) if I started distributing free copies of Neil Diamond's music without his permission, which, incidentally, I don't have. So for now, my American road-trip music-video spectacular will be enjoyed by me, my family, and a few of my close friends.

10. Time Traveler

Movies you create with Windows Movie Maker are unique because they can be easily stored on small media such as floppy disks or CD-ROMs. CDs are especially useful because you can store a fairly long movie on one and it is easy to tuck away somewhere.

Here's an idea that takes advantage of that ease of storage: Create a video time capsule of your family, your business, or anything else that is important to you. Save the movie on a disk and then store the disk away somewhere that is both safe and out of the way. This could include a bank safe deposit box, a family album that you don't look at very often, or even a cabinet at a relative's house. Leave it there; forget about it for ten or fifteen years. Eventually, you'll stumble across it and you'll have hours of enjoyment as you relive old times, people, and places long forgot.

If you want to make a video time capsule, keep these things in mind:

✔ CDs are great for compact storage but they also have a shelf life that varies from 10 to 25 years. They deteriorate over time, and if a CD sits for too many years, the data on it may be lost.

✔ Time marches on but technology races. Ten years from now, floppy disk drives probably won't be around anymore, so even if your movie does fit on one, I don't recommend using it. We can only hope that computers will still have CD drives for a while.

✔ Software that can play movies you create with Movie Maker is hard enough to find now; imagine how scarce it will be in the coming years. You will do yourself a favor if you download a copy of Windows Media Player from Microsoft and include it on the disk with your movie.

Now all you have to do is decide what to film for the time capsule. Big events such as a first day at school or a major religious ceremony are nice, but also consider making a simple "day in the life" video. You may find that a movie about your day-to-day life will bring back a wealth of memories when you review it many years from now.

Chapter 20

Ten Tips from a Pro Videographer

By Billy O'Drobinak

Bill O'Drobinak is a professional camera operator who has worked in the motion picture and television industries for 20 years. He has shot motion pictures for all the major studios, with such credits as Starship Troopers, Austin Powers: The Spy Who Shagged Me, Bowfinger, The Parent Trap, *and many others. Bill also shoots many independent professional video productions for the home video market, as well as his own projects for his company Gamba Productions.*

• •

In This Chapter

▶ Protecting your equipment and recording

▶ Avoiding light flares

▶ Understanding exposure and focus settings

▶ Making wise choices

▶ Rehearsing and editing

• •

*T*he goal of good video production is for your viewers to be totally *unaware* of the camera or sound production techniques used by the videographer. By incorporating some basic tips into your video production, you should notice a dramatic improvement in your footage, and others will pay more attention to your subject matter and less to your shooting technique.

Aside from the basic operating instructions outlined in each different video camera manual, you need to remember many other considerations that can help you achieve better shooting results and avoid unwanted picture-quality problems. A camera is only as good as its operator.

Before shooting any video, remember that the information in your camera's owner's manual is as important as anything. Cameras differ in many ways. Starting with the instructions may seem obvious, but many video problems result from owners not knowing how their own camera works. They either haven't read, or thoroughly read, their owner's manual. Many times, the obvious is the first thing overlooked. It happens. Read the manual, and know it.

Protect Your Lens

One of the most delicate and important components on your video camera is its lens. Almost all video cameras have zoom lenses, which means that more than one glass element is included in its construction. You want to be aware of its care. Some factors can harm a lens and thereby deteriorate its optical clarity and crispness, and these factors are not mentioned in most manuals.

Avoid keeping your camera in any extreme temperature, cold or hot, for a prolonged period of time when you are not actually operating it. If you have to do so, don't pull it out of one extreme temperature and immediately put it into the opposite extreme climate, especially if either climate is very humid. Make the transition from one temperature to the next gradually.

A sudden change of climate from very cold to very warm (or vice versa) can sometimes cause liquid condensation to build up between the glass elements inside a lens. This can temporarily fog up your lens, rendering your camera unusable until the condensation evaporates. Sometimes it will go away quickly and sometimes it can take a while. Repeated occurrences of this can deteriorate the sharpness of a lens. In some cases, the evaporated condensation can leave very fine dust particles, causing a film on the inside elements of a lens. A buildup of this film can, in extreme cases, distort the sharpness or clarity of your lens. Saltwater condensation is especially dangerous because of the salt film left after evaporation. Salt grains left between the moving glass elements can scratch the surface of the lens.

Lenses can be cleaned only by taking them completely apart, and for most commercially sold video cameras, this service is not feasible. Most cameras are built with tight seals encasing the lens to avoid this problem, but no camera is completely immune to condensation if it is subjected to rapid and extreme temperature and humidity fluctuations.

In general, avoid any contact of any material with the front exposed element of your lens. This is to avoid scratching or pitting the front of the lens, which can cause points of your image to look slightly out of focus, or distorted. Furthermore, the front glass element of your camera's lens usually has a protective coating glazed over it. This coating is there to help protect the lens from *flaring* (see the next section) and can be damaged or scratched easily if the owner is not careful.

Scratches in the coating can cause minute color or exposure shifts (or both) within your image. Use only a very clean, soft, nonabrasive lens cloth or tissue to wipe the front of your lens, and avoid using any lens-cleaning fluid unless you absolutely have to. Minimize the number of times you have to wipe the lens clean. It's better to blow clean the dust with compressed air or a lens brush, but because your breath contains too much moisture, avoid using it to blow dust away. Lens-cleaning accessories are available at most photographic-equipment stores.

Avoid Light Flares

Many people get footage that has some weird light streak, white spots, or rings that move within their frame, whiting out or destroying some of their images, and they don't know why. Sometimes what appears to be a white fog or haze covers the entire image, making it look overexposed. These image mutations are often caused by a light halation, or *flare*, that occurs when intense light directly hits the surface of the lens.

Almost all manufacturers of lenses put a protective coating over the front element of the lens to help reduce flaring. This helps diminish flaring with some of the smaller or softer light sources you shoot, but most large light sources can flare a lens. It is easy to avoid flaring your lens if you remain aware of the light sources illuminating your subject matter.

The sun is a major cause of flares, such as those shown in the video clip in Figure 20-1. Obviously, if you point your camera at the sun, well, you know what happens. You can see it through the camera. But not all flares can be seen when you are actually shooting. Sometimes they rear their ugly head later when you are at home trying to enjoy your footage. Remember that if any of the sun's rays hit the lens directly, even if it's just barely catching the front element from the side, you stand a good chance of a flare occurring.

Flares

Figure 20-1:
This clip of Mount Rushmore, shot facing west in the late afternoon, was flared by the late-day sun.

Try to keep the front element of your lens in the shade. Some video cameras come with a small rubber ring extending from around the front of the lens to help shadow the lens. You can easily create this, or add to an existing shade, with the use of photographic black paper tape. It's black tape similar to household masking tape, probably available at most photographic and hardware stores. You want to use this paper tape because the gum of the tape does not stick to the surface that you are adhering it to, as other, heavier adhesive tapes tend to do. Just take a piece of the tape and wrap it around the front of your lens, forming a cone that extends out past the front edge of you lens. Remember to look at the widest lens on your zoom to make sure that your homemade shade is not sticking into your field of view.

If you don't have a shade of any kind with you, use your hands to shadow the lens when you are shooting, much as you would hold your hand over your eyes when looking at something in the bright sunlight.

Be aware that the sun reflects very brightly and harshly. Look at all the surfaces, such as windows or shiny metal, that are in the direction of your shooting to make sure that you are not seeing the bright light of the sun reflected toward your lens from one of those surfaces. A light reflection of the sun bouncing off one of these reflective surfaces can also cause a flare.

What holds true of the sun also holds true of bright, bare bulbs whose element is casting light directly on the front of your lens. Indoors, keep your lens shaded from the light sources that are bright and bare, such as a light without a lampshade, the same way you would protect it from the sun.

One last point to remember is that a large amount of soft light coming toward the lens can cause flaring in the form of a *whitewash,* or hazy white film over your image, causing it to look as though the image is overexposed. This usually happens when the lens is right next to a bright surface that reflects or emits a large amount of soft light. Leaning over the front of a white car while shooting on a sunny day can cause this. So, if it's not actually in your frame, avoid shooting close to any bright panel of light, such as a lamp shade, TV, and so on that is at an angle where its light can fall upon your lens.

Protect Your Recording

Besides practicing good photography, you need to be aware of some technical concerns to help get the best quality recording on your tape (if your camera uses tape for storage). Any substance that gets onto the recording head inside your camera can cause video *dropout,* or *glitches,* as well as lost bits of sound. The video glitches look like static, blank, or mutated pieces of your images that show up when you are playing back the tape. After a video dropout is on your master tape, there is no getting rid of it. You won't see it while you are recording; you can only take steps to try to prevent it.

One important thing to do is protect your camera from harmful elements. In a humid environment, moisture can get inside your camera mechanisms and sometimes on the recording head itself. This moisture can cause video dropout and, in some cases, shut down your electronic mechanisms altogether. Dust, dirt, or sand can easily find their way inside your camera if you do not protect it. And all these can get on your video recording head and cause dropout or glitches in the image.

If you are going to work in an environment with these conditions, simply wrap the camera in a lint free cloth or some other material that breathes but protects it from the elements. Be careful to shield the tape chamber from unwanted blowing or falling dust and debris when you open it to change or insert your videotape.

Used tapes can be stretched or damaged and can also cause video glitches. If you really want to prevent this from happening, use a new, high-quality video-tape instead of a recording over an old one. Video records best onto a blank videotape. Even if you choose a used tape, make an effort to erase or record black over the old material.

Some other steps that you can take to protect your video include:

✔ Keep the recording head clean with regular service or by using a head-cleaning cassette, available at many retail video-equipment stores.

Make sure that any head-cleaning cassette you use is approved by your camera's manufacturer for your specific camera. Even though your digital camcorder may use tapes similar to analog camcorders (such as Sony's Digital-8 cams), a special head cleaner may be required.

✔ Watch out for troublesome subject matter. Light, color, and pattern can all affect the quality of your recorded image.

✔ In extreme red light, the focus on subjects can appear to be less crisp than they are in daylight or typical indoor lighting conditions. Shooting bright objects, especially red or white in color, can sometimes cause them to "bleed" into the other part of your image.

✔ Shooting at screened windows and doorways, or at materials with thin striped patterns, can cause a herringbone effect, which means that the pattern moves or vibrates on your recorded image. Usually, you can't tell with the naked eye whether this will be a problem. If you have any questions about your subject matter in this regard, simply shoot a test first to see whether you'll have a problem.

✔ Avoid an extreme contrast between the light and dark elements in the frame. Your camera has more trouble trying to balance the exposure when you shoot a very dark subject in the same frame next to a very bright one.

✔ Remember that in low-light situations, images become less sharp, picture and color quality degenerate, and the image looks grainy (you can see the little dots that make up the image). Obviously, do what you can to make sure that you have enough light to get a decent exposure.

Make Wise Lens Choices

Many times, you cannot control the distance between your subject matter and where you place the camera. When you do have a choice, however, you'll want to keep some things in mind.

The wide-angle lens sizes on your zoom (the low numbers — 16mm, 18mm, 21mm, 28mm) used at a relatively close distance (say, between 10 and 20 feet away), allow you to keep almost all of your subject matter in focus. When shooting with these lenses, you do not have to worry as much about your subjects going in and out of focus. With a wide-angle lens, the depth of field (range of sharp focus) is greater and therefore more forgiving than it is in the longer (telephoto) lenses. So, if you're hand-holding the camera, when you can, don't zoom in; move closer!

Note: Many camcorders label their zoom control using the letters *W* (Wide angle) and *T* (Telephoto).

Another consideration of the wide-angle lenses is that they do not transfer as much *shake* to the image, in the hand-held mode, as longer lenses do. Because their field of view is so much wider, they seem to absorb more of the unsteady movement, and when you're hand-holding the camera, achieving less shaky footage is much easier with these lenses.

Longer, telephoto lenses (50mm, 75mm, 100mm, and up) are the most flattering when shooting an actress or actor close up. The longer the lens, the greater tendency it has to soften the image while still being in focus. This makes shots look prettier. Wide-angle lenses tend to distort at a close-up range and are definitely not flattering.

Long lenses also diminish the amount of background that is viewable or in focus. Using the longest end of your lens tends to give the subject a feeling of isolation (separated from its environment), as well as making it seem far away.

If you intend to fill your frame with your subject matter, with no background, and it is not a human face, you are better off using a wider lens because that end of your zoom lens creates crisper images. If you filled your frame with a shot of a wall of roses and shot the exact same frame with both the 20mm lens size and the 100mm lens on your zoom, the 20mm image would, in almost all cases, look sharper and clearer.

Don't Abuse the Zoom Lens

Most professional movie-makers try to avoid zooming, and some cameramen simply *refuse* to use it. Four words best sum it up: *Use the zoom sparingly.*

Excessive zooming in and out can have a dizzying effect on your viewers and often adds little to the quality of your shot. If you want to move into a close-up from a wide angle, stop recording, zoom in and refocus, and then start recording again. Or stop recording, walk up closer, and then start recording again. Either of these choices is a more pleasant way to move in to get a closer look at your subject.

Many times when you zoom in to the long end of your lens, the choices your auto-focus feature make will often change as the subject matter in your frame changes. This invariably means that you will experience some "fishing" for focus by your auto focus feature, making your subject matter go in and out of focus. One way to avoid this erratic focus is by zooming in on the subject that you wish to shoot *before* you start recording, and find the focus. Then, shift to the manual focus setting, which locks the focus where you just set it. Then, zoom back out, start recording, and zoom in to your subject, knowing it will be in focus when you get there.

Once in a while, using the zoom is acceptable if it occurs smoothly. Usually, it is easier to be smooth while zooming out than while zooming in, because at the end of a zoom, a wide-angle lens is easier than a telephoto lens to hold steady. Following are some tips for successful zooming:

✔ Be gentle on the button when operating the zoom control. Don't jump on the start, and try to slow down as you finish your zoom. This is not easy and definitely requires a delicate touch (and lots of practice).

✔ Control the zoom by using a ¼-inch piece of foam between your fingers and the zoom control. The foam dampens your touch, which helps "feather" your stops and starts so that they are not jerky or abrupt.

✔ Short zooms are less offensive. If you must zoom, set up your shot to make the length of the zoom as short as possible.

Understand Manual Exposure and Focus Settings

Most video cameras have a manual as well as auto setting on the camera's iris control and focus settings.

The *iris* controls how bright or dark your image looks. Most of the time, leaving this setting at the auto choice is acceptable and easier to use. But sometimes, setting your own exposure is better.

Most cameras' auto iris setting sets the exposure based on an average of all the subject matter in your frame. Sometimes, this setting does not capture the proper exposure on the elements in the frame that you want to focus on. A perfect example is shooting a full moon in a night sky. The automatic setting reads all the black sky in you field of view, which is the majority of your picture, and opens the iris all the way. This method, however, overexposes the moon (a very bright object) so that it becomes just a white spot with no detail on its surface. If you set the iris control to manual and slowly close down the iris, you will begin to see the surface of the moon appear in your image.

The reverse happens when you shoot toward a person or object in front of a white sky or other bright surface. The person or object becomes dark, like a silhouette, because the camera is exposing for most of the bright sky behind the subject. By dialing open the iris in the manual setting, your dark subjects will become brighter, bringing out their detail. Of course, the sky behind them will get brighter, but it is already all white anyway!

It is desirable to *never* see an unwanted focus shift in all your footage. Your auto-focus feature is a handy tool, for sure. It is very difficult to manually see and therefore know you are in perfect focus by looking through the eyepiece at that little blue image! Even trying to tell focus from one of those flip-out video screens, especially outside, is not easy. So, auto focus is a good feature to use most of the time. Just remember this: Your auto focus does a lot more swimming in and out of focus when zoomed into the longest lenses. Watching this occur as the camera pans from one subject to the next can be very disturbing to the viewer.

At the widest end of most video camera zoom lenses, you can often set your focus at about ten feet, turn off your auto focus feature, and keep everything from about five feet to across the street, and further, in focus. If you keep your subject matter in that range (don't let it get closer than arm's length), everything will stay in focus and you won't have to worry about your auto focus ruining your shot by suddenly swimming while you are recording.

One good use of the zoom feature on your lens is to help you make focus choices. Try this exercise:

1. **Zoom all the way in on the subject you want while the focus control is set on auto to make sure that is in focus.**

2. **When the camera finds the focus for your subject, immediately reset your focus control to manual.**

   Resetting the control to manual keeps your focus set at the distance of your subject.

3. **Zoom out to a wider frame size and reposition your primary subject anywhere in your frame.**

   The subject remains in focus.

Position the Camera Carefully

Most people just shoot from their eye height toward the subject matter, usually right from the place where they first see it. Experiment with the point of view from which you shoot the camera. Different angle choices can affect the way a person or object looks, or improve the overall quality of your shot.

For example, shooting a beautiful woman from a low angle, up close under her chin, looking up her nose with a wide-angle lens is usually a good way to make her look unattractive. To flatter a woman, it is usually best to not shoot her closely with a wide lens, or from an angle lower than her eye level.

Shooting down from above a subject tends to diminish its size, whereas shooting up from a low angle tends to make objects and people seem larger or taller than they really are. Low angles are often good for capturing the point of view of kids and small animals.

Be aware that where you place your camera affects how your light sources hit your subject. Think about how your subjects can best be illuminated. Experiment looking at different ways the light hits your subject and which looks better to you. Remember that, most of the time, it is a good idea to be able to see well into at least one eye of your subject so that your viewer can catch the expression in your subject's face. Heavy top light from the sun or other sources usually brightly exposes the face. However, because of the direction the light comes from (overhead), many people's brow or forehead shadows the eye sockets, and your subject's eyes can look like black holes. Avoid this kind of contrast when shooting faces. In the same bright outdoor light, a softer, more even light can be achieved under a tree, for example, or in the shadow of a building. Other factors to keep in mind are the following:

- Your soundtrack is definitely affected by your camera position. The best sound recording for a talking person is achieved from an angle anywhere inside of fifteen feet. (This subject is further discussed in the next section.)

- Another thing to remember is to make a choice about your background. Don't let your background be accidental. Even if you're just choosing from one of the four directions right where you are standing, think about the choice that is best for your shooting.

✔ Try to place your subject matter against a background that is not too distracting, one that does not make it hard for you to see or focus on your principal subject, and, if possible, one that adds information to your overall image about what you are videotaping.

✔ Choose an angle that makes it easy for you to physically operate the shot. Many times, a shot is missed because the operator loses balance or bearing while following the subject. If you have to walk around a tripod while panning with a fast-moving car, for example, plan your steps. It is usually best to put the camera where you think the shot will end up and then move your body backward, in whatever way is comfortable, to the beginning position where the shot will start. This gives you an idea ahead of time of where you are going and how you will get there.

Make Sound Audio Choices

You want to hear your subjects as well as you see them. Obviously, in most cases it is a good idea to have the microphone close to the subject being recorded. Therefore, moving in closer for a better sound recording is often more desirable, as opposed to zooming in with a longer lens from further away. Keep the following ideas in mind:

✔ Try to balance the sound sources that you can control so that distracting noises do not interfere with, or detract from, the sounds you want your viewer to hear.

✔ Avoid having an unwanted noise coming from directly behind the subject you are trying to record. Background noise is diminished if it is off to the side or behind the camera. When you are trying to record someone speaking outside or in a public area, sometimes just walking around a corner or turning and shooting 180 degrees in the opposite direction can reduce the amount of background noise.

✔ Shield the camera from strong winds to help eliminate unwanted rumbling noises on the soundtrack. Temporarily affixing a piece of very light foam over your microphone can do a lot toward eliminating unwanted wind noises on your soundtrack without losing volume in your recording.

Many cameras are equipped with a port to plug in an external microphone. If you have this capability, get a good microphone with as long a cable as is recommended for proper operation.

Sometimes, being close to your subject with your camera is not a good idea, and sometimes you simply can't be. In such situations, running a microphone with a cable from your camera is useful. If you will be far away while shooting a close-up of your subject, a microphone can be planted and remain unnoticed in one of many places where a camera cannot go. The sound you achieve from running a cabled microphone out to within 10 feet (or as close as possible) of your subject isolates your audio focus the same way that zooming in to a close-up isolates the image you want to see. If you don't have a stand, place the microphone on a cloth or piece of foam to avoid vibration noise, and remember to place it where it will not get bumped or moved while you are shooting.

Stabilize Your Images

In the professional movie-making world, a hand-held camera is used selectively, and usually to create a particular style. One characteristic common of the hand-held style of camera work is that the shaky movement invokes feelings of disorientation, and subconsciously is very unsettling to the viewer. Creating this unsettling feeling is often one of the reasons that a hand-held camera style is chosen. But that mode of operation is usually not preferred because a shaky camera distracts some of the viewer's attention away from the material. Unless you are trying to disorient your viewers, a stable, smooth-moving camera that follows your action and remains level with the horizon is the preferred style for most movie making.

Ironically, the home video maker is usually walking around with a camera in hand, shooting all his or her material in this fashion. The commercial video camera makers, being quite aware of this inherent problem for the amateur videographer, invented the image-stabilization feature, now available on almost all the new digital video cameras on the commercial market. They know that a smoother image makes for better watching, and I recommend using this feature all the time. But the new feature still does not eliminate all the unwanted image movement that occurs during hand-held operation. There are some simple things to remember and some easy ways to help the average videographer with this problem.

Most manuals never mention this, and the average home videographer is not aware of the fact that the most distracting camera movement occurs when the video image frame dips on the right or left side, going "out of level" to the horizon, similar to the clip shown in Figure 20-2. Left-and-right lateral movement, called *panning*, and up-and-down movement, called *tilting*, are far less noticeable to the average viewer because that is how human vision works. Most of our vision is level to the horizon. (*Level to the horizon* means that if you were shooting at the ocean from a coastline, the top and bottom lines of your frame would be parallel to the line of the ocean on the horizon.) We don't walk around with our heads tilted to one side or the other. Keep frames level to the horizon unless a specific visual effect is being attempted; otherwise, it will subconsciously disorient the viewer.

Figure 20-2: In this shot, the camera was clumsily tilted to the right, causing the subject to go out of level.

Attempt to smooth out your camera moves and stabilize the horizon during those moves, and maintain a level horizon when shooting a nonmoving "static" frame.

Obviously, using a tripod with a moveable head is one way to keep your images more stable. If this is not available to you, make an effort whenever possible to place the camera on a stable surface while you shoot, or lean on a solid object or against a wall to keep your arm and body motion to a minimum. You can still pan and tilt, but by wedging your camera against a solid surface while you operate it, you can eliminate much unwanted camera shake.

Get into the sling of it

If your shooting demands a lot of hand-held operation, you can eliminate some camera shake by assembling a simple sling for your arm. Take an adjustable strap and attach some sort of small sling for your elbow to rest in when your arm is bent up toward your face, as it would be if you were pointing a camera. Put the strap around your neck as you would any other sling. Adjust the size of the loop so that when you rest your elbow in the sling, your neck and shoulders carry the weight of your arm with the camera in it. With your elbow wedged against your body and the sling holding the weight of your arm and the camera, you can walk around hand-holding the camera much longer, and much of the shake that comes from the muscle fatigue of just trying to hold the camera still can be diminished.

One simple way to help keep your horizon level is to tape a small bar level (with three sections: left, middle, and right) to the top of your camera so that you can easily glance at it when using the swing-out monitor screen available on many video cameras now. Even if you have to look through an eyepiece while shooting, the level is a good reference tool for composing frames.

When mounting this level, make sure that the camera is sitting on its base, flat on a level surface, which you can predetermine by using a level. The level should be placed perpendicular to the shooting direction of the lens so that when you lean the camera to the right, the bubble moves out of the center toward the left side, and vice versa. Then, while you are shooting, you can glance at it to help you maintain your horizontal level. After awhile, you will become accustomed to how that means you should hold your camera; as a result, even when you are not glancing at the level, your operating will become increasingly better.

Rehearse Whenever Possible and Edit in the Camera

Your videography skills can best be improved with practice. Even the most seasoned videographer rehearses his or her camera moves when possible. Try to do the same.

Experiment with the settings and operation before you even go out so that you are aware of your camera's capabilities and limitations as well as your own.

If you are shooting moving people or objects and have the ability to record a practice take of what they are going to do, by all means do so. You can then decide ahead of time, before you do your final recording, whether you can improve your shot in some way.

If you are shooting with actors or friends, you have the opportunity to take advantage of rehearsing, whereas documentary-style, or spontaneous shooting, does not allow you that luxury. For documentary-style shooting, think about what you will be videotaping. Practice shooting camera moves that you may use when the time comes, using other similarly moving subject matter just to practice your camera operation. Here are some more ways to hone your skills while simultaneously making better movies:

- ✔ Edit in the camera whenever you can. Try to have your camera pointed, focused, and ready to operate before you press the Record button. And when you finish each shot, stop recording before you stop operating, or swing the camera away. These two things will help you edit out, ahead of time, unwanted slop footage at the head and tail of your shots.

- ✔ Anytime you are going to reposition yourself for a better or new angle, stop the camera for all the running around in between. You won't want to watch it later and neither will anyone else.

- ✔ Make decisions about what you are going to shoot and what you want to see before you press the Record button. Doing so helps you decide your angles and choose the best way to shoot your material. It also helps prevent you from shooting a bunch of unwanted footage.

Sometimes you'll have to keep rolling because you are capturing spontaneous activity and you don't know what is going to happen next. Even then, however, you can start and stop the scene while holding the camera still and framed on your subject.

Chapter 21

(Not Quite Ten) Creative Special Effects

In This Chapter

▶ Compositing

▶ Using fake blood

▶ Using contact lenses

▶ Moving the camera, not the subject

▶ Making sci-fi effects

▶ Messing with perspective

*O*ne thing that makes the art of video and movie making different from other forms of visual art is the ability to show the viewer actions in real time that he or she wouldn't otherwise be able to see in real life. Movies can take you into the heart of a black hole, onto the bow of the *Titanic*, or into the middle of a Civil War battle. Movie makers use special effects to create many of their on-screen illusions.

Some critics have bemoaned the way in which effects-laden (and expensive) blockbusters have taken over mainstream film in the last quarter century. Others believe that the art of effects has broadened the canvas on which movie makers paint. However you feel about the movies produced by Hollywood these days, you will find that some well-placed special effects can enhance some of your movie projects and be a lot of fun. And, fortunately, you don't need a multimillion dollar budget to add a few fun surprises to the movies you create in Windows Movie Maker.

Compositing (Not)

Many special effects shots you see in movies use a process by which one piece of film (called a *matte*) is superimposed on top of another so that they look as though they were photographed together. This process is called *compositing* because you are creating a composite scene from multiple pieces of film. Consider some of the space battle scenes from the *Star Wars* movies. Each spaceship model was filmed individually and then each ship's matte was composited together, along with mattes containing laser blasts, explosions, and the star field that fills the background.

Windows Movie Maker doesn't do compositing, exactly. However, you can take advantage of the ability of Movie Maker to cross-fade between clips to create the illusion of a subject fading in or out of a scene. Just shoot a "before" clip and then have your subject step in and shoot an "after" clip. To make this work, you must observe the following:

- ✔ Use a tripod. There is absolutely no way you can hold the camcorder still enough to achieve the smooth transition that you need between clips.

- ✔ Do not reposition the camera between clips. If you accidentally bump the camera between shots, retake the first shot to ensure consistency.

- ✔ If you are working outdoors, shoot the clips one right after the other to ensure that each one has the same lighting. Make sure that no person or object off-camera is casting shadows on either clip.

- ✔ If your camcorder has a remote control, use it rather than the Record button on the camera to start and stop recording. Doing so eliminates the possibility of you jiggling the camcorder when you push that little red button.

The first shot you take may look something like Figure 21-1, and the second may look like Figure 21-2.

Figure 21-1:
First shoot a "before" clip like this.

Figure 21-2:
Next,
position
your subject
and shoot
the "after"
clip.

After you have both of your clips, import them into Movie Maker, place them on the Timeline, and create a cross-fade transition between the two, as shown in Figure 21-3. The cross-fade will give the appearance that your subject is gradually materializing in the scene, a là the transporter in *Star Trek*. You may need to experiment a bit with the length of the transition to get it just right. If you would rather give the appearance that your subject simply popped into the scene, use a simple straight-cut transition instead. Instead of gradually materializing, the subject pops in. Think of Jeannie from *I Dream of Jeannie* magically jumping from scene to scene with the blink of an eye and you'll get the general idea.

This type of pseudo-compositing using transitions is one of the few effects you can do using the Movie Maker software. Most of your effects must be implemented in the production process while the camera is rolling.

You can use transitions in the manner described here to make subjects *disappear* from a scene as well as appear in one. Just shoot your "before" clip with the subject in place and the "after" clip after the subject has been removed.

Fake Blood

Whether or not you are appalled by the growth of violence in films and on television, it's always handy to know how to make a really good batch of fake blood. Guess what? Ketchup is *not* the best substance to use. Nor is tomato sauce. In fact, nearly all tomato products are inadequate for use as fake blood because their particular shade of red is too bright. And in the case of ketchup and tomato sauce, the consistency just isn't right, either.

Cross-fade

Figure 21-3:
A cross-
fade
transition
makes your
subject
appear to
materialize
in the
scene.

What you need is a substance that flows smoothly, but not as quickly as water. It needs to be nontoxic to ensure the safety of everyone on your film crew. The best thing I have found is corn syrup, available inexpensively at any grocery store. Corn syrup is clear or has a slight yellowish tint, so use red food coloring to achieve the correct shade for your batch of blood. Corn syrup also seems to have a favorable consistency. Furthermore, because corn syrup is nontoxic, it is safe to use around people and animals (although it probably creates an increased risk of cavities if you eat it).

Please don't splatter red-colored corn syrup on your best Armani suit or on your mother's white carpet. The stuff will stain just about any fabric it touches, so you should choose costumes and other on-scene materials that are compatible with the syrup or are disposable.

You may need to experiment with the color a bit to get it looking just right, but don't be too concerned about the translucent nature of the red corn syrup. This feature actually helps it look shinier on video. Also, of course, you can add chunks to your blood with chocolate chips and other edible objects. Knock 'em dead!

In-Camera Effects

Remember that thick paper thing that came with your camcorder? You know, that packet of pages that said, "Read this before you even breathe on your camcorder!" That was your camera owner's manual and it's probably worth a good review when you want to do some special effects. Why? Digital camcorders tend to be high-end units, as consumer camcorders go, which means that most of them are packed with special features.

Among the special features you're likely to find in your camcorder are in-camera special effects. Specific effects and the way you use them vary from camera to camera, but some common effects include:

✔ **Still compositing:** Many cameras allow you to snap a still photo and then superimpose it on top of moving video. Usually, you do this by enabling the *still* mode and snapping the photo of your still subject. The still photo is stored in the camera's built-in memory, and when you record video, the still is superimposed over the top of it. Some cameras are "smarter" than others, but this generally works pretty well if you shoot a still of your subject in front of a blank, white background before shooting the video.

✔ **Psychedelic effects:** They're almost certainly not referred to as "psychedelic" in your camera's manual, but you probably have a bunch of built-in effects that would look at home in a rock music video. These can include trails, luminescent shadows of bright areas in the scene, and blurriness.

✔ **Black and white:** Any good digital camcorder should have a black-and-white mode. Black-and-white video is perfect for that noir detective film you plan to make, or other situations in which color is not desired for artistic purposes.

✔ **Sepia tone:** Some camcorders have a mode that alters the shutter speed and applies a pseudo-sepia effect to the video to give the appearance of a very, very old movie. This feature is perfect for the Buster Keaton wannabes.

✔ **Negative image:** When you are filming your own sci-fi epic, switch the image to a negative-image mode whenever you want to film a scene from the eyes of the android bent on destroying all that is good and normal in your world.

✔ **Solarize, pastel, mosaic, and others:** Most cameras offer lots of special color modes that, although they seem neat at first, are actually things that you will use seldom if ever. Consult your camera's documentation to find out which effects it offers.

✔ **Night vision:** Some digital camcorders from Sony include a feature called Night Shot that allows you to film in total darkness (Figure 21-4). The feature uses infrared technology to produce usable images even in total darkness. This effect is great for that wildlife documentary you've always wanted to make on the nocturnal creatures in your yard.

Figure 21-4: Sony's Night Shot technology allows me to shoot this video in total darkness.

The Eyes Have It

It has been said that a person's eyes are a window into his or her soul. This is especially true in the case of actors in a movie, who will be watched closely by your audience. When you are filming subjects closely, pay special attention to their eyes and watch for common problems:

✔ **Squinting:** Is your lighting too bright? Try to shield your actors' eyes from direct sunlight and intense light sources.

✔ **Redness:** What can I say? Keep some eye drops handy.

What do eyes have to do with special effects, you ask? If you are working on a sci-fi or horror project, consider getting some special contact lenses for your actors that give the eyes an unnatural color. These seemingly simple items can significantly change the way your audience perceives the subjects in the film.

Colored contact lenses aren't cheap but they are widely available. Consult your local optometrist or visit an online supplier such as Bodytech (http://www.bodytek.com/).

Move the Camera, Not the Subject

One of the most common special effects techniques used in movies, both low and high budget, is to use miniature models to replicate much larger subjects. Spaceships, cityscapes, monuments, battlefields, and other difficult-to-film subjects can often be recreated using models.

A problem you may encounter when shooting models involves movement, especially if you are shooting in front of a background and can't pan on forever. The object may be difficult to move smoothly and realistically. Why not move the camera instead? Fashion a dolly with wheels to which you can mount your tripod, and use it to roll the camera around your set. Motion can be simulated by moving the camera just as well as by moving the subject matter, often with more desirable results. This technique may require some experimentation on your part but can save you a lot of trouble on those really difficult shots.

The Final Frontier . . .

Access to high-tech video equipment such as digital camcorders and software such as Windows Movie Maker can make the creative juices flow in all of us. You get the bug and before long, you go beyond the standard school plays and weddings and start creating your own creative films.

Have you made a science fiction movie yet? All you really need are some willing actors, a decent script, a few props from the toy department at your local department store, and voilà! You're ready to launch into space.

Before you do launch, however, have you considered how you plan to depict spaceships flying through space? What were you planning to use for the starfield in the background? A starfield seems like a simple thing to create, but simply punching holes in a sheet of black construction paper won't work nearly as well as you think. The texture of the paper will probably show up on film, especially if you use bright lights to illuminate your spaceship models. Furthermore, the holes will not have the luminescence that stars should.

For an effective starfield, use a sheet of black velvet and decorate it with sequins for the stars. The velvet will absorb almost all light that shines on it, allowing you to use more intense light on your subjects. The sequins, on the other hand, will reflect light brightly enough that on film they will appear as tiny points of white light, and they may even twinkle a little bit.

Forced Perspective

Visual effects pros are often confronted with the problem of trying to make a miniature model look life size or a life-size item look tiny. They often accomplish this using a technique called *forced perspective*, in which visual tricks and camera angles are used to mask the actual size of subjects on camera.

How does it work? Two main concepts are at play here:

- ✔ Normal perspective in the human eye means that closer objects appear larger than distant ones.
- ✔ A camera has only one "eye" and thus no depth perception.

Because the camera cannot perceive depth, it is relatively easy to fool it into perceiving distances incorrectly. Figure 21-5, for instance, shows a shot of what looks like a train parked in front of a factory. In actuality, the locomotive and cars in the foreground are models that stand about three inches tall, whereas the factory and rail cars in the background are real. By carefully positioning the subjects and the camera, I have forced the perspective of the camera.

Figure 21-5:
In this shot, I use forced perspective to fool the camera into thinking this train is parked right in front of the factory building. They are actually more than 100 yards apart.

Figure 21-6 shows how the modeled scene actually looks in relationship to the factory and rail yard behind. It's crude, perhaps, but effective.

Figure 21-6:
The camera's eye is easily deceived by a simple model scene constructed on a card table.

Forced perspective can work the other way, as well. Continuing with the train theme, model railroaders often use the concept of forced perspective to make their indoor train layouts look larger than life. As a model train rolls past a modeled scene that includes mountains, buildings, trees, and other details in the background are made artificially smaller to appear more distant.

Can you make this work in your movie projects? Absolutely. You can use progressively smaller models in the background to give the illusion of a much larger scene. In fact, you may find this type of forced perspective easier to implement because it does not present the same focus problems that a shot like the one shown previously in Figure 21-5 can present.

Note: Forced perspective works only if your subjects are perfectly positioned and your camera angles are just right. Expect to spend hours setting up a single shot, because it's going to take some experimentation on your part.

Chapter 22

Ten Online Resources

In This Chapter

▶ Filmmaking resources

▶ Copywriting your films

*I*t has been said that if you can't find it on the Internet, it probably can't be found. This may be a slight overstatement, but the online world definitely contains a lot of information, as well as source material. This chapter looks at some Internet resources that you may find useful.

Yahoo! Directory of Amateur Filmmakers

```
http://dir.yahoo.com/Entertainment/Movies_and_Film/Filmmaking/
Amateur/
```

So you say you want to make a film project but you're fresh out of ideas? You may find inspiration by looking at the work of other amateur filmmakers. The art of amateur film has exploded in recent years, thanks in large part to the video boom. High-quality cameras are now widely available and reasonably priced, and with some elbow grease and a bit of creativity, you can create some astounding amateur video productions using only your digital camcorder.

Yahoo!'s directory includes links to dozens of amateur film groups. Some specialize in film, some specialize in video, and some shoot their movies any way they can. The groups vary from school-sponsored projects to semi-professional production companies. Each is unique, with the only common thread being a love for the filmmaking art.

What can you expect to find in the many amateur filmmakers listed in Yahoo!'s directory? You may find:

✔ **Creative inspiration:** You're not looking to steal film ideas, but sometimes the act of simply losing yourself in the work of another movie maker can inspire your own creative juices.

 ✔ **Local filmmaking groups:** Is there a local group of amateur filmmakers in your area? You may find one here. Working with a local group can help you hone your own skills, and some groups host local online film festivals where you can see what other filmmakers in your area have created.

 ✔ **Online film festivals:** If you're proud of some of your work and want to share it with others, look for an online film festival that features work from independent, nonprofessional artists such as yourself.

Like A Story

http://www.likeastory.com/

Like A Story calls itself a "Center for Creative Expression," which without question it is. The site contains some archived articles and other items of interest to the amateur filmmaker, but the very best of this site can be found in the various discussion forums that are hosted.

Forums at Like A Story are moderated. Specific forums topics include:

 ✔ Set building, cinematography and lighting

 ✔ Computer graphics and animation

 ✔ Sound

 ✔ Movie trailers and film shorts

 ✔ Make-up

 ✔ Script writing

 ✔ General special effects

 ✔ "Blood and goo"

 ✔ *Star Wars* topics

This is an abridged list. If you're interested in special effects, Like A Story is an excellent place to visit, especially because the low-budget mindset of most of Like A Story's members probably suits your own limited movie budget quite well.

Creative Planet

http://www.creativeplanet.com/

Fancy yourself a movie or television professional? Immerse yourself in the industry by hanging out in some of the same online communities that the pros do. Creative Planet is one of those communities.

The Creative Planet Web page organizes its content into categories in much the same way as many popular Internet search engines do. Categories contain links to other Web sites, news, and movie-making resources. Categories you may find interesting include:

- **Arts/Crafts:** Here members discuss various aspects of the movie-making art.
- **Equipment & Materials:** See what gear the pros use for photography, editing, sound, lighting, and more.
- **Events:** Find out when and where film festivals and other movie events are taking place.
- **Technology:** What's new in movie making? You'll find it here.
- **Training & Education:** If you want to get serious about making movies, consider going back to school.

Creative Planet is also home to community areas where discussion forums allow members to communicate with one another. One forum, "Guerrilla DV Filmmaking," should be of special interest to you because it's for people who have digital video cameras and perform post-production editing on their computer.

Overall, Creative Planet is very much geared to the film and video professional, but even amateur filmmakers are sure to find some interesting stuff here.

Reel Clothes

http://www.reelclothes.com/

Okay, this one might be a bit over the top for amateur filmmakers using Windows Movie Maker to fashion simple online movies. But if you want to add a touch of class and excitement to your dramatic productions, check out Reel Clothes. Reel Clothes purchases used costumes and props from film studios and then re-sells them thrift-shop style to the public.

Reel Clothes guarantees the authenticity of the items it sells, claiming that all of them are obtained directly from studios and production companies. Items are delivered with a certificate of authenticity, which ensures both that the items are authentic and, perhaps more important, that they are not stolen. Listed are movies from which costumes and props were obtained.

Over the top and expensive? Perhaps, but if you're a film enthusiast and also need a specific prop or costume for your own movie project, genuine "Hollywood" items are hard to beat.

If you ever consider buying an item that was supposedly used in a specific movie, walk away if the item does not come with a certificate of authenticity or other substantial proof of origin. And when you buy an item, keep that certificate in a safe place to protect the collectibility and value of that item in the future.

MusicDownloads.com

http://www.musicdownloads.com/

One of the biggest mistakes made by many amateur filmmakers is not spending enough time producing and preparing high-quality audio for their film projects. It's an easy mistake to make but one that you are ready to avoid.

One thing you can do is to seek out high-quality soundtrack music. Web sites such as MusicDownloads.com make finding great music that costs little or nothing to download easy. MusicDownloads.com serves new, up-and-coming artists (or at least artists who *hope* to be up-and-coming), meaning that they are often eager to let you download free, legal copies of their music in MP3 format. And as you know, MP3 files can easily be imported into Movie Maker and placed into the audio tracks of your movie projects.

Actually, not all the music you can download at MusicDownloads.com is from small bands and it's not all free. Some music expires after a certain amount of time, and some of it even requires a special player to listen to them. Thus, make sure that you review the license or terms of use for any music you try to download. If it can't be played in any MP3 player and it has an expiration period, you probably won't be able to import it into Movie Maker.

The Hollywood Edge

http://www.hollywoodedge.com/

Video and film producers don't have time or resources to record every single sound effect that they need in their projects, and neither do you. Do you need to include the sound of a car crashing over a cliff, or a stampede? How about something simpler, such as a barking dog or cracking whip? Do you really have the ability to record all those sounds yourself? No, you probably don't. So you'll do what the pros do and cull some sound effects from "stock" material.

The Hollywood Edge is an excellent resource for sound effects and other audio files. Most sounds are offered in MP3 format, meaning that they will be high quality and easy to import into Movie Maker and use in your own projects. Much of the material available at The Hollywood Edge has some licensing restrictions, but they do offer an extensive collection of free sound effects that can come in very handy. Just look for the link to free sounds.

LicenseMusic.com

http://www.licensemusic.com/

LicenseMusic.com is another excellent source of audio for your movie projects. At this site, you actually license music for your creative projects. This means that you'll have to pay for the music, but at least you will not be saddled with the guilt of using music illegally.

LicenseMusic.com's database is searchable using some interesting criteria. You can search for music that matches a certain mood, genre, or tempo and then you can narrow that search further by using criteria such as artist or region.

When you have found a song you think that you might like to license, you can click a link to listen to a streaming full-length sample. If you like it and want to calculate a licensing price, you have to register. Licensing music is, alas, not cheap. Expect to pay several hundred dollars for a license. But if you have a movie that you plan to distribute widely and want to ensure that you aren't infringing on the rights of other artists, this is an excellent way to get some high-quality music legally.

 One of the problems associated with registering e-mail addresses with Web sites is their tendency to generate high volumes of junk e-mail *(spam)*. If you want to keep spam to a minimum in your primary e-mail account, sign up for a free e-mail account from Hotmail or any other free e-mail provider and use that e-mail address whenever you register with a Web site.

U.S. Copyright Office

http://lcweb.loc.gov/copyright/

It is an inevitable part of movie making that you will have to deal with some copyright issues. When a person creates a work, whether that work be a book, painting, song, Web site, or movie, the creator is assumed to own it unless some long-winded contract states otherwise. In other words, you own your movies and you control who is allowed to use them.

You will have important questions about copyrights. Rather than try to answer them all here, I point you in the direction of the United States Copyright Office's Web site (Figure 22-1). Here you can find out your rights, others' rights, and how (and whether) you should register your works with the Library of Congress.

AAA Free Clip Art

http://www.aaaclipart.com/

Countless Web sites exist that offer free clip art. Most clip art is small, usually intended to be used as small icons on a screen. However, some clip art images are larger and some are even photographs. You may find that free clip art resources such as AAA Free Clip Art contain some useful images that can be imported into your movie projects.

Clip art is generally offered in GIF or JPEG format, making your life easy because Windows Movie Maker can import them directly. So, for instance, if you need a photograph of the Taj Mahal but all the flights to India are booked, you can probably find one in AAA Free Clip Art. The site actually serves as a directory to hundreds of other clip art sites around the Internet.

Figure 22-1: The U.S. Copyright Office is your first and best place to research copyright issues.

Note: The only problem with most clip art is that it looks like, well, clip art. Clip art galleries often contain photographs, and for movie projects, I generally suggest that you stick to those.

Windows Movie Maker Web Site

www.microsoft.com/WindowsMe/default.asp

Microsoft itself can be an excellent source of information on using Windows Movie Maker creatively. Its Web site devoted to Movie Maker can be quickly accessed from within Movie Maker itself by choosing <u>H</u>elp⇨Windows Movie Maker on the <u>W</u>eb. Internet Explorer will open, your Internet connection will be dialed (if necessary), and you will be connected directly to Microsoft's online world.

What kind of information can you expect to find at the Movie Maker Web site? Look for the following:

✔ Software and device driver updates

✔ Movie Maker project ideas

✔ Technical assistance and support documents

✔ Links and information about other online Movie Maker resources

You are not the only person in the world using Windows Movie Maker to create movies. Thousands of other people are doing the same thing and many of them get together in the Windows Movie Maker newsgroup hosted by Microsoft. There they discuss tips and techniques for making better movies, "how-tos" for installing and configuring hardware, and more. The Movie Maker Web site should list information about how to find this newsgroup, which you can access using Outlook Express.

The Movie Maker newsgroup can also be a good place for you to promote some of your movie projects after you put them online. Other people are doing the same thing, so why not? In fact, you may want to search through the various posts to this newsgroup to find projects that other people have made. Reviewing other Movie Maker movies can provide both ideas and inspiration as you work on your own.

Newsgroup postings are public, so don't post anything that you do not want the whole world to read.

Chapter 23

Ten Software Tools You Won't Want to Do Without

*W*indows Movie Maker is a great tool, but if you really want to turn your computer into your own private movie studio, you'll want to equip it with additional tools. Windows Me comes with some valuable tools, including Internet Explorer, Outlook Express, and Paint, but these applications will probably not suit your every need. This chapter shows you ten programs that you may find it hard to do without.

Graphics Editor

I listed this one first because it's the most important, no question about it. If you plan to use any still images in your movies — and you will — you need a good graphics editor. A good graphics editor will let you resize images, recolor or retouch an image, convert image files into a format that can be imported into Movie Maker, and more.

Many graphics editors are available for Windows, including:

- **Adobe Photoshop:** This is the industry standard for graphics editing. It's the program that most professional publishers use to edit, retouch, resize, and distort graphics that will appear in books, magazines, and other printed materials. In fact, the various graphics throughout this book were edited using Photoshop. Unfortunately, Photoshop is expensive. As of this writing, the retail price for Photoshop is a cool $609. A lighter-featured Limited Edition is available for a much more affordable price of $95. Visit www.adobe.com/.

- **Adobe PhotoDeluxe:** Another graphics editor from Adobe, PhotoDeluxe comes free with many digital cameras and scanners. If you simply want to buy it, you can get the Business Edition for $79 or the Home Edition for a paltry $49. Visit www.adobe.com/.

- **Deneba Canvas:** Canvas is more than just a graphics editor; it can also perform page layout, author Web pages, create illustrations, and do just about anything else a budding desktop publisher can hope to do. Prices range from as little as $85 to as much as $375, depending on which version you get and how you buy it. Visit www.deneba.com/.

- **Microsoft PhotoDraw:** Some versions of Microsoft Office 2000 come with a graphics editor/illustrator called PhotoDraw. It does not have as many features as some of the more advanced editors such as Photoshop but it has many tools that you will find useful as you prepare graphics for use in movie projects. Most people don't buy PhotoDraw by itself (they usually get it with Office), but if you really want it, it can be had alone for $109. Microsoft offers discounts and package deals from time to time, so it's worth checking its Web site (www.microsoft.com/) to see whether any special offers are available.

Audio Editor

Do you want to achieve fine audio in your movies? I'm sorry to say it, but you're not going to get high-quality audio for your movies from the tools in Movie Maker or any of the other programs that come with Windows Me. I strongly recommend that you obtain a third-party audio editor so that you can:

- Edit the length of various types of sound clips
- Convert various audio formats into ones that can be imported into Movie Maker
- Filter unwanted sound artifacts
- Dub multiple audio tracks over each other
- Distort sounds to create sound effects

Table 23-1 offers a selection of audio editors for Windows.

Table 23-1		Audio Editors	
Program	*Publisher*	*Web URL*	*Price*
Cool Edit 2000	Syntrillium Software	www.syntrillium.com	$69
n-Track Studio	FASOFT	www.fasoft.com	$35
SuperSonic	Morton Software	www.gosupersonic.com	$39.95
VoiceOn	ManDorG Software	mandorg.cjb.net	$10
Wave Flow	Xavier Cirac	www.waveflow.com	$25

Good CD-R Software

Recordable CDs can be a reliable and affordable way to share large movie files with your friends, family, and other associates. And just about every CD recorder you can buy comes with some software to help you create — or *rip* — CDs. Unfortunately, the "free" software that comes with CD recorders is almost always quite feeble, lacking the ability to record audio CDs or format CDs that can be used on a Macintosh.

I heartily recommend that you invest in some better CD-R (Compact Disc-Recordable) software. Companies that offer advanced CD-R software include Adaptec, Adaptec, and Adaptec. (And you thought operating systems were competitive!) Adaptec makes a program called *Easy CD Creator 4 Deluxe,* not to be confused with the garden-variety *Easy CD Creator 4* that probably came with your CD-R burner. Easy CD Creator 4 Deluxe includes a number of useful features over and above the free version, including:

✔ Decode MP3 files into CD Audio so that they can be played in any CD player

✔ A tool for creating CD labels

✔ The ability to format CDs that can be used on a Macintosh

That last bit is pretty important. If you have some Mac-using friends with whom you would like to share some of your movies, your CDs should be properly formatted. In the CD Layout Properties dialog box, you should choose "JOLIET" for the file system. This will also, by the way, allow you to use filenames longer than eight characters.

HTML Editor

Would you like to publish some of your movies on the Web? Sure you would! But you're going to need a program that lets you create HTML *(HyperText Markup Language)* files, the files behind nearly all Web pages. In Chapter 16, *Creating an Online Screen Room*, I show you how to create a Web page the old-fashioned way: by typing out raw HTML code in a text editor such as Notepad.

If you don't feel like typing all those lines of monotonous HTML tags, you may want to try using an HTML editor instead. An HTML editor is a program that lays out all the elements of your Web page on-screen in a sort of WYSIWYG (What You See Is What You Get) format, even though the best any program can provide is an approximation of how a Web page will look on the computers of your visitors. Still, you may find it easier to style your text, insert pictures, and create links to your movie files. Figure 23-1 shows an HTML editor that I like to use called WebExpress.

Table 23-2 lists some popular HTML editors.

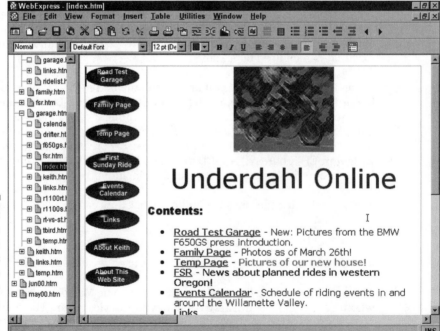

Figure 23-1:
A program like WebExpress can make Web page creation a snap.

Table 23-2	HTML Editors	
Program	*Publisher*	*Web URL*
FrontPage	Microsoft	www.microsoft.com/
HotDog	Sausage Software	www.sausage.com/
PageMill	Adobe	www.adobe.com/
WebExpress	MicroVision	www.mvd.com/

FTP Client

Windows Movie Maker includes a built-in tool that helps you upload movies to Web servers. If that tool works for you every time, congratulations. Microsoft's developers pegged your target perfectly.

Alas and alack, most of us sometimes have a hard time uploading files using Movie Maker. Some Web servers must be accessed a certain way and others are unable to accept .WMV files (the default format that Movie Maker movies are saved in) at all.

What can you do if you have problems uploading movies to the Web with Movie Maker? First, read the instructions or FAQ file for the Web site or server to which you are trying to upload the files. They almost certainly contain special instructions on how to upload files to the server. And you stand a good chance that those instructions will tell you to use an FTP client, such as the one shown in Figure 23-2.

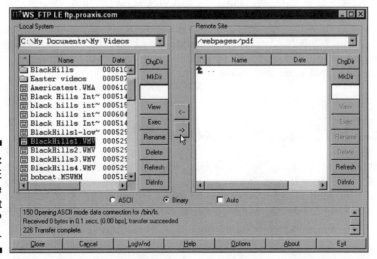

Figure 23-2: WS_FTP LE is one of the most popular FTP clients.

FTP stands for *File Transfer Protocol*, a protocol used on the Internet for (surprise) transferring files. But that doesn't concern you right now. What *does* concern you is finding a good FTP client, installing it, and learning how to use it.

Perhaps the most popular FTP client for Windows is WS_FTP LE, available from Ipswitch (www.ipswitch.com/). Best of all, if you are using the program for noncommercial purposes, it's free! Other free clients include CoffeeCup Free FTP (www.coffeecup.com/), FreeFTP (members.aol.com/), FTP Commander (www.vista.ru/), and SmartFTP (www.smartftp.com/).

Desktop-Publishing Software

Want to promote your movie? How about create some neat packaging for your CDs or video tapes? A desktop-publishing or page-layout program can help you fulfill these goals. Furthermore, most desktop-publishing programs today also help you create Web pages, meaning that you may be able to kill two birds with one stone, so to speak.

Some popular desktop-publishing programs include:

- **Adobe PageMaker:** Adobe's PageMaker is a well-rounded and high-quality product. But at $499, it's not cheap. (www.adobe.com/)

- **Deneba Canvas:** Also described earlier under "Graphics Editors," Canvas can produce some truly astounding documents. (www.deneba.com/)

- **Microsoft Publisher:** Publisher comes with some versions of Microsoft Office 2000 or can be purchased separately. (www.microsoft.com/)

- **QuarkXPress:** One of the most popular and respected page-layout programs, QuarkXPress is also expensive at $849. (www.quark.com/)

Desktop-publishing programs are usually expensive, so you may find that this is something you prefer to do without. But if you want to create high-quality, professional-looking documents, there is no substitute.

WiMP Download Package

Where and how will you be sharing the movies that you create with Windows Movie Maker? However you go about distributing your movies, you need to be sure that your audience will be able to view the movies. In other words, they have to have a current version of Windows Media Player, or as some of us like to call it, WiMP.

When you share movies online, providing your audience with the latest version of WiMP is easy. Simply include a hyperlink to Microsoft's Web site, where your viewers can download the software they need. The URL for the WiMP download site is `www.microsoft.com/windows/mediaplayer/ download/default.asp`. Provide a link to this site so that people who need the Media Player can quickly get this taken care of.

Note: Microsoft even has a little logo that you are welcome to use on your own Web site for a link to the WiMP download site. You can download the logo and read its terms of use at `www.microsoft.com/windows/windowsmedia/ en/create/logo.asp`.

Besides providing a link on your Web site, you should also have copies of the actual download files handy. Then, if you share a movie on a CD-R, you can include a copy of the WiMP installation file on the CD. You may want to obtain copies of WiMP for other operating systems as well, including Windows 3.1 and Macintosh. Download sizes range from approximately 7.3MB (megabytes), for the latest version 7, to less than 3MB for the Macintosh version.

You should not sell copies of the Media Player or distribute it to anyone but your friends and family when you share movies with them. This would be a violation of Microsoft's terms of use agreement.

Screen-Capture Software

Have you ever wondered how we get pictures of the Windows Movie Maker program and various dialog boxes onto the pages of this book? We do it with screen-capture software, programs that can take a snapshot of the current Windows Me environment.

Why is screen shot software useful to you? There are two main reasons why you may find it useful:

- ✔ If you want to give people instructions on how to do something on the computer but they live or work far away, a movie made in Movie Maker may be the best way to do it. Use the screen-capture software to take pictures of things on-screen that you want to show in your movie, assemble a movie using those stills, and add some narration to provide verbal instructions.

- ✔ Movie Maker's Record dialog box has a "Take Picture" button but sometimes it doesn't work very well. The pictures come out blocky or improperly colored, and getting a picture of the exact frame you want may be hard. With screen-capture software, you can play a movie, pause it at exactly the frame you want, and "capture" a picture.

The screen capture program I use is called Collage Complete, from Inner Media, and is shown in Figure 23-3. When you start a capture, the program disappears until after the capture has been completed. Capture programs usually have an adjustable countdown to give you a bit of time before the actual capture takes place.

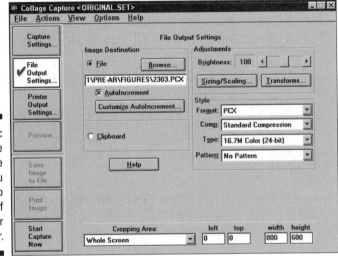

Figure 23-3: Collage Complete allows you to snap pictures of your computer.

Screen-capture software usually allows you to capture screens in a variety of formats. Make sure that you capture them in a format that can easily be imported into Movie Maker, such as JPEG or bitmap.

Collage Complete is available from Inner Media (www.inner-media.com/). Other programs include 20/20 (www.hotfreeware.com/), AnalogX (www.analogx.com/), and PrintScreen 2000 (www.sssware.com/).

Advanced Video Editors

Windows Movie Maker is an excellent tool for amateur video editors such as yourself. And, of course, you can't beat the price. It's also hard to beat the compact size of movie files created by Movie Maker, no matter how much you spend. This is especially important if you plan to share movies online, where smaller files help conserve precious bandwidth.

But there are some things that Movie Maker just can't do, so a time may come when you will want to try using another video editor. For instance, if you have a hard time capturing good video from your camcorder using Movie Maker, you may want to try another editor.

Why can other programs often capture higher-quality video? Movie Maker compresses video as it imports or records it, meaning that it makes your computer's processor work much harder during the import/record process. If your processor isn't fast enough, Movie Maker will capture poor audio and video, especially from a digital camcorder connected to a FireWire card.

If you have another video editor that captures video as AVI or MPEG files, you can use it to get the video onto your computer and then import it into Movie Maker. Many FireWire (IEEE-1394) cards and some digital camcorders come with free video-editing software. Figure 23-4 shows Ulead's VideoStudio 4, which came free with our SIIG FireWire card.

Some popular video editors include:

✔ Adobe Premier (www.adobe.com/)

✔ Pinnacle Systems Studio DV (www.pinnaclesys.com/)

✔ MGI Software VideoWave (www.videowave.com/)

✔ Ulead VideoStudio (www.ulead.com/)

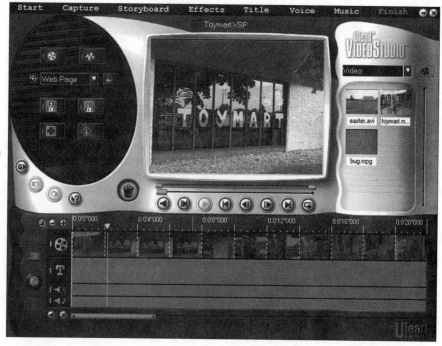

Figure 23-4:
Programs like Ulead's VideoStudio can be used to record video, which you can then import into Movie Maker.

MP3 Encoder

If you plan to use music or other audio in the soundtracks of your movies, the best place to store that audio is on your hard drive. Unfortunately, many of the most popular audio formats such as CD Audio and .WAV take up a lot of disk space. A better way to store it is in MP3 format. MP3 — short for MPEG audio level 3 — retains near-CD quality sound, but MP3 files are about one-twelfth the size of regular CD Audio.

An MP3 encoder records existing audio into MP3 format. This makes the files easier to store on your hard drive, and MP3 audio can be easily imported into Movie Maker for use in your projects. Table 23-3 lists a few MP3 encoders that are currently available.

Table 23-3	MP3 Encoders	
Program	*Publisher*	*Web URL*
MP3 Toolz	Softuarium	www.softuarium.com
MPAction Rip'n'Coder	Birdcage Software	www.birdcagesoft.com
StreamRipper32	Oddsock.org	www.oddsock.org

Some audio editors have built-in MP3 encoders. See the section on audio editors, earlier in this chapter, to see whether one program can suit all your audio needs.

Appendix

Equipping Your Movie Maker Studio

* *

*W*indows Movie Maker is just one tool in your personal movie studio. Granted, Movie Maker *is* the focus of this book, but if you want to make excellent movies, you need the right equipment on hand and working properly. This appendix helps you select and use some of the equipment that Windows Movie Maker can take advantage of.

The Joys of Digital Video

When digital still cameras were first introduced a few years ago, they were wildly expensive compared to good ol' film cameras. On average, digital still cameras remain quite a bit more expensive than their film counterparts. You would expect digital camcorders to suffer from the same malady, but thankfully, digital camcorders tend to be only slightly more expensive than analog formats such as VHS, 8MM, or Hi8.

More important, with digital camcorders you get a lot for your money. Unlike digital still cameras, which struggle to match the image quality of a good film camera, digital camcorders generally have far superior image quality to analog recorders. And unlike analog recordings, which deteriorate slightly every time you view them, digital recordings maintain their original high quality forever. Digital camcorders also tend to have features that used to be found only in the most expensive analog camcorders, such as:

- **Image stabilization.** Camcorders use electronic or mechanical systems (or both) that take some of the movement and jerkiness out of your video when you are holding the camera by hand.

- **High-quality digital sound.** Most digital camcorders record sound in AFM or PCM sound for optimum quality.

✔ **Digital special effects.** Digital camcorders often have built-in special effects such as special transitions, fade-in/out, negative or solarized exposure, black-and-white or sepia tone modes, and other special auto-exposure modes.

✔ **Still photo capability.** Many digital camcorders can also take still photos. This is handy because it means you have to take only one camera rather than two with you on vacation.

✔ **Manual focus and exposure control.** Although most people rely on auto-focus and automatic exposure control, being able to control these things manually when you need to is nice. Many digital camcorders allow you to do this.

And don't forget the most important advantage of digital camcorders: With a FireWire adapter, you can easily capture and edit video on your PC with Windows Movie Maker!

Goin' Camera Shopping

The selection of digital camcorders grows daily. Which one is best? Most of the cameras on the market today are quite good, and a simple search on a Web site that allows camera owners to provide feedback (such as www.cnet.com) reveals an overwhelming majority of satisfied customers. With few bad choices, the main factor affecting your purchase will likely be the amount of money you have to spend. Digital camcorders are already widely available for as little as $400, but even if your budget is in the thousands, you'll find many cameras from which to choose.

Sorting out the DV alphabet soup

The spec sheets of digital camcorders contain many obscure and cryptic terms, acronyms, and codes that can make choosing a camera difficult. The following sections sort them out.

Storage formats

You probably know that analogcamcorders use many different kinds of media for storing video. Some camcorders use regular VHS tapes such as those in your VCR, whereas others use smaller tape formats such as VHS-C, 8MM, or Hi8. Digital camcorders also have different methods of storage. Three main formats exist for digital camcorders:

✔ **DV:** These camcorders store video on a unique tape called a *digital videocassette.* DV is the most common format for digital camcorders.

✔ **MiniDV:** MiniDV tapes are similar to DV cassettes but smaller. This smaller size makes the entire camera smaller and less bulky.

✔ **Digital 8 (D8):** A few digital camcorders (most of them are from Sony) record digital video onto Hi8 tapes. Hi8 tapes have the advantage of being cheaper and more widely available than DV or MiniDV tapes.

Sony also offers a digital camcorder that uses a re-writable compact disc rather than a tape for storage. Unfortunately, the "Discam" tends to be very expensive and, with current technology, can record only about 20 minutes of video on a disc.

Note: Some cameras include a secondary storage media such as a SmartMedia or CompactFlash card. These are used only for storing still images that you take with the camera, not video.

Connector types

Unless you want to watch videos only on that tiny little LCD screen that comes with the camera, you'll want to connect the camcorder to other devices such as your computer or a VCR. At a minimum, most digital camcorders have connectors for:

✔ **IEEE-1394 (FireWire):** A FireWire port provides a fast connection to your PC, which is critical if you want to edit video using Movie Maker. Some camcorder manufacturers have their own names for this port, calling it such things as *i.link*, *DV link*, or *Lynx* port.

✔ **RCA Video:** Standard RCA-style connectors include a red connector for audio right, white for audio left, and yellow for video. RCA connectors allow the camera to be connected to virtually any VCR and many TVs.

Some digital camcorders also have connectors for:

✔ **S-Video:** Also called S-VHS, S-Videoconnectors allow a high-quality connection to an S-VHS VCR. S-VHS provides much higher video quality than standard VHS. Note that the S-Video connector transmits only video; you'll still have to use RCA jacks for sound.

✔ **RS-232 (Serial):** Some Panasonic camcorders can be connected to a standard 9-pin Serial port on your computer. Unlike FireWire, virtually every PC has at least one Serial port. This can be handy if you don't yet have a FireWire adapter, but unfortunately, Serial ports are too slow to allow efficient video capture by Movie Maker.

Should you buy online or off?

Dozens of online retailers would like you to buy your digital camcorder on their Web site rather than at your local electronics store. They entice you with incredibly low camera prices, but are these deals too good to be true? When evaluating a purchase, make sure that you check the many "hidden" costs associated with the camera. Does the online retailer charge an exhorbitant shipping and handling fee? Are accessories reasonably priced? Is an extended warranty available and, if so, is the price reasonable? What is the return policy? Has the retailer been in business for a while or will it disappear from the face of the Earth when you need to make a warranty claim?

A local retailer can offer some advantages. No shipping charges are involved, the accessories may be priced affordably, and the warranty and service policies are probably quite a bit more liberal than those offered online. Of course, the camera itself may cost hundreds more, the store's selection may be limited, and if you live in an area that has a sales tax, you may end up spending as much on tax as you would have on shipping charges from the online store. Still, it is an option worth researching because you need to add up *all* the costs of buying your camera to ensure that you're getting the best deal.

Television standards

If you've traveled around the world much, you've probably noticed that electrical plug-ins vary from country to country. But did you also know that different parts of the globe have different standards for television signal formats? Most of Europe and Asia use a system called *PAL* (*Phase Alternating Line*), by which the signal is provided at 25 frames per second with 625 lines of resolution per screen. The Americas, on the other hand, use a system called *NTSC* (*National Television Standards Committee*), which delivers 30 frames per second at 525 lines of resolution.

Why does this matter to you? If you're buying all your equipment from a local retailer, it doesn't matter at all because it will sell only TVs, VCRs, and camcorders that use the local format. But if you're shopping online, make sure that you get a camcorder that uses the right system. For instance, if you live in the United States and buy a PAL camcorder, the video you record with it won't play on any of your TVs or VCRs.

Divining the ultimate digital video camera

You've done your research and understand some of the basic jargon of digital camcorders. How do you decide which one is best? Here are some recommendations:

✔ Don't put too much weight on digital zoom claims. Optical zoom is good, because it uses the glass lenses of the camera to zoom in on a subject. But digital zoom just enlarges the pixels of the captured video, meaning that if you zoom all the way in with that "300x digital zoom," all you'll see are a few blocks of pixelated color. Lame.

✔ Get a camera that uses a Lithium Ion battery. NiCad batteries are a pain to recharge and don't last very long, and disposable alkalines are too expensive.

✔ Know that although an LCD panel is nice, it also uses more battery power than a conventional viewfinder. Bigger LCD panels tend to add a lot to the price of a camcorder but can also provide greater detail.

✔ Remote controls rule. Some camcorders come with remotes that not only control playback but also let you start and stop recording remotely, as well as control the zoom.

✔ Keep an open mind about the shape and size of a camcorder. A smaller, flatter camera may not look like the bulky units that pro videographers carry, but it will be lighter and easier to carry around with you.

Accessorizing for any occasion

Rarely does a camcorder come with all the equipment you actually need. Sure, the box probably includes everything you need to turn the camera on and record a few minutes of video, but in addition to the camera, you'll probably have to buy a grocery list of other items:

✔ Extra blank tapes

✔ Spare battery or two

✔ UV filter to protect the camcorder's lens from damage

✔ Camera case

✔ Tripod

Those are the basics. In addition, you may also want to obtain an accessory light, a better microphone, and some other lenses and filters for your camera (if available).

Roasting Your PC's Marshmallow with FireWire

If you want to get video from your digital camcorder into your PC, you need a FireWire card. FireWire — also called IEEE-1394 — is a type of adapter card that provides another plug-in on the back of your computer, kind of like a serial, PS/2, or USB port. But unlike those other ports, FireWire is fast. We're talkin' up to 400 million blazing bits of data per second; that's more than 30 times as fast as USB. Smokin'!

Whew. Sorry about that. As I said, FireWire is fast, and fast is an Official Good Thing when you are trying to transfer something into your PC that requires a lot of bandwidth. Digital video needs a lot of bandwidth, which is why all digital camcorders on the market today have provisions for connecting to a FireWire port.

Microsoft would prefer that I not tell you this, but Apple is ahead of the game on this one. FireWire was invented by Apple, although that doesn't mean that you have to buy a Macintosh to take advantage of this technology. If you don't mind reading a bunch of Macintosh propaganda, you can learn more about FireWire directly from the source at `www.firewire.org`.

FireWire adapters can be used for much more than just connecting digital camcorders to your computer. Other FireWire products include printers, scanners, external hard drives, and removable drives such as CD-recorders. And because a single IEEE-1394 adapter can link up to 63 devices, you can expand your computer as far as the rev limiter on your credit card will allow.

Before you buy . . .

Chances are, your PC did not come with a FireWire adapter built in. If you're not sure, check the manuals that came with the computer. The easiest place to check is the diagram that every computer manual has showing you each and every button and port, along with a description of each one. If you don't see anything about a FireWire or IEEE-1394 port, you probably don't have one.

Go ahead and check. I can wait.

Ready? Good. If you're still reading, my guess is that you didn't find a FireWire port and now you realize that you're going to have to buy one yourself. Prices vary widely, from as little as $70 on up into hundreds of dollars. Regardless of price, look for a few key features:

✔ **More than one 6-pin FireWire port per card.** Many have three.

✔ **A bus-type that is compatible with your computer.** In most cases, your FireWire card needs a PCI bus, but if you are working with a laptop computer, you probably need a PCMCIA adapter.

✔ **Support for other FireWire devices.** Some FireWire adapters are specifically designed for digital camcorders and won't support other FireWire devices such as disk drives, scanners, and printers. Get an adapter that supports everything to ensure maximum upgradability in the future.

✔ **A 6-pin to 4-pin cable.** A good FireWire card should have at least one cable included in the package. IEEE-1394 cables are kind of expensive and hard to find if you have to buy one separately.

✔ **OHCI compliance.** In order to capture digital video with your FireWire card in Windows Me, the FireWire card must be OHCI (Open Host Controller Interface) compliant. Check the card's documentation for this before you buy it.

✔ **Bonus software.** Many FireWire adapter cards come with software specifically aimed at you, the digital camcorder owner.

While you're at it, make sure that your computer is ready to accept a FireWire card:

✔ **Make sure that you have an available PCI slot.** Making this determination requires that you open the case. If you're not sure what a PCI slot looks like, check with a local computer store or expert.

✔ **Check the system requirements.** The system requirements of most FireWire cards for RAM and processor speed are well below the requirements for using Windows Movie Maker, but it's still worth a check. System requirements should be available from the retailer before you buy an adapter.

Installing a FireWire card in your PC

Putting a new FireWire card in your PC is a two-step process:

1. Install the hardware.

2. Set up the software.

Simple enough for ya? Okay, there's actually a little more to it than that. First, take a look at the hardware side of the process. Installing an adapter card (also sometimes called an *expansion* card) in your computer requires you to open the PC's case and get your hands dirty.

The parts inside the case are pretty delicate, so if you've never replaced hardware inside a computer, you may want to leave this procedure to a trained professional at your local computer store. It is all too easy to cause hundreds of dollars worth of damage inside your computer simply because your screwdriver slipped or you had a little bit of static electricity built up in your finger. With that in mind, be prepared for a lot of warnings in this section, beginning now.

Before you turn a single screw, make sure that opening up your case and replacing components won't void your warranty. Consult the documentation that came with the PC just to be sure.

If you've decided that you can handle the installation, take a deep breath and follow along.

1. **Open the box containing your new FireWire adapter and read all the papers and documents that come raining out from inside.**

   Fill out the registration card, answering all those very personal questions about your income, household size, occupation, and hobbies.

2. **Mail in the registration card.**

   Doing so will activate the adapter's warranty and will probably also result in more junk mail and phone calls from telemarketers. Consider yourself warned.

3. **Shut down your computer and turn the power off but leave the computer plugged in.**

   Keeping it plugged in will ensure that the computer remains properly grounded as you work.

4. **Open the computer case (being sure to check the PC's documentation to make sure that you remove the correct screws).**

5. **Double-check that you have an open PCI slot (assuming that a PCI slot is required for your FireWire adapter).**

   Figure A-1 shows what a typical PCI slot looks like.

PCI slot

Figure A-1:
I'm in luck!
This
computer
has one
open PCI
slot left.

Even if you confirm that you have an open PCI slot, make sure that some other stuff isn't in the way. Space can get pretty tight inside your computer, and an otherwise open slot may be blocked by cables or parts on other expansion cards. Don't try to force an adapter card into a space where it won't easily fit.

6. **Touch a bare metal spot on the computer case with your finger.**

   Touching metal will ground you so that you don't damage sensitive computer components with the static electricity built up in your body. A tiny "shock" from your finger will instantly fry thousands of microscopic semiconductors in your computer and the adapter card.

7. **Remove the block-off plate in front of the PCI slot that you plan to use.**

   The plate is held in place by a single screw. When you remove plate, keep the screw handy.

8. **Carefully remove the adapter card from the silver anti-ESD (electro-static discharge) bag.**

   It probably looks something like the card pictured in Figure A-2.

Hold here.

Figure A-2: This IEEE-1394 adapter card is typical of modern PCI FireWire adapters.

Hold the adapter card by the metal end piece so that you're not touching any of the circuits. And remember what I said about static electricity? Ground yourself as often as possible.

9. **Line up the adapter card and make doubly sure that nothing is in the way.**

   Make sure that the gold-colored contacts on the bottom of the adapter card correspond to the openings in the PCI slot.

10. **Gently press the card into the PCI slot.**

    You may have to wiggle the card fore and aft slowly to work it into the slot, but don't press too hard or you'll crack the computer's motherboard. Cracked motherboards are An Official Bad Thing(tm).

11. **When the card is seated in the PCI slot, secure it to the case with the single screw that you removed when you took off the block-off plate in Step 7.**

12. **Re-close the lid on the PC case.**

You did it. Congratulations! Now all you need to do is fire the computer back up and configure your new adapter in Windows. But before you do that, go ahead and plug your FireWire cable into the back of the adapter card, as shown in Figure A-3.

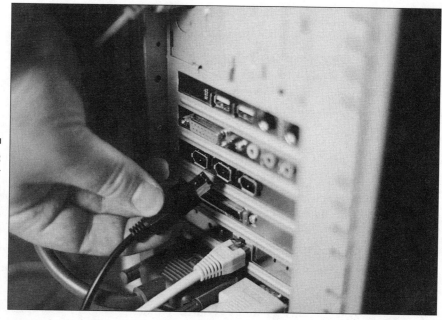

Figure A-3:
Plug your
FireWire
cable into
the adapter
card now
because it
may be
hard to get
at later.

Setting up IEEE-1394 support in Windows

Any piece of hardware you want to use on your computer — including your
new FireWire adapter card — must be recognized by and configured in the
operating system (Windows). Not so long ago, this process required setting
dozens of tiny *dip switches* on the hardware, followed by installation of software called a *driver* that helped run the hardware. Then you spent hours
trying to figure out why it didn't work, and you would read and re-read the
instructions about a dozen times. Your mouse stopped working. Friends
would come over and offer useless advice while drinking all your beer. Dogs
and cats started living together, and all was not right with the world.

Finally, someone at Microsoft noticed that hardware engineers universally
lack the ability to write intelligible instructions. So they developed a system
called Plug-and-Play (PnP for short) that greatly simplified the process. With
PnP, Windows recognizes any new hardware you install, automatically
resolves hardware conflicts, installs appropriate driver software, and makes
any other configuration changes that are necessary.

PnP was introduced with Windows 95 but it didn't always work exactly as
advertised. Cynics labeled the system "Plug-and-Pray" because it was pretty
much a miracle if it actually worked. Thankfully, those days are past and PnP
works with virtually any hardware in Windows Me.

The first time Windows restarts after you install your new FireWire card, you
should see a dialog box similar to Figure A-4.

Figure A-4:
Windows
has detected
a new
FireWire
adapter
and is
configuring
it.

Windows will show you a few more dialogs and then you'll probably have to restart the computer again. Just follow all the instructions on-screen and you should be fine.

But what if Windows didn't detect the FireWire adapter, and you didn't see the dialog box shown in Figure A-4? That could be a sign of trouble with the card, or not. To be sure, try this:

1. **Click Start⇨Settings⇨Control Panel.**

   The Windows Control Panel appears.

2. **Double-click the Add New Hardware icon.**

   The Add New Hardware Wizard appears, with instructions for letting Windows try to find your new hardware. If Windows detects the new hardware, it should begin installing it. If not, you'll probably see a dialog box similar to Figure A-5.

3. **If the FireWire adapter is listed, choose Yes, select the adapter, and click Next; otherwise, choose No and click Next.**

Figure A-5:
Windows
didn't detect
a FireWire
adapter
on my
computer.
Hmm.

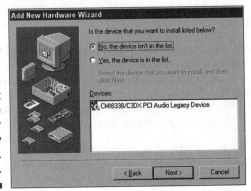

4. **If you chose "No" in Step 3, you should now be asked to let Windows search for *legacy* hardware (items that are not PnP-compatible).**

   Otherwise, follow the on-screen instructions to begin installation.

Chances are, if you went through the previous steps, there is something wrong with your computer or the FireWire adapter. IEEE-1394 devices are relatively new on the PC scene, which means they should pretty much all be PnP compliant.

Wiring FireWire with a proper cable

To use your new FireWire (IEEE-1394) adapter, you need a cable that connects your camera to the card. Most adapter cards come with at least one cable in the package, but if one wasn't included with your adapter, you'll have to buy a cable separately. Choose carefully, because FireWire cables have two different types of connectors:

- ✔ **6-pin connector:** The on the back of your FireWire adapter card are usually the larger 6-pin connectors.
- ✔ **4-pin connector:** Most digital camcorders have a 4-pin FireWire port.

Your equipment may vary, of course, but chances are you need a FireWire cable with a 6-pin connector on one end and a 4-pin connector on the other.

Murphy's Law of PC Cabling says that the cable will always be two feet shorter than what you actually need. The best thing to do is estimate the length of FireWire cable that you need and then buy one that is at least twice as long.

Using TV Tuner and Video Capture Cards

A decade or two ago, many personal computers used a regular old television set for sound and display. Why the switch to more expensive PC-only monitors and individual speakers? Well, the picture quality of most TVs is acceptable when you're staring at it from across the room, but seated a few inches away from it (as you do when using a computer) and trying to read fine text, eye strain becomes a serious problem. Thus, even though computer monitors use the same basic technology (cathode ray tubes) and are the same shape as a regular TV, they provide far superior image quality and clarity.

One thing that makes PC monitors superior to regular TVs is the way the pictures are drawn. A single frame of NTSC video is divided into 525 horizontal lines across the screen. When a television draws those lines, it first draws every other line and then goes back and draws the lines it skipped on the first pass. This type of display is called *interlaced*, and TVs draw 60 of these "half-frames" per second. But computer monitors are called *progressive* because they draw all the lines in a single pass. The lines are progressively redrawn 30 times per second. When you see a monitor advertised as *noninterlaced*, that actually means that it is progressive.

Now that the quality of TV sets have been so improved to make them suitable computer monitors, you're probably thinking how great it would be to turn your monitor back into a TV. Sure! Why not? In fact, some experts argue that modern PCs are already better suited to up-and-coming digital broadcast technologies than regular televisions ever will be.

If you want to use your computer to watch TV or other video, you need to have a functioning picture and sound (I assume you've got this one covered already) and a video capture or TV tuner card.

Using a capture card

You're probably wondering what use a capture card would be to you as you use Windows Movie Maker. With a video capture card, you can connect your VCR or DVD player to your computer and capture video from tapes or discs. And, of course, if you really want to watch TV on your computer, some capture cards will allow you to do that, too.

Capture cards can be either internal or external. If you buy an internal capture card, it probably fits in a PCI slot, much like a FireWire adapter. External capture devices may connect through a parallel, serial, USB, or even FireWire port. To record video from a video capture card in Movie Maker:

1. **Make sure that the video capture card is installed and functioning properly; also ensure that any devices you want to capture video from — such as a VCR or analog camcorder — are ready.**

2. **Launch Windows Movie Maker and click Record.**

   The Record dialog box opens.

3. **Note the video device and audio device listed in the upper-left corner of the Record dialog box; if your capture card is not listed, click Change Device.**

4. **In the Change Device dialog box, choose the capture card next to Video.**

   If it doesn't appear in the list, double-check to make sure that the card is working properly.

5. **Click Configure next to Video.**

   You should see a Properties dialog similar to Figure A-6. Your actual dialog may vary a bit, depending on the brand and type device you have. You may want to come back and experiment with these settings later on as you capture video using the capture card.

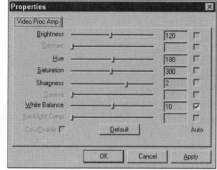

Figure A-6:
Adjust
video quality
settings
in this
dialog box.

6. **Click OK twice to return to the Record dialog box; click Record to begin recording.**

7. **If you are capturing video from a VCR or DVD, press play on the device to begin playing it.**

8. **Click Stop when you are done.**

   You will be prompted to save the video you just captured.

Recording from a TV tuner card

Some video capture cards also function as TV tuners. A tuner is that component in a TV or VCR that receives signals and interprets them into appropriate channels. Without a tuner, your TV is, well, just a monitor. But with a TV tuner card installed in your PC, your computer monitor becomes a TV!

You can record video in Movie Maker from a TV tuner card just as you would from a video capture card. Switch to the TV tuner software that came with the card, select the channel you want to record from, and then record video using the Record dialog box in Movie Maker.

Early testing has revealed that Movie Maker doesn't work well with many popular TV tuner cards. If you find that Movie Maker will not record video from your tuner card, try closing the TV Tuner software and simply choosing the tuner device in Movie Maker's Record dialog box.

Don't Forget a Good Microphone

As thrilling as digital video may be, it's easy to overlook the sound that needs to go along with that high-quality video. If you want your movies to be complete, you need to record the best sound possible. To do this, you may want to get a better microphone for recording "on location" with your camcorder.

Most camcorders have external plugs for accessory microphones, although in some cases, you will have to buy a microphone from the same manufacturer as the camera itself. If your camcorder has an accessory shoe on it, check to see whether the manufacturer offers an "intelligent" microphone that plugs into the shoe. Intelligent microphones actually synchronize with the camcorder's zoom feature, so ensure that the sound you record comes from your actual subject rather than something closer but out of the picture. Consult the camcorder's documentation to see what your options are.

A common problem with the built-in microphones on many camcorders is that they can pick up noise from the motor driving the tape inside the camera. If you notice a steady, low-frequency hum or whine in the background of your videos, a microphone that can be held away from the camera may solve this problem.

While you're at it, get a decent-quality microphone for your PC, too. Do you really want to record your dramatic narration with the cheapo mic that came with your sound card? I didn't think so. Perfectly adequate microphones are available for as little as $10, but if you can afford to spend a couple hundred dollars, a "studio quality" mic will provide the best quality.

One more thing: If possible, support your microphone with a boom or stand. Hand-held microphones pick up a lot of unwanted noise from hand movements, and a boom eliminates much of this. What's that? You say you can't afford a microphone with a boom? I see an old broom handle and a roll of duct tape in your future . . .

Index

• *E* •

Notes

Notes

Notes

Notes

Notes

Notes

Notes

Notes

Discover Dummies Online!

The Dummies Web Site is your fun and friendly online resource for the latest information about *For Dummies*® books and your favorite topics. The Web site is the place to communicate with us, exchange ideas with other *For Dummies* readers, chat with authors, and have fun!

Ten Fun and Useful Things You Can Do at www.dummies.com

1. Win free *For Dummies* books and more!
2. Register your book and be entered in a prize drawing.
3. Meet your favorite authors through the IDG Books Worldwide Author Chat Series.
4. Exchange helpful information with other *For Dummies* readers.
5. Discover other great *For Dummies* books you must have!
6. Purchase Dummieswear® exclusively from our Web site.
7. Buy *For Dummies* books online.
8. Talk to us. Make comments, ask questions, get answers!
9. Download free software.
10. Find additional useful resources from authors.

Link directly to these ten fun and useful things at
http://www.dummies.com/10useful

For other technology titles from IDG Books Worldwide, go to
www.idgbooks.com

Not on the Web yet? It's easy to get started with *Dummies 101*®: *The Internet For Windows*® *98* or *The Internet For Dummies*® at local retailers everywhere.

Find other *For Dummies* books on these topics:

Business • Career • Databases • Food & Beverage • Games • Gardening • Graphics • Hardware
Health & Fitness • Internet and the World Wide Web • Networking • Office Suites
Operating Systems • Personal Finance • Pets • Programming • Recreation • Sports
Spreadsheets • Teacher Resources • Test Prep • Word Processing

IDG BOOKS WORLDWIDE
BOOK REGISTRATION

Register This Book and Win!

We want to hear from you!

Visit **http://my2cents.dummies.com** to register this book and tell us how you liked it!

✔ Get entered in our monthly prize giveaway.

✔ Give us feedback about this book — tell us what you like best, what you like least, or maybe what you'd like to ask the author and us to change!

✔ Let us know any other *For Dummies*® topics that interest you.

Your feedback helps us determine what books to publish, tells us what coverage to add as we revise our books, and lets us know whether we're meeting your needs as a *For Dummies* reader. You're our most valuable resource, and what you have to say is important to us!

Not on the Web yet? It's easy to get started with *Dummies 101*®: *The Internet For Windows*® *98* or *The Internet For Dummies*® at local retailers everywhere.

Or let us know what you think by sending us a letter at the following address:

For Dummies Book Registration
Dummies Press
10475 Crosspoint Blvd.
Indianapolis, IN 46256

BESTSELLING
BOOK SERIES